This book is dedicated to MANCHESTER CITY, the KK family, my family, and especially my loving wife, Suzanne, (to use the posh word), of 58 years, partner, soul mate, co-editor, artist, cartoonist. If there's a term beyond 'long suffering' then that applies, in droves. Love you x.

Also, thanks to all the consultants, doctors, nurses, and staff in the NHS (Please don't let Farage get his hands on it!) at the following hospitals and health centres – Leigh, Wigan, Atherton, Wrightington, Bolton, Preston, St. Helens, Pemberton, and Haydock, who've patched me up over the years. Some proceeds from this book will be donated to Diabetes UK.

No part of this book may be reproduced, sold or utilised in any form or transmitted in any form and by any means, electronic or mechanical, including photocopying, recording or by any information storage and retrieval system without prior permission in writing from the Publisher.

©David Wallace 2025

The right of David Wallace to be identified as the author of this work has been asserted to him in accordance with sections 77 & 78 of the Copyright Designs and Patents Act 1988.

King of the Kippax
25 Holdenbrook Close

Leigh, Lancs, WN7 2HL

emaill: kotk.fanzine@gmail.com

A CIP catalogue record is available for this book from the British Library

ISBN: 978-0955-7056-4-9

Designed by Graeme Alderson

INDEX

Preface	3
Forward	5
1. Introduction	8
2. Sellers	12
3. Home Sales	20
4. Pre Season	24
5. Glasgow & North East	34
6. Yorkshire & Lincs	40
7. Merseyside	48
8. Lancashire	53
9. Greater Manchester	59
10. Cheshire, Staffs & North Wales	65
11. South Yorkshire & Derbyshire	72
12. West Midlands	77
13. East Midlands	83
14. Anglia & Suffolk	87
15. South West & South Wales	93
16. South Midlands	99
17. North London	105
18. East & West London	110
19. South London	118
20. South Coast	124
21. Europe 1	131
22. Europe 2	142
23. Outlets	151
24. Highs & Lows	156
25. City Fanzines	162
26. Ian Cheesman	165
27. Epilogue	167
Subs & Sponsorship	171

PREFACE

This is the third KOTK book we've attempted. The first was 'Century City', which covered the remarkable 1957/58 season, when City both scored and conceded over 100 goals, issued in 2007. Second was 'Us and Them', which featured City against every other club from 1891/92 until 2010/11, issued in 2011. Both sold in limited numbers, and are now out of print.

Inspired by Tom Parish's KK sellers anecdotes in KK300, and a photograph book put together by our daughters Marnie, Kaye and grand daughter Heather on 35 years of KK, we thought it might be of interest to acknowledge the sterling work and support of all the KK sellers over the years.

Here we go then with 'Selling King of the Kippax, in the Golden Age of Football Fanzines, 1988 to 2024…..' We pondered on how to reflect on 35 years, and 300 issues of producing and selling the fanzine, which is half a lifetime. How best to document events which saw Manchester City, with our fine history, drop to the third tier of football, for a brief period, then rise, after the Sheikh Mansour takeover in 2008, to the pinnacle of World football.

It would be impossible to reproduce a 'best of' selection of the many articles produced by our wonderful contributors, but surely the experiences of selling the fanzine, at the many grounds we've visited, and the highs and lows of the games played, and surrounding events, might be of interest?

The main features of the fanzine over the years have been the 'from the heart' articles from our contributors, (many included in the 'Us and Them' book), plus looking backwards (How Was It For You?), and forward to games (It's A Fix') including ground diagrams, toons, occasional photos, programmes, and match tickets, which this book may include.

Thanks to all contributors, subscribers, to Noel Bayley for the foreward, and Ian Cheeseman for the article, and Tony Petrie for some proof reading. Special thanks to Sue, and the family, for all the help and support in this latest venture. To Manchester City for the 'character building' and for providing us with the best and most successful period in our history, which at my time of life, is most welcome. To all Blues, and all those who have sadly passed, particularly Tony Grayson, Alan Rowbottham, and all others who have missed the recent glory years, and others who have seen some of them. To all the football clubs and fanzines, who've inspired and kept us 'on our toes'. To all the media, mainly local, particularly, Jimmy Wagg, Chris Bailey, Ian Cheeseman, Andy Buckley, Fred Eyre, Gary James, David Clayton, James H Reeve, Joanne Lake, Stuart Brennan, and Emily Brobyn for their support.

To Graeme, our Geordie layout fella, the printers, interviewees, all the supporters clubs, especially our local Astley and Tyldesley and Scandinavian branches, outlets, our sellers particularly Tom and Steve Parish, Ged and Carin, who stayed with us until the end. To everyone who have said hello on the street, purchased and contributed to the fanzine, and to those who've provided support and hospitality, David (RIP) and Susan Bookbinder, Arsenal fans Roger and Maureen Hewlett, Joe and Dolly O'Neill, Colin (RIP) and Margaret Brinkley in Spain, Graham (RIP) and Marion in France, Dave and Kay Pugh in Conisbrough, Kaye and Brian in Newport, and especially Raymond and Chrissie (R and C). who regularly treated us to London shows, meals, and the Chairman's Club at the Etihad, where we have, in over twenty games, a 100% win record. There are no words to express our appreciation.

Also to ex Chairmen, Peter Swales (RIP) in the early days was fine, Franny Lee (RIP), who defined me as "The man they can't shut up"; John Wardle and David Bernstein, who, considering some of the criticisms they may have suffered in the fanzine, have always been absolutely brilliant.

Very special thanks to the club, Sheikh Mansour, Al Mubarak, Soriano, Danny Wilson, Paul Dickov, Fanzone Danny and Natalie, Pep, and the players, for the touching and emotional send off they gave us at the Spurs home game in 2023, after we announced that we're finishing publishing the fanzine. Apologies to anyone we may have missed out.

I'm sure that all other fanzine editors and sellers, might have similar stories, and hope that this book may provide the inspiration and format, for them to put fingers to keyboards. Good luck, enjoy.

Dave Wallace, Summer 2025

FOREWORD

■ North Stand Fanzine corner (l to r) Noel Bayley, Frank Newton, Pete Gregory, Mike Kelly, Wayne Norris, Danny Wallace, Tony Seal.

Looking back to the 1980s today in the Summer of 2025, I am struck by one thought: how long ago it all seems. For Manchester City, the decade really got going with the hope of John Bond in Autumn 1980 and a rare Cup Final in May 1981. The rest of the decade saw City yo-yo between First and Second Divisions with two relegations and two promotions. But it wasn't just City who were in the doldrums; English football was too, as was the country in general. It isn't a coincidence that Margaret Thatcher was the Prime Minster for the whole of the 1980s and the ramifications of her tenure are still being felt today, both politically and socially.

The 1980s also bore witness to the Bradford Fire in May 1985 and the Heysel Stadium disaster just 18 days later. It was easier to blame ordinary fans than it was to blame club chairmen and their respective boards. For too long fans had been caged behind fences, herded into pens on terraces and in railway stations and marched to football grounds that were often decrepit but, unlike the government, the fans didn't have patsy newspaper editors to make their case for them. Yet football fans had been largely voiceless for as long as the game had been played.

By the time of the Hillsborough Disaster in 1989, things had started to change. Self-published magazines like *Sniffin' Glue* that celebrated the punk scene while embracing its do-it-yourself ethos had originated in the 1970s. Although football fanzines such as Bradford City's *City Gent* and the general *When Saturday Comes* and *Off The Ball*, had started up in 1984 and 1986 respectively, the concept wasn't widely recognised. Although widely available now, *WSC* was only available by subscription or by nipping down to Sportspages, just off Charing Cross Road.

Meanwhile at Maine Road, a fanzine called *BluePrint* appeared during 1988 while City were plying their trade in the old Second Division. Although basic by today's standards, it was a real game-changer. That September, *King Of The Kippax* appeared. What a change these publications made from dreary old programmes… What a time to be alive!

Several months later, in April 1989, I ventured out to Ewood Park to launch my own fanzine, *Electric Blue* – on a day when Mel Machin's City were battered 4-0, but the day is remembered as being the day of the Hillsborough Disaster. Although we didn't know it then, things were to change very quickly - and drastically.

Football fanzines back then were kitchen table affairs, held together with bubble gum and string. Well, not quite, but it was all Letraset and typewriters, Tipp-Ex, trusty roller, and Pritt Sticks, with a kindly friend doing some after-hours photocopying!

Times change and so does the technology and, while most people have a computer at home now, it wasn't like that then. Computers were expensive and took up a lot of space, together with scanners and printers. As the technology improved so did the fanzines' format, but they remained a labour of love, rather than "scurrilous rags" which was how one local paper described the results of late nights and hours of blood, sweat and tears that only a fanzine editor or their partner would recognise!

I remember a conversation I had once with the late Tom Ritchie, editor of *City 'Til I Cry* when he wondered if we, City fanzine editors, would each be able to create an issue in the style of one of our rivals. I thought it would be an interesting exercise and yes, you would be able to mirror another fanzine's style, but not its editorial content as that is driven by and reflects the nature and character of the individual editor, rather like a newspaper's house style.

BluePrint was ahead of the game not just because they appeared first, but because they knew someone with a camera and printed clear photos. Everybody might have a camera in their pocket nowadays, but before smart phones became de rigeur, the only time you were likely to see a camera would be if you were on your holidays or on Christmas Day.

King Of The Kippax's unique selling point was of course its drawings, whether they were contemporary cartoons or stadia diagrams.

So I was left with a puzzler as I neither knew anyone with a camera nor a cartoonist, so I just went with the flow and in the beginning, before I came up with a semblance of a running order or style, everything bar the kitchen sink went in!

As the tail lights of the 1980s disappeared and the dazzling headlights of the

1990s came into view, City fans were well served with the aforementioned "big three" fanzines. Other fanzines followed (see chapter 23), jostling for space on the Maine Road forecourt and in "Fanzine Corner," and for some time we must surely have offered the biggest fanzine selection at any club.

The club took a dim view initially, confusing fanzines with pirate programmes of the past and reminding supporters that the programme was the official news organ of the club! And yet they tried to get in on the action by launching *The Citizen* via the Official Supporters Club – a professionally typeset publication which looked like a thinly disguised attempt to either cash in on the fanzine boom or to try and put us out of business. Not that it fooled the fans as it did neither, and folded after just two issues!

Without a doubt, the 1990s was a golden era for the fanzine movement. Every club had at least one publication, although it came as something of a surprise when Liverpool and United fanzines appeared. "What have they got to complain about?" we asked. And yet, when it came down to it, putting loyalties aside, their fans had some of the same issues that we had, particularly with the onset of the Premier League and its associated issues: Sky TV, unsociable kick-off times, ticket allocations, prices etc. etc.

And still, several decades on, many of those issues still remain but almost all of the fanzines have long gone, ushered out together with the Pink Final, voucher sheets, the 'End Is Nigh' man and hot dog sellers and replaced, in part, by online forums, podcasts, vlogs, radio phone-ins and fans' TV channels.

Of the aforementioned big three, *BluePrint* was the first to disappear, just as it had been the first to appear, having had a couple of changes in editorship while my own fanzine survived a legally enforced name change (to *Bert Trautmann's Helmet*) and lasted for 14 years.

King Of The Kippax must surely have set some sort of record for longevity, continuing for 35 years until 2023, establishing itself as an institution along the way. It's truly remarkable that it first saw the light of day at a Second Division match at Oakwell and its 300th coincided with City being confirmed as World Club Champions.   **Noel Bayley, August 2025**

1. "SITTIN' ROUND HERE TRYIN' TO WRITE THIS BOOK"

Some background...

THE EDITOR From the 1980s, I'd sometimes go to games with my work mate Eddie. He could sit through matches passively. I can't, I sing, shout, rant, rave, curse and swear, kick every ball, head every header, and save every save. I get totally absorbed, too easily wound up, and have hardly mellowed over the years, still having sleepless nights after a loss, and would definitely kick the cat if we had one (though I don't like cats anyway). For me it's an emotional experience, for which I'm often told by Sue, (who, annoyingly, win, draw or lose always remains philosophical, although she wouldn't dare to go as far as saying "it's only a game") to calm down and "watch my language". I know it's ridiculous, but that's just me, and apparently, thousands of City and other football fans are similarly, unashamedly afflicted, for which I offer no apology.

FAMILY In 1988 we were in our early 40s and had just moved house, from Astley to Leigh, (after living in Swinton and Pendlebury, Sheffield, Conisbrough, and Keyingham) due to the arrival of baby number four, after a ten year break. Our children were Marnie (19), Danny (17), Kaye (12), and Alex (2). I was working as a mechanical engineering project manager at Amec, then Manchester Airport, Sue had left work at Lewis's to look after young Alex. All of whom have been roped

in to lend a hand at some point, (and I constantly remind them that they don't know what it's like to have an embarrassing dad, like I did!) including Sue's mum Marie, who did some typing early doors, and her dad Bill, who sometimes sold.

FAN ON THE BOARD I was appointed as such in season 1994/95, when we didn't sign or sell a player. Brian Horton was manager, and I attended parts of Board meetings, where it became apparent that Board members were on a different planet. Example being: Club Secretary - *"We have to keep the ticket office open on match days because sometimes fans forget to bring their season ticket books."* Director: *"Can't we just tell them to f*ck off?"* Obviously, I put him right on that one. The FOTB appointment was retired at the end of the season, when I persuaded the Board to agree to 'Points of Blue' meetings, later replaced by City Matters, where all the same old problems seem to be still in place.

HITTING THE HIGH NOTE? Fanzines often claim to be into music, and fashion as well as football, well two out of three ain't bad! Music certainly brightens up our lives, and takes our minds off things. We've put on a few KK Karaoke nights over the years, including testimonial evenings for Ian Brightwell and Paul Lake. Whilst on the mic, all troubles can be forgotten. Current venues are the Atherton Arms, with big Steve, and the Cart and Horses, Astley, with Jenny, where landlord Tom is a massive Blue. My taste is fairly mainstream, certainly compared to buddies  Mick Thompson and Gary Phillips, Rock Royalty. My current top ten includes 1) Edie (The Cult), 2) Baby Blue (Badfinger), 3) Comfortably Numb (Pink Floyd), 4) Times Like These (Foo, Foo Fighters), 5) Behind Blue Eyes (The Who), 6) Thunderstruck (AC/DC), 7) Run to The Hills (Iron Maiden), 8) Seven Seas (Echo and The Bunnymen), 9) Cats in the Cradle (Harry Chapin), 10) The Passenger (Iggy Pop), and much more.

"SATURDAY'S THE DAY WE PLAYED THE GAME?" Or every other day and time of the week, unlike in the old days 3pm on a Saturday? Except for which ever day Christmas or Boxing Day landed, (we once played Plymouth Argyle home and away on those days in 1946/47!) also games were played on Good Friday and Easter Monday or Tuesday. F.A. Cup replays? Wednesday afternoons at 3pm pre floodlights, and winter games often played at 2.30pm to finish before it went dark or evening games at 5.30pm. However, with the current TV schedules, it's gone beyond all reason, and has affected sales.

HOW WAS IT FOR US? The KK fanzine years went from 1988 until 2024, 35 years or so.. Early state of play was - City were in Division 2, England fans were banned from Europe after Heysel, Thatcher was PM, Colin Moynihan was Sports minister, we were threatened with ID cards, away fans were excluded at Luton, we were fenced in, stewarding and policing left a lot to be desired, hooliganism was rife, and reporting in the media did not reflect the views and behaviour of match going fans. Football fans were all branded as hooligans and it got so bad that if you went for a job interview, you couldn't admit to being a football fan. The Football Supporters Association was formed in 1985, where fans of most clubs found they had common issues, and fanzines started to blossom, to give fans a voice and especially, bring out the humour rather than extolling the violence. There were about forty zines produced when we started, rising to about three hundred at the peak. I had a responsible job, wasn't exactly a youngster, but I was inspired by the editor of 'Just another Wednesday', Martin Gordon, who was of a similar age and a Doctor no less, with no 'overgrown schoolboy' inhibitions. Blueprint was the first City fanzine to which I originally contributed, but I started KK due to 'editorial differences' as The Beatles may have declared, after they split?

LOWS AND HIGHS In 1988 we were in Division 2, hoping for a return in our second season in the division to the First. City went on an incredible journey, with promotions, relegations, even dropping to the lowest point in our history, 12th in the third tier in 1998. Then the rise began, in 1999, eventually regaining Premier League status, moving to the Etihad, then the Sheikh's takeover, and with shrewd investment and management, to eventually become the Centurions, multiple Premier League, F.A. Cup and League Cup winners, Domestic Quadruple, and Treble winners, European Super Cup and Club World Cup Winners, truly "the best team in the land and all the world". No longer irony!

WHAT'S IT ALL ABOUT ? It's the story of travel to games, by train and coach in the early days, then by car, ferry, boat and plane in Europe, visiting service stations, pubs (limited due to my diabetes and driving duties). Surviving punctures, crashes, breakdowns, roadworks, speed cameras, struggling to park, humping bags of zines to grounds, meeting fellow Blues and rival fans, friendships, camaraderie with ordinary fans, contributors, subscribers. observing and sometimes chatting with players and ex players, rock stars, managers and ex managers, comedians, DJs, radio and TV presenters, politicians, MPs, Knights of the Realm, broadcasters, Chairmen, ex Chairmen and authors. Ducking and diving, dodging stewards, police, facing abuse, threats, libel, slander, praise and ridicule from fellow and rival fans, and ex players and club officials, particularly when considered 'persona non grata' (as I was supposed to be happy that we'd dropped to the third tier) plus the threat of being sued always hanging over us like the sword of Damocles. It all went with the territory, the good by far outweighing the bad, but we could, of course, dish it out!

SALES Peaked at about 4,500 with KK17, not even our best issue, in 1991, whilst gradually reducing over the years to around 800 in 2023. Home sales peaked at about 1500, aways at 450. Subscriptions peaked at around 400.

THE JOURNEY We realise it's probably not as exciting or as interesting as relating tales of being chased or chasing rival fans down back alleys or whatever, or seeing it 'going off' in a pub, or rail or service stations. We hope, however, most football and fanzine folk can identify with this journey. It's as exhaustive and comprehensive as our memory which can play tricks, and notes allows, but in mitigation, I am 81! So, here we go with stories from the KK fanzines, with a few ground diagrams, toons and the odd pic chucked in to break things up, with the story of 'Selling King of the Kippax, in the Golden era of Football Fanzines' with a few extras. Enjoy.   *Dave and Sue Wallace, Summer 2025*

2. SELLERS

Initially I was the lone seller, then with my mate Tony Grayson, and eventually one by one, game by game, others volunteered, coming and going during the 35 years, ducking and diving from stewards, police, and club officials, braving the British and European weather, the wind, rain, hail, snow and very occasionally sunshine, out there at Maine Road, the Etihad, and grounds up and down the country and abroad, just for the fun of it. After all, whilst there wouldn't be a fanzine without the contributors, there's little point in producing it if it can't be sold.

Here are the hardy souls, none accustomed to selling a fanzine at first, and we doff our caps to everyone who volunteered over the years to sell.

I was first joined by **TONY GRAYSON**, RIP who had inspired us to start the fanzine in the first place, and suggested that we sell before home games, then in the Kippax tunnels at half time and outside the Kippax after games. Tony sadly died in 2006 at the young age of 54, and it is so sad that he missed the good times.

Eldest son **DANNY**, who wasn't coerced (honest) but volunteered, and sold KK from the early issues until he found better things to do, being involved in martial arts and UFC fighting.

The rest of the family, have all been roped in at some time, including **BILL**, Sue's dad, daughters **MARNIE, KAYE**, niece **RUTH**, grandson **JOE** and youngest son **ALEX**. Last but not least **SUE** has been there from the early days, once baby sitting duties were relieved, at Maine Road, and on Joe Mercer way at the Etihad until Covid put paid to ground sales.

Elder brother **FRANK** was there from the start at Maine Road, at the North stand corner and the Etihad on Joe Mercer way with his own clientele, carrying on selling until well into his 80's, until Covid struck.

TONY SEAL, Chadderton's finest, sold for a short time at Maine Road.

LOUISE BURGESS/ DEEKS/COX, Lytham-based, hooked up with the KK team very early on just after KK3 hit the streets at Sunderland, and was a brilliant seller, and so supportive. Sometimes standing in for the Ed on Soccer AM. Now spends her time with Aussie hubby Ken, between Australia and the UK, still a massive Blue.

RICHARD BURGESS, Louise's younger brother, often joined us, and was amused when we sold at Ipswich in the snow and I went over the road and advised "It's practically tropical over here". He's now a 'Big Cheese' at the BBC.

GED ISAACS, long time seller, sold from the early days after meeting the Ed on the long train journey to Brighton in 1989, and carried on until the very end. Often driving the KK team, sometimes separately with Mick, Jason and Carin.

GIDEON SEYMOUR was also on that train and became a top seller for a number of years at Maine Road and away games.

BIG DEAN MCDERMOTT, was an occasional seller at Maine Road.

DAVE FREEMAN, a Coventry Blue, musician, who co-wrote Annie Lennox's 'No More I Love You's, sold in the Isle of Man.

STEVE WELCH, sold briefly at Maine Road, before starting his own fanzine 'Main Stand View', with his dad Alex RIP.

JOHN KEOHANE was a stalwart seller from the Maine Road days selling at home and away games, travelling in the KK mobile.

WAYNE NORRIS joined the selling team early on, and one of his proudest sales (although a freebie) was passing KK8 through the open window of Eddie Large's car in the Nottingham Forest car park after the 1-0 loss in 1990. Wayne now lives in Australia, regularly returning to the UK to watch the Blues.

NICK LEESON, yep him, sold a few at Fulham in 1999/2000 season.

HALIFAX STEVE RIP, volunteered to sell in Europe, when we couldn't make it, particularly at Poznan.

SEAN RILEY, long time KK contributor with his HWIFY match day experiences, travelled separately with his missus Jane, Wilkie and others, and was an occasional seller.

JOHN JACOB was a prominent seller from the Maine Road days at the front of the ground right through to his Ashton New Road sales pitch, and some away games plus mentoring Andy and Stephen Woodhouse in the art of selling. When we were on a freebie at Anfield on our wedding anniversary, we arranged to meet at the Carr Mill pub on the East Lancs Road to hand over some zines for him to sell. We couldn't believe it when he sailed right past us, but we managed to catch up at the ground! John became a steward at The Etihad

CARIN BOWMAN added another female touch to proceedings, and brother Spencer helped out on occasions.

FLAT CAP MIKE, nicknamed as such as he was critical of Alan Ball's flat cap, on the radio. Mike was a born salesman who upset a local resident at Highbury (away entry was via a row of terraced houses) when shouting KK on the street outside, being berated by an angry woman householder. She obviously, didn't realise she lived next door to a football ground. Mike sometimes drove us to away games.

DANTE FRIEND sold KK in particular at Crystal Palace in the Q/F of the League cup in 1995, before producing his own fanzine 'The Fightback' (considering KK to be an old folks fanzine!). He was involved in the 'Free the 30,000' campaign, and currently with the 1894 group at the Etihad, and considers the Eds as his 'surrogate parents!

PETER BRODIE RIP, a born salesman joined us at The Etihad as he said he had "time to kill" before kick off, taking up a spot at the South stand area of the ground, after encouraging a group hug before taking up his pitch. Peter, was a member of the Laurel and Hardy Appreciation Society.

ANDY and **STEPHEN MOOREHOUSE**'s dad David approached us at the Etihad advising his sons wished to sell KK as Steve had a mate who sold 'United We Stand' (boo!) and he wanted to get in on the fanzine selling act. The boys reduced the average age of zine sellers, and sold around the main and south stand areas, and some away grounds, until other commitments took over.

STEVE HUSBANDS volunteered to sell at the Etihad, as he had a short window before assisting his dad into the ground, before kick off.

NOELLE ATKINSON RIP, sold at Maine Road on occasions, and travelled with the team in the KK mobile, to certain away games.

WAYNE X, musician (drum and bass) was a short term contributor and seller, but became disillusioned after the 2008 takeover.

STEVE and **CATH KNOTT** are great friends, who sold briefly at Bournemouth.

MICK THOMPSON, Rochdale Blue, big rock music fan, sold at Maine Road.

STEVE PARISH, the Blue Vicar, once surprised us, turning up at Crystal Palace, as he didn't usually attend away games. Steve then became the longest serving and most successful KK seller home and away, often driving, and is still going strong..

TOM PARISH was a comparative newcomer, making his debut at Fulham and has since never looked back, making his pitch in front of the Colin Bell stand entrance his very own. Tom is easily recognisable with his height and 'Jesus' like appearance. Competes with his dad for most sales, and often drove us to games.

JIMMY GARDNER, an Evertonian, and mate of son Alex's is the sort of guy who gets where water can't. He's got some bottle, selling KK before and after his team lost 5-1 to City at the Etihad in season 2003/04!

NOEL BAYLEY often travelled in the KK mobile, sold in particular at a reserve game when we were unable to give him a lift to Southampton, along with his own fanzine Electric Blue, later Bert Trautmann's Helmet.

Happy days then, massive thanks from the Editors to each and every one, who championed the cause.

- Ged Isaacs

- Noel and Dave

- 'Flat Cap' Mike Sutcliffe

- Kaye Price

- Tom Parish

- Alex and Marnie

■ Ruth Kelly

■ Danny Wallace in Beefeater gear

■ Steve Husbands

■ The ED & Sue

■ Steve Parish

■ Joe and Dave

■ Dave and Louise

■ Richard Burgess

■ Rogue zine seller Nick Leeson

■ Steve Welch

■ Spencer & Caron

■ Steve & Andy Woodhouse

■ Peter Brodie

■ Chris Sievey RIP (Frank Sidebottom) The Ed, Mick Thompson

■ John Jacob

■ Sean Riley

■ Big Dean McDermott & partner

18

■ Dave Freeman, Lisa, Gideon Seymour

■ John Keohane

■ Steve & Cath Knott

■ Ged & Dante

■ Wayne Norris & son Simon

■ Tony Grayson

1. HOME SALES

Once the zines were collected from the printers, later delivered (luxury!), it was all hands to the pump. Boxes were unloaded from the car and transferred into the garage, numbered, then zines counted and checked for quality. They were then bagged up, ready for home game selling, taking into consideration, whether it was first, second or third day of sales, and praying for good weather, especially hoping for no rain or snow, as everyone would then scurry past, and no one wanted a 'frost bitten' fanzine.

MAINE ROAD

From 1988/89 until 2003, 15 years. We'd drive to the ground, setting off in ample time to give us a good hour before kick off for selling, picking up older brother Frank in Clifton on the way, and sometimes John Keohane; park up, deliver to Colin Lund's Soccer Shop on the corner of Claremont Road and Maine Road, and the loyal sellers would then pick up the bags of zines, and take up their positions.

■ Platt Lane stand opened 1993, new Kippax stand opened 1995, plus temporary stands (Gene Kelly's 'Singing in the Rain') at each corner.

It was street parking initially, and on one occasion, the 3-3 Derby game, I ran out of zines, flagged a taxi down, was driven back to the car to pick up more stock, then driven back to my selling spot. Later we secured a parking place on the Kippax car park, but after being booted off, we moved to the St Edwards school play ground, both dead handy for nipping back to the car to replenish supplies, or dumping the used bags, and cash!

Main selling spots were outside the North stand, and at the front of the ground near the souvenir shop, in the Kippax tunnels at half time, and outside the Kippax after the game, We generally rubbed shoulders with other fanzine sellers. Initially I sold on my own, later being joined by all the volunteers.

We were often hassled by the Police and club stewards, until we obtained a letter from the council, which clarified that as we weren't a periodical, and didn't have a stall, we were OK to sell outside on the street. The club objected to us selling inside, particularly when we became more critical due to our awfulness both on and off the pitch, sometimes having our bags of zines confiscated, so it was a case of ducking and diving.

■ Oldest seller brother Frank only one with a buyer! (Pic thanks to Richard Foster)

Amongst the comments, most of which were complimentary, was this one, every home game, from the Blue who, after walking past the souvenir shop, scarf and poster sellers barked at us outside the souvenir shop selling point "Making money out of City". (If he only knew the trouble we went too?)

We also sold in the Kippax tunnels at half time, and post match outside the Kippax, usually receiving choice comments after yet another dismal performance on the pitch.

One particular low, by the stewards, was at home to Bradford City in season 1996/97, when we had the bags of zines taken off us. I finished up having a strop, going back to the car and listening to the game on the radio, it was a 2-0 win.

We also sold to the queues of Blues, waiting patiently, or not, for away tickets, generally, early on a Saturday morning. Sometimes we sold on the coaches before they set off for away games, then we'd dash to Piccadilly station, to catch the 'special train'. Any opportunity to sell fanzines were taken, we couldn't afford to wait for fans to seek us out, we had to be one step ahead.

ETIHAD STADIUM

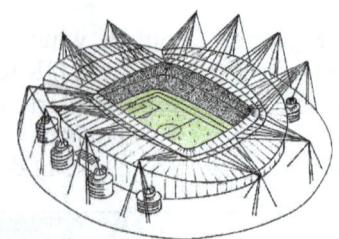

The Etihad was a much bigger selling challenge than Maine Road due to the vastness of the ground, and surrounding area, which needed sussing out early doors, i.e. where the crowds came from, who bought, where to pitch.

■ The Etihad, opened in August 2003, south stand extended in 2015, and North stand anticipated in 2025.

It was a similar journey, via Clifton, but different route, than to Maine Road, We initially parked in the North car park, later in Mary D's and finally in the East car park, and it was always a trek to get to our spots as the bags got heavier as the zines got bigger and bigger.

Sales pitches were established with Sue, and sometimes Ged, at the top of Joe Mercer way, Steve P. at Commonwealth Way, Tom P.. outside the Colin Bell stand, Steve Husbands sometimes near the Mercedes garage, Peter Brodie RIP, Steve and Andy Woodhouse outside the South stand. My pitch was on Ashton New Road near the lights, for a while aided by John Jacob.

As the South stand car park was kindly donated to away fans. It was therefore a walk from Ashton New Road to the East stand, although sometimes I was allowed the short cut through the car park.

After selling, we'd queue up for bag and personal effects searches, before entering the ground, usually arriving late and annoying those on our row. Tom and Steve sold at half time, and at the end of the game we'd leave early to get to our selling spot on Commonwealth Way, further away since we were moved due to the 93.20 club, thus missing the end of games, weather permitting, whilst Steve and Tom competed with each other around Joe Mercer Way.

By now there were only ourselves, *City till I Cry*, and briefly *One Million Miles* left, and we were soon the only remaining zine.

We obtained a letter from the club permitting us to sell inside and outside the ground, but were still often challenged by stewards who hadn't been briefed. On one occasion my bag was nicked by a young female scrote, who I had to chase after down JM Way, to retrieve the bag and give her a piece of my mind!

On another occasion, the evening game v Everton It was a hot night, I'd been selling for an hour, and was uncomfortable (at 78 years old). I trudged over to the turnstiles with the remaining zines in a back pack which the steward ordered me to take off, which was tricky. I asked if he'd just peer into my bag, which he refused so we exchanged pleasantries, with him advising he'd "let me in this time". Turns out some bright spark at the club had decreed that only A5 size bags would be allowed in, even though most merchandise sold in the store was A4 or bigger?

Next home game, we were in the Chairman's lounge, on our 50th wedding anniversary, and treated like Royalty by the club, as we beat Liverpool 5-0. Next home game was Palace. I'd had a hypo the night before, but, after selling, had to walk all the way round from Ashton New Road to Commonwealth Way, and queue up for twenty minutes, whilst the roar went up for our first goal. The same stroppy steward spotted me saying sarcastically, "my favourite supporter", and I countered with, " yes I hope you're not going to be daft again". Annoyed , he said, "right you're not going in". Naturally I lost my temper, instead of remaining cool, calm and collected, and eventually I did get to my seat but by half time. City, obviously inspired by my presence, went on to win 5-0. No sympathy from 'Steve Graham look alike' Ken, who sits next to me, who advised - "It's 'cos you're a gobshite". A bit harsh, but we had a laugh, as I had to agree, after a bollocking from Sue, for being cantankerous?

I did, often, become an unofficial Club Ambassador, though I was often asked the way to the pubs, certain stands, the megastore, ticket office, Asda, and particularly the away end. In exasperation, I once produced a cardboard sign to clarify, and an away fan exclaimed "all that money, and they've got a cheap sign like that!" A Blue then tore it down, as he objected having to walk all round the away car park, but after I protested, he bought a fanzine. I was once asked if I was the 'Real Renegade!'

Again it was always a pleasure to chat to fans whilst selling, but one of the strangest comments came from a Blue, Wigan home 2006/07, full of bravado in front of his mates but at a safe distance, who came out with this little gem, "do you have a map of how to get to Old Trafford in there, after all you're there every other week". Side splitting, but I didn't see him the following week at Reading!

THE MINICOMS STADIUM

The Mini Coms stadium was utilised for reserve games, which we occasionally attended. We were made to park in the North car park, a quarter of an hour's walk away. The empty stand close to the pitch was for VIP's only, so we 'plebs' were seated on the far side, with not one, but two running tracks between us and the pitch, so we were a 'javelin's throw' away from the action. The floodlights pointed in the opposite directions, so it was not a pleasant experience, and we hardly bothered selling. Games were then transferred to the Academy, which became the Joie stadium where the Women's team also played. We did attend a few games, but the logistics of parking and the trek to the ground, with health issues worsening, meant we rarely attended and when we did we never bothered selling.

4. PRE-SEASON & FRIENDLIES

Gone are the days when City would action summer tours, to accessible places like Europe, Scandinavia, the Isle of Man, Ireland, and even filling the coffers of our less fortunate neighbours, the likes of Stockport, Tranmere, Oldham, Port Vale, and Bury, which are included in the relevant club sections. From 1991/92 until 2014/15, City travelled to Florida, the I.o.M, Scarborough, Scotland, Ireland, Hamburg, Carlisle, Rochdale, Ballymena, Barcelona, and Morecambe.

1991/92 FLORIDA

(Despite the above, this was a one off!)

THE ED March 1991, and the rumours were spreading regarding City's possible Summer Tour. Maybe a trip to Scandinavia, Hong Kong or a Tournament in Spain. Then the news broke, in early April, of the 'Alan Hudson Transatlantic Soccer Classic', it was renamed later, but it was to be held in Florida, in the US of A, no less.

For most, including ourselves, it was a pipe dream, especially if you've never been abroad before on holiday, or seen the Blues play on foreign soil, though everyone seemed to be going to the USA in those days.

It appeared in the Derby home programme, a package deal being advertised, and again in the Sunderland programme. It somehow got us thinking, we'd love to go, but only if we could get a cheaper deal, and we could ALL go. A package was put together that we couldn't refuse, and we were IN. Brilliant! We must've been mad, but what the hell?

The whole thing gathered momentum, it was unstoppable. The tournament included, Celtic, City, Wednesday, and Forest, and would be held in Tampa. What a great idea by Alan Hudson the ex-Chelsea and Arsenal player, one event a year leading up to the World Cup to create interest for the Yanks. Soccer fans going over there in friendship and fun, what could be better?

The KK Florida special was underway, no turning back now, we had to book early, although we knew there were slight doubts about the official sanctions. Dates of games were advised, deposits paid, and the final instalments settled in mid-May. Then the whole world caved in. Phone call from Colin Lund, "Are you sitting down? It's off. They're trying to change it to Bermuda".

The following Thursday in the souvenir shop, Eddie Phillips was giving people their deposits back for the official trip, so the penny finally dropped, hopes dashed, chins on the floor, KK Florida special scrapped (although partly utilised in KK 18). The real reason was unclear, but the Sunday People printed a story which suggested that the US Soccer Federation wouldn't sanction the tournament, worried that the crowds wouldn't come, which would affect Tampa's or even the USA's chances of hosting the 1994 World Cup, or Alan Hudson not clinching sponsorship deals. There was also talk of a personality clash between Hudson and Rodney Marsh, who was the Tampa representative on a World Cup Task Force, who decided which tournaments would take place in the USA, though Hudson was invited to a meeting which he didn't attend.

Anyway, we decided to go ahead. Sue, Me, Danny, Kaye, Alex, Joy, Richard, Louise and Gideon. Joy had superbly sorted our two hired cars, Buick's no less with air conditioning. We stayed in a luxury villa in Clearwater with its own pool, but were a couple of hours away from Disney World, and other theme parks. So we would need to set off at 7 am to arrive at 9, to beat the queues. We attended a Tampa soccer match, surprising ex Blue Steve Kinsey who was sitting on the bench, and turned round in astonishment when we chanted his name, plus a Philadelphia Phillies baseball game, and took in the sights. We met up

with Rodney Marsh, and arranged an interview (KK 19), so all in all it was a great experience, with no City games to complicate matters, and it gave us some articles for KK's 18 and 19, including a Q and A with Rodney.

I later met up with Alan Hudson in a pub in Stoke, then went back to his house, which was sparse, to chat and watch the play off final between Leicester and Blackburn (0-1), with his son and a relative. His wife or ex-wife, called round, and they had a row at the front door. I didn't publish the interview, but it was pretty clear that Alan wasn't capable of organising the Florida competition, as Rodney suspected.

CARLISLE UNITED
■ Brunton Park. My first visit was in season 1983/84, 0-2. Two friendlies in the KK years, 1988/89 and 1991/92, both unattended.

Awayday Zine Land of sheep And Glory.

1994/95 ISLE OF MAN

DAVE FREEMAN "Summer 1994, and when the tournament was announced, Brian Wardle persuaded us to go, then backed out at the last minute, leaving The Ed, who drove, myself, partner Lisa, and Gideon to make the trip. On the way out on the ferry from Fleetwood, it had been very hot. Blues were out on the decks, sunbathing, singing, with some lads drinking beer down a funnel through a plastic tube, and passing out in the heat. One lone rag fan with his Cliff Richard T-shirted wife were spotted. They were off to a wedding, unwittingly booked on a Blue boat.

We were able to watch the boys train, have a chat with the City IOM supporters club members, plus Brian Horton and Tony Book, and then enjoyed the nightly entertainment. The Ed had produced an A5, KK number 38 and a half which Gideon and myself sold at the games.

The tournament was held in an Athletic stadium, a bit inappropriate. First game was on the Friday night, against the IOM team, Nicky Summerbee scoring on his debut with City winning 4-1. Next afternoon Oldham beat them 7-1, and in the final City lost 3-0 to Oldham who lifted the Okell trophy.

Homeward bound was quiet, except for the bar which was noisy, with people sleeping off the weekend. We'd had our footy on the beach, plus, been to a grunge bar, seen the squad train, then took photos, had chats, and overall, apart from the final result, a good weekend. A few extremists vandalised the promenade and some telephone boxes but the weekend was mostly harmless and friendly.

We attended an IOM supporters club meal and race meeting plus the Ed managed an interview with Rick Wakeman, who introduced Norman Wisdom to him, but we missed the Frank Sidebottom show."

1996/97 SCARBOROUGH

COLIN SMITH OF ASTLEY "I found out about this game on teletext on the Saturday morning and asked the Mrs if she fancied a day at the seaside, "Why, who are City playing" she asked? So off we went to

Scarborough. Arrived at the McCain stadium at 2pm, just as the team arrived, so obtained a couple of free tickets off Alan Kernaghan. After chatting to other Blues, including Michael Brown's dad, very helpful stewards took us up to their main stand and into their club for a couple of beers. Strong City team but 0-0 at half time, against a 'Boro side including ex-rag Andy Ritchie. On the way to the loo, I passed the away changing room and could hear Alan Ball effing and blinding at those who'd played in the first half. Ball was screaming at the players about their poor first half performance, and had a real go at the strikers who had been particularly poor. He replaced Kavelashvili with Quinn for the second half, but despite Kinkladze and Ian Thompstone scoring, it finished 2-2, named by KK as a 'Desmond', a description adopted by the mainstream media!

Back to the dressing room window for part two. Ball continued his tirade at the team, much to the amusement of other travelling Blues, and a couple of stewards. I didn't think this was the way to speak to International players two weeks before the start of the season but time will tell?"

(Ed: It certainly did!)

Awayday Zine *The Seadog Bites Back.*

1996/97 TOUR IN SCOTLAND

THE ED City played Livingston (4-1), Stirling Albion (0-0), and Falkirk (1-1). We drove up for the Kilmarnock game and, after Alex (10) refused to stay in a B & B ("I'm not staying in someone's house!") booked in at a hotel I'd stayed at when working on site at Rockware Glass Irvine in the 1970's, It hadn't changed at all! We won the game 4-0. Rugby Park was a fine modernised stadium, there was a big City turnout, maybe 1,500 to 2,000, the locals were friendly, and we actually won in style, so it was obvious we were going to go into the next division which was unfortunately the Third and not the First tier!

I sold some KK 60s at the end of Wallace Road! There were a group of reds in the stand opposite (even though United were playing not too far away, at Lancaster) hoping for a City loss. They all left disappointed at 3-0, and I was surprised they didn't face a City 'welcoming party.'

On the way home at the Services, we chatted to City director Ian Niven who gave me a look when I said I was confident for the new season, advising me that we'd only had one decent manager recently, that being Howard Kendall!

Awayday Zine *Killie Ken (Keeps you in the know!), Paper Toses.*

2000/01 IRELAND

JOE "Dolly, son 'Podge' and I travelled over to Belfast and Windsor Park, home of Linfield. Blues were overwhelmed with the hospitality of the Linfield fans, being introduced to the delights of the city's watering holes.

Linfield were the first opponents in the two-match tournament, ground surrounded by houses bedecked with loyalist regalia graffiti.

Inside the ground we felt safe amongst more than 3,000 Blues. To the right the spectacular Cavehill mountain looked down on the lush pitch on a warm and clear day. We were full of infectious optimism for the new season. Around us are Blues of every age and accent including a surprising number of locals, glad of this rare opportunity. Two stalwarts of the P. and W. branch unfurl a flag, and it's announced that the match ball is sponsored by the wonderful Ballymena branch, many of whom make the long trip to Maine Road for every home match and keep the faith in a hostile sea of red hysteria. It's easier to be a 'cowboy in Rochdale' than a 'Blue in Ballymena'. These are real fans, and fixtures like this are one small way City can acknowledge their incredible fidelity. Tommy Wright on his return to his home town played the full 90 minutes as City ran out 4-0 winners, with goals from Goater, Kennedy, Horlock, and the new 'slim Bob' Taylor.

On to Drogheda, which is down south in the R.O.I. It's a typical Irish town full of booming bustling, and affluence in a chaotic way, too small for the number of people and not planned with the motor car in mind. The place is full of Manchester City fans, and locals tell us how glad they are we're back where we belong. An hour before kick-off the chippies are full of Blues, one of whom

burns his finger on a chip, but he feels no pain, responding to my son with some advice which he has no intention of heeding.

"When you're older, don't go to foreign countries, get drunk and make a fool of yourself"

The ground, United Park is a throwback to times gone by. Both sides are available to spectators; the two ends are occupied by the Galway supporters club Tricolour and eager ball boys. The ground is full to its 4,000 capacity. First half was the Mark Kennedy show and Prior had a goal disallowed for offside. News came through that Goater's injury at Windsor Park meant he would need surgery and would miss the first month of the season. SWP came on, making an immediate impact, and the breakthrough came with his goal. Then in a quiet spell, chants of ,"big fat, big fat Bob, big fat Bobby Taylor", rang out and Bob smiled ruefully! Then it was "Feed the Bob and he will score", until the final version, "Starve the Bob and he will score". It finished at 1-0 and the announcement that "everyone was welcome to post match refreshments in the club bar", got the biggest cheer. We'd enjoyed a happy couple of days in Ireland, and looked forward to City embarking on a new, frightening, and exciting experience.

(Ed - we sadly missed this one as we had to finish KK87

HALIFAX TOWN/FC HALIFAX

Just a couple of friendlies in seasons in season 1999/2000 (2-0). Whitesnake's *'Here I Go Again'* and *'Is This Love'* played pre-KO. Despite a half empty terrace, stewards were getting Blues arrested for encroaching in gangways painted with yellow lines, though no one was standing within twenty metres of each other on the terrace, plus there were two individual pitch invasions. Then in season 2001/02 a 2-1 win, KK96 celebrated Keegan's arrival, and the news came through that we'd signed Eyal Berkovic, boosting sales.

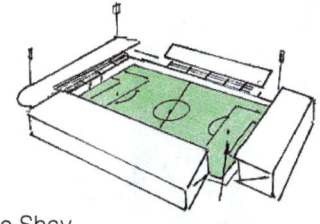
■ The Shay.

Awayday Zine Shaymen Down South.

2002/03 HAMBURG

THE ED I didn't fancy the trip at first, but with the "part time supporter" jibes and all that, it became irresistible, so Ged and I got a late booking with International Travel, Spike's/Tony O' Neill's outfit (once rags' top boy?) and flew out on the Saturday morning. Back on Sunday afternoon, foggy at Liverpool, but ok. 370 on the plane, lots of banter, early in the morning. "But you've all got your wits about you", said Katie, the steward.

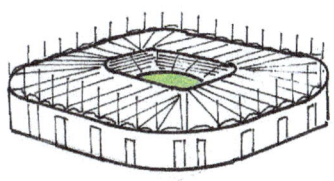
■ Volkparkstadion.

We waited a few hours for our rooms, met up with our room mate Steve Turner, and lazed in a bar, so missed the boat party laid on by Dirk Hansen from the Hamburg supporters club. There were stories of bother on the Friday night after St Paulli's game, but OK for us. Lovely hot day, picked up two £6.50 tickets from a kiosk. Hero's welcome for Kev, superb stadium, beer swilled in sight of the pitch, but the German anthem was sadly booed, and 5-1 chants (after England's win). Game not much to write home about and a 1-0 loss.

We sold KK104 in two currencies, three Euros or two English pounds. "You have a very good team." a Hamburg fan said to me after the game. We had a stroll down the Reeperbahn at night. Sunday morning, we had time for a few drinks down by the lake, where there was some sort of cycling event going on, (Lycra shorts??) and a superb drumming band. There were plenty of German youths milling about, wearing Iron Maiden T-shirts. We bumped into Ian

Cheeseman, then it was the 5pm flight back, but 150 Blues were still in the bar at 5.15 pm so, inevitably, the flight was delayed. One Blue was chucked off the plane for misbehaving, but overall, it was a decent trip, and I was back in time for Karaoke at The Britannia in Swinton at night. Big Blue Landlord, Garry though, was still on his way home! Apparently, the official club coach trip was a shambles and Blues were offered a refund.

ROCHDALE

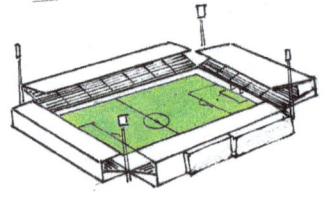

It was a nice hot night in 2002. Not an all-ticket match, but Ged picked some up by fluke as he actually went to collect Hamburg tickets, so we were ■ Spotland. able to dodge the queues. Kick-off was delayed for half an hour or so, Rochdale being delighted with the attendance. City won 6-0. Other friendlies were played in 2003/04, won 4-0, and 2006/07, won 3-2.

Awayday Zine *Exceedingly Good Pies.*

MANSFIELD TOWN   ■ Field Mill. Just the friendly in 2003/04, which Ged attended as we weren't back from holiday.

Awayday Zine *Follow The Yellow Brick Road.*

2006/07 BALLYMENA UNITED

THE ED Tommy Wright was their manager. It was my first ever visit to the Emerald Isle September 2006, where all my dad and his family came from. EasyJet flight booked by Steve P. (who didn't make the trip) from Liverpool, for about £40. I was chauffeured round by KK subscriber N. Irish Blue Allan Wilson, then wined and dined with his mum and dad. We went up to Giants Causeway to surprise Ged and Co, who'd belatedly decided against it, afterwards going straight to the ground. Sold a few KK143's, and it looked like a sell-out of about 5,000 with plenty of Blues in attendance. A marching band entertained, taking me back to the Beswick prize band and Sylvia Farmer days at Maine Road. The game was a bit of a struggle. Pearcy came on in the second half and we finally won it with two late goals. Post match, the players walked round applauding the crowd, which was good PR. Alan dropped me off at one of my relatives in Belfast, Sharon, whose hubby Noel is a 'big cheese' on Irish TV, but a Spurs fan. Sharon ("sons are studying in Manchester, but support United") then took me on a whistle stop tour of the city and I flew home on the Wednesday afternoon after a great trip, hoping City would do it again, sometime.

2009/10 GLASGOW RANGERS

THE ED A fellow Blue, Andy Williams, had kept in contact with ex Blue and Glaswegian John McTavish from the City team of the fifties, who assisted with regard to my Century City book in which he featured. Andy advised that John would be interested in attending the game, and could we help?

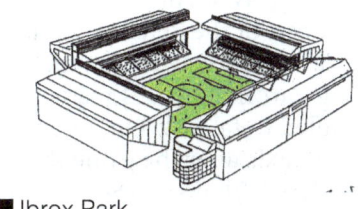
■ Ibrox Park.

Sue and I drove up on the day, and met Danny Wilson and Bernard Halford at the ground who provided us with a ticket for John who we'd arranged to meet. We also met up with Mark Dingwall, editor of 'the Gers' fanzine Follow, Follow. Swapped and sold KK180, plus ace KK contributor and seller, Louise Deeks and her young son Freddie joined us. She'd warned him that City might not win, as home friendlies usually benefitted the home team! Inevitably the game was a disappointing 3-2 loss, but not a big deal, and we enjoyed our chats with John who was excellent company. We stayed over at Louise's house in Helensburgh, for a pleasant stay before driving home to face the new season.

2009/10 BARCELONA

THE ED Off we went from the Blue Camp to the Nou Camp, home of the European Champions Barcelona, who'd just beaten United in the final, inspired by their rookie manager Pep Guardiola, and star man Lionel Messi, with the type of football "that could never be successful in the Premier league?" What a momentous trip it was, organised by Steve P. We set off

■ The Nou Camp.

on the Tuesday evening from Liverpool airport with a fair smattering of Blues including Mrs Onuoha and one of her daughters. Nice hotel, hot of course in Barca, in fact the hottest day of the year. We enjoyed a little bit of sightseeing, including the Olympic stadium and museum, which were fantastic.

Then it was down to the Goa beach bar to meet up with resident Blue Patrick Knowles, (his claim to fame is being in the famous 1968 pic at Newcastle at the side of his hero Franny who had just scored the 4th goal) for drinks, chats and songs with fellow Blues. Patrick had hoped to organise various events, but was generally thwarted. Then it was off to the game, with drinks and snacks in a local bar, with time to give the locals a rendition of "Barca 2 United 0, Barcelona, Barca 2 United 0, Barcelo-o-na…" which went down well, one Catalan advising that we'd win the League that season? We were on the top tier, half way line, with the Barca fans, and after an impressive light show, their players were introduced individually.

What a performance from City. Martin Petrov scored the goal against the run of play. Weiss did well as did Shay Given and Dunney (as announced!) and the rest of the defence. Could there be a better place than the awesome Nou Camp to receive a text that the rags had lost at Burnley, whilst we were beating Barcelona 1-0? I made the announcement, but with little response from the baffled Catalans! "Oh, I never felt more like Singin' the Blues!" Hardly any buses or taxis after the game though which made it a late, late, night, and my feet suffered. Thanks to Steve for picking up some plasters on the Thursday morning at the local chemist, (Steve stayed on for another day) for a quick patch up before the flight home. Again, in good company, and the prick in the united shirt got plenty of stick I'm pleased to say.

2011/12 INTERNATIONAL DUBLIN TOURNAMENT

THE ED We set off on the Friday morning at 9am, with friends Joe, and Dolly driving, down to Holyhead to catch the packed mid-day ferry over to Dublin's fair city. After settling at the hotel, we ate then ambled over to the Temple bar area, and enjoyed some good music in the Thunder cafe. I'd braced myself for The Irish Rover, Seven Drunken Nights, Wild Rover, Fields of Athenry etc but we rocked along as we were treated to Crowded House, Floyd, Neil Young etc.

Saturday, first game v Airtricity at the Aviva, an impressive stadium but with a very shallow end behind one goal. It's hemmed in by houses and the railway line so it was not possible to walk all round. There was a smattering of Blues, plenty of Celtic fans behind the goal and in the top tier doing the Poznan, and booing Vlad Weiss mercilessly.

■ Aviva Stadium.

It was 0-0 at half time, when a goofy kid said "Manu are better, all you've got is money", so he got a mouthful. 3-0 at full time. Second game, after an impressive display of drumming from the locals was Inter v Celtic, which Inter won.

Post match we purchased, from some enterprising youngsters, some toilet rolls sporting Fergie's head, which were later, put to good use! We beat Inter 3-0 to lift the trophy, and after the games we drove up to Draperstown, stopping off at the services, where a car load of Irish rags commented, after spotting our City scarves on show, "we'll do you next week at the Charity shield". "Oh, like you did in the semi - final?" "Oh yes, you'll dine out on that for the next 50 years". We were hoping for a 6-1 win like in 1968, but had to wait a wee bit longer for that to arrive! We stayed at Dolly's mums, then visited my relative Sharon and her husband Noel, before driving up to catch the ferry across to Stranraer, and home. It was a very pleasant trip with good company.

2014/15 DUNDEE

THE ED Ged drove Jason and myself, there and back on the day with no real incident of note and not many sales. It was interesting to clock that the Dundee and Dundee United grounds are practically next to each other, and the Dundee supporters crossed over the road rather than walk past United's ground!

It was a 2-1 loss, one of their goals coming from a penalty, initially saved by Willie Caballero, but their player netted the rebound. We sold a few KK215s, leftovers from the previous season.

Awayday Zine Derry Rumba.

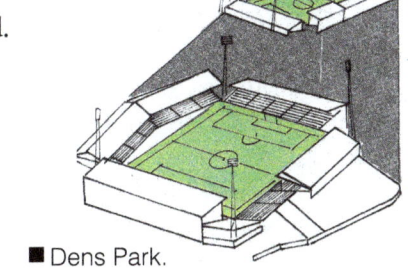

■ Dens Park.

MORECAMBE

Selling KK at the end of the game at Christie Park which City won. One sad bastard walked past, at a safe distance, and pulled open his jacket to reveal the despicable, antiquated, rag logo. "Envious?" he said. "F*ck off". Why anyone would drive up from London to watch City reserves, just shows their mentality.

5. GLASGOW & NORTH EAST

Unlike the HS2, we kick off 'up Norf', travelling up to Glasgow, Darlington, Newcastle and Sunderland

DARLINGTON

Just the one visit to division 3s Quakers, in the F.A. Cup 2nd round in 1998/99 season. It was a freezing cold evening in December on a Friday Sky TV night, and Tony G. and I travelled up after work selling KK74 in the back streets around the ground.

City went a goal down after 16 minutes, ex Blue Gary Bennett doing the biz, with Blues chanting "Where's our City gone?" Paul Dickov (77) rescued us in the 1-1 draw, and Michael Brown scored the only goal in the replay in front of only 8,595 at Maine Road.

■ Darlington, Feethams, vacated in 2003 for the ill-fated Arena.

Away Day zines *Mission Impossible, Where's the Money gone, Darlo, It's Just Like Watching Brazil, Mission Terminated.*

GLASGOW CELTIC

First KK visit was for the Wednesday night pre-season friendly in 2008. Tom drove, in the rain, and we had a look at the Scottish football museum at Hampden Park, before moving on to Parkhead, which was very impressive. Celtic's "You'll Never Walk Alone" anthem, was met with "Just like Manchester, your city is Blue!" We went ahead through Petrov, but they pulled one back for 1-1.

Our first competitive game came in the Champions league, group stage 1st leg in season 2016/17. Celtic 3 City 3. Dembele (3) opened, Fernandinho (11) equalised, then Sterling (20 OG), Sterling (28) making amends, for 2-2. Dembele (47) put them ahead again but Nolito (55) in for the injured KDB, made it 3-3.

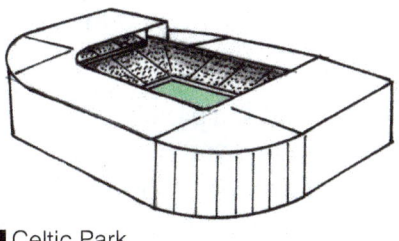

■ Celtic Park.

We had a good drive up in Tom's car. We queued for almost two hours in the rain to pick up our tickets, at the designated location. It would've been nice if the club had sorted the hall out so Blues could have sheltered from the weather. We parked in a side street, had a snack, picked up a Souvenir programme produced at £5 (a bit different from the friendly in 1970 at Hampden Park, which was one shilling (5p), but the incessant rain inhibited sales. City showed character to come back in the match and whilst the draw was a little disappointing it was great to be part of a fantastic atmospheric evening, City fans, in loud voice, more than holding our own. I wouldn't have missed it for the world. Slight delay on the way home when a puncture had to be fixed but overall, an uneventful trip.

2nd leg December 6th (a 'dead rubber' as City had already qualified, and Celtic couldn't advance to the knock out stage) City 1 (Iheanacho 8) Celtic 1 (City loanee Roberts 5) 51,297 with 2,924 Celtic.

Away day zines *The Shamrock, Not the View, The Celt, More Than 90 Minutes, The Thunder, CQN Magazine, Bhoyzone, Hail-hail, Welcome to Paradise, Once A Tim, The Hoddle, Over and Over, Jungle Drums.*

MIDDLESBROUGH

First KK visit was in season 1991/92, a 2-1 loss to 2nd division 'Boro, in the League Cup round 4. Smogsville lived up to its name with the ground enveloped and visibility severely restricted, but the fog lifted for the second half as we watched the Blues exit the competition. (To add insult to injury, we also lost 2-1 up there in the 3rd round of the F.A Cup). It was a good

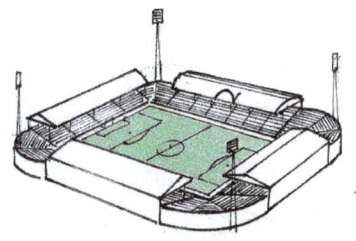

■ Ayresome Park, my first visit was in season 1981/82 with my father-in-law, a 0-0 end of season bore draw.

run generally, with a Little Chef stop off on the A19. Parking was usually on the street, and selling was usually OK. Can't think of any highs, plenty of lows, including August 1992 (KK25) Quinny sent off, and Paul Lake's career ending injury.

First KK visit to the new Riverside was in season 1995/96, and a 4-1 loss. We always parked in a car park right next to the ground and partook of what was splendidly on offer in the burger vans!

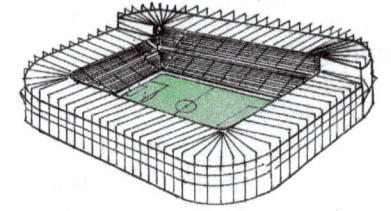

■ The Riverside, opened in August 1995

At half time Ged and I were accosted by two Blues who disliked the front cover of KK48 which showed Alan Ball having enjoyed the 4-0 and 6-0 defeats at Liverpool, plus they were annoyed at the front cover of KK 49 which apparently didn't give any credit for Ball being 'manager of the month' for November!

I can't remember many highs, but the low was certainly the 2008 last game of the season which we lost 8-1 after the previous day's 'Save our Sven' rally at The Etihad. The weather was scorching when we set off, but was freezing when we arrived at Smogsville. Blues were dressed inappropriately in shorts and T-shirts, whilst there was a heavy police presence as they were worried that there would be a reaction to the pending Sven sacking. At 0-6 we decided enough was enough and left, with Louise who'd come down especially from Scotland. City fans accidentally knocked a copper's helmet off and the police went berserk wading in with their batons. Disgraceful. Despite the loss, City (down to ten men) qualified for the UEFA league on the baffling 'Fair Play' ruling, but the darkest hour was just before the dawn. We were told by the cops at the next visit in October 2008, that they had expected a pitch invasion, and as they made their way to the front they were being tripped and kicked by City fans so it all went off.

New Years Eve, 2006, and a steward accused young KK seller Stephen Woodhouse (15) of trying to get in on a junior ticket as "there's too much of this going on, and it's denying the club valuable revenue". I was just about to resolve the situation, amicably, by unleashing a torrent of abuse on the unsuspecting jobsworth, when Steve handed over his mobile phone to the steward, and Steve's dad, Dave, a headmaster, cooly and calmly, confirmed to our man, the youngster's age, who was then allowed in, to sample the delights of a 0-0 draw. More than one way to skin a cat! Lesson should have been learnt.

For the 2010 FA Cup 3rd round, it was a nightmare drive, snowing over the M62, looked dodgy at Saddleworth Moor and bad at the Riverside. It was an early Mancini game and a 1-0 win as we identified him, on the front cover of KK176, as a magician, which he must have seen, as he later refuted the honour!

Away day zines *Fly Me to the Moon, Ayresome Angel, Bread and Boro, The Boys from Brazil*

NEWCASTLE UNITED

First KK visit was in season 1994/95. It was generally a day trip but we did stay over on a couple of occasions. We'd often stop off at the Leeming services, sometimes Washington services where we once bumped into media blokes Paul Hince and Andy Buckley. It was always a pleasure to pop into the Back Page memorabilia shop, and to say hello to Mark Jensen, who edited '*The Mag*', and also visit the Trent House pub to meet with the young editors of '*Half Magpie, Half Biscuit*' zine, or spotting '*Auf Wiedersehen Pet*' TV stars outside the Gallowgate end. We'd often say hello to Geordie KK subscriber Blue Jackie Marr with her City logo tattoo on her leg, accompanied by her Magpie-supporting hubby.

■ St James' Park. My first visit was in season 1959/60, the last away game of the season, when after 11 unsuccessful away trips, I finally saw us win 1-0!

Parking was okay on the street or in local car parks. In the early days we sold outside the away seated section by the West stand and also at the away standing bit in front of the main stand. When the ground was redeveloped, we were able to sell under cover, before heading for the lift to access the away seats, up with the gods. We were advised by stewards that we'd be arrested if caught selling inside, but City fans once threw smoke bombs onto Geordie fans below, which was much less dangerous!

AC/DC's *Thunderstruck* was once played pre match, and the programme advised that "City were "living in United's shadows for as long as virtually any living fan can remember". I recall the KK93 front cover celebrating our last trophy, the League Cup win over Newcastle in 1976, which antagonised the locals who responded with such original comments as "I wouldn't wipe my arse on that". The cops advised us to move on for our own safety!

The League Cup 4th round replay, evening 2-0 win in 1994/95 season, was both a high and a low. I'd had a tough day at work, and drove up afterwards with Tony G. We had trouble parking, but managed it eventually, Tony did, however, break the 'golden rule of selling', unintentionally, by asking a copper if it was OK to sell. "Don't know Sir, I'll check". He rang someone up at the club, then advised "Sorry Sir you're not allowed to sell, you'll have to move away".

I went round to the other side at the away seated area and post-match had an altercation with a London Blue who told me I was "talking shite" about London Blues' ticket problems, (for which they boycotted the zine) and the cops intervened, which put a slight dampener on our magnificent win. I was compensated the next day as I popped into City's offices in Hart Road, as 'Fan on the Board', and Brian Horton poured me a glass of champagne. I pompously advised him not to underestimate Palace in the next round (which we lost 4-0!).

For the snow bound 1-0 win of 2001, we stayed in Whitley Bay with the

'Bernard Buckley Barmy army', and John Dignum's Bolton branch for company. After the game we attended the late-night cinema and, on the way back to the hotel in the early hours, I was cautiously driving along the icy promenade when we were stopped by the police and I was breathalysed. "You don't look like football types," we were told after we said we'd been to the match. Little did they know! I'd had a decent meal at the Whitley Bay hotel and drank very little so tested negative. "Why did you stop us?" I asked. "You were driving erratically". Later Sue said knowingly "they must've thought you'd have to be drunk to drive erratically! Ouch!

The real high came in the penultimate game of the 2011/12 season when we stayed over on the Friday night. We travelled over to see R. and C. at their posh hotel, with the team bus parked outside, though the team were staying elsewhere. but the nerves were tangible. Yaya scored the goals, and Blues celebrated the win, exiting the ground singing and dancing, whilst hoping that United didn't beat Swansea by a big score (it was 2-0). This meant we just had to beat relegation candidates QPR who hadn't won away all season, in the last game at home to clinch the title on goal difference if United won at Sunderland. A formality? We stopped off at Leeming services, bumping into Dante Friend, who'd predicted weeks ago we'd win it on goal difference.

Away Day Zines The Mag, Half Magpie Half Biscuit, Talk of the Toon, The Giant Awakes, The Number Nine, Toon Army News, True Faith, Talk of the Tyne, Jim's Bald Heed.

SUNDERLAND

Tuesday March 14th 1989. I was working on a Kelloggs high bay warehouse project at Wrexham, and the Kelloggs City boys, all Mancs, said they were setting off in their hired minivan at 12 noon if I fancied it, but as I didn't have a ticket, decided to opt out. Then I was miffed as the crowd was only 16,000. Vinny Tovey did the HWIFY report, as City clocked up a fine 4-2 win.

■ Roker Park My first visit was for the FA Cup 3rd round tie in season 1982/83, a 0-0 draw., (2-1 win in the replay). Low crowd of 21,516, but I was impressed with the Roker Roar.

First KK visit was in season 1988/89, a 1-1 draw, Kendall's last game in charge. Always there and back in the day, or night! Street parking was available; I don't remember many problems selling.

First KK visit to the Stadium of Light was in August 1997, when we opened up the new stadium, on a Friday night, a 3-1 loss, driving up with John K, F.C. Mike, and Ged. After a traumatic summer, indeed I missed out on the last game of the previous season against Reading, as I was recovering from what turned out to be Diabetic Amyotrophy Radiculo Plexopathy, after months off work.

We'd drive up, sometimes stopping at Durham services, then parking on the street, or local car parks. We once parked at the Grange pub where we met KK subscriber and Sunderland resident City fan Dave Bambrough. Mackem fans were usually Ok, complaining about how many ex-United 'has been players' they'd bought and how David Moyes was their worst ever manager, also wondering about how many we'd put past them that day.

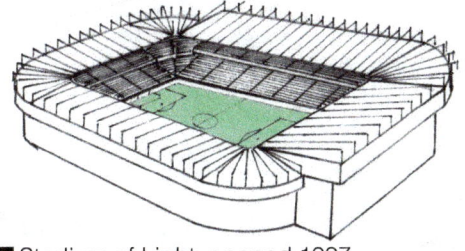
■ Stadium of Light, opened 1997

City fans were housed behind the goal until the ground was redeveloped with an extra tier added on to the opposite stand, with lift access for us old codgers! Selling was sometimes tricky.

Season 2007/08 we met up with Steve and Tom at Birch services, but the £35 parking fee was extortionate, so we drove separately to a hotel off the motorway in Yorkshire, where I parked and we continued in Tom's car. Nice 2-1 win, but needless to say when we arrived back to my car, I'd left the ignition on and the battery was flat. Luckily, I was on a little hill so Tom and Steve were able to roll it down and thankfully it started.

Season 2008/09 August 31st and the takeover announcement was made, with City to become the 'biggest club in the world'. SWP's return, and our 4th consecutive win, 3-0 this time. We encountered fog then rain, but optimism was high, though we often lost up there in the following years. Last league visit was in 2017, a 2-0 win, when they were eventually relegated. Good to see them back!

Away day zines *Wise Men Say, A Love Supreme, We're All Going To Wembley, Roker Roar, The Black Cat, The Sunderland Fanatic, Sex and Chocolate, It's An Easy One For Norman, It's The Hope I Can't Stand, The Wearside Roar, Where Else We.*

WEMBLEY

For the Carabao Cup final in 2014 we stayed over in Uxbridge and caught the overland train to Wembley. The area was rammed with Sunderland fans who'd stayed overnight in London. The predominance of the red and white colours was intimidating, but they were all great, and we obliged by taking selfies of their fans, at their request, as we tried to sell KK213. We felt better when we went to the City end, but were shocked when Sunderland went ahead and nearly made it two. "Not from there Yaya" shouted the Blue behind us, as he smashed in a worldie, before Nasri made it 2-1 and Navas got a late 3rd to settle our nerves.

6. YORKSHIRE & LINCS

Over to Barnsley, Bradford, Grimsby, Huddersfield, Hull, Leeds, Lincoln, Scunthorpe, and York.

BARNSLEY

Route was over the M62, down the M1, peeling off at the (strange) Barnsley/Manchester sign and down to Oakwell. First KK visit was in season 1988/89, a 2-1 win. This game is etched in my memory as it was the launch of KK 1, 20 pages for 50p. On the previous Thursday I'd picked up about 200 zines in the pouring rain from Manchester University where

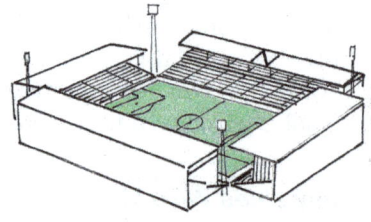

■ Oakwell, my first visit was in 1969, for the English League v the Irish League, to see Mike Summerbee and Franny Lee play.

they were printed, (on the Q/T) and I wondered how on earth I would sell them. I drove over on a sunny September day, stopping off at Woodall Services where I bumped into Mark and Stuart, young Blues who I'd often been to City away games with. I showed them KK1 and asked if they fancied giving me a lift selling, but they looked non plussed!

Trevor Morley chips the ball over advancing Barnsley 'keeper **Clive Baker** to net City's 85th minute winner.

I parked up on the grassy slope outside the away end, ideal for selling. Wandered down to the turnstiles, almost bottled out and went in, but went back to the car. I had a chat with Mike Kelly, Blueprint editor, took a deep breath and sold a few to puzzled Blues. We won the game 2-1 to kick start our promotion campaign.

I sold after the game with the win aiding sales, about 80 in total, which was remarkable, helped towards printing costs, and we were off and running. I also received a nice letter from their club further to the game.

There were a couple of games with incident, 1996/97 when City fans chanted "We'd rather be in Barnsley than Barbados", referring to absent Chairman Francis Lee, also the game in March 2000 when City fans rioted at half time due to the food outlets being closed.

KK Contributor, Andy Schilling attended with his brother and five-year-old daughter: "Half time, we eventually gave up, queuing for refreshments, and went back to our seats, where we saw the signs of violence erupting at the far end of the stand. I returned to the refreshment area to get a drink, but on the way, I saw a Policeman being trampled on by the retreating crowd. Once the crush had stopped, he was helped to his feet, dusted down but clearly shaken and in some pain. I think he was one of the Manchester police who travelled with us. A small group of about six of us stood around him in an attempt to protect him from further injury. When the South Yorks police riot mob arrived to rescue him, they kindly repaid our good deed by whacking us with their batons. The injured officer attempted to protest our innocence but was dragged off by his colleagues. After the mayhem I saw a pregnant woman crying and two children separated from their parents. I don't want to stop taking my daughter to away games, but displays like this make it difficult to take such a risk".

In the pre-season friendly in 1996/97 Gary Fleming Testimonial, it was a 2-2 draw and in the 2009/10 friendly it was a 1-1 draw, with Barnsley fans singing "You're gonna win f*ck all". At the time, despite the investment, that looked highly probable!

Season 2000/01, a night match and we set off at 4.30 pm. The M62 was down to one lane, due to an accident, and there was a massive traffic jam, so we rang and warned Steve, Ged and co to exit asap. We arrived at 8pm just as Shaun Goater scored. Though we usually had a good relationship with Barnsley, Sue and Carin were stopped from selling at half time, both by the stewards and the cops

Another visit was in July 2008, when we beat EB Streymur 2-0, in the UEFA Cup 1st qualifying round, the Etihad being unavailable due to a Bon Jovi concert. The M62 was chocker, so we took the scenic route, parked up next to the sports hall for a snack and a drink. I noticed a house next to the ground with United posters in the window, but not sure if they were intact after the game? City fans were allocated the East stand which was soon filled and Blues overflowed into the North stand, on a pleasant evening.

Awayday Zines South Riding, Better Red than Dead, Dizzy Heights, Yoo Reds.

BRADFORD CITY

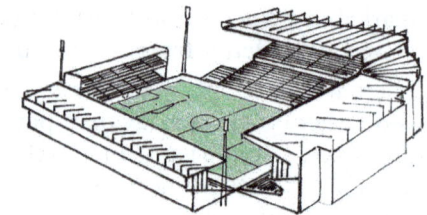

First KK visit was in season 1988/89, and the crucial match in which we needed to draw in the last game of the season, as we'd tossed away a 3-goal lead in the previous week at home to Bournemouth. Tickets were like gold, but we were OK thankfully. We set off early, with Wayne Norris, and true to tradition roadworks on the M62 were to cause delays, which turned out to be the incredibly important job, on this heavy traffic day, of painting white lines! We made our way through the police cordon and ticket check, parked up and were in the ground by 2.15. Ex City manager John Bond, who'd previously said on TV that we wouldn't get promoted, was interviewed pitch side close to the City away end, and was loudly booed causing the interview to be curtailed. Blues were all

■ Valley Parade, my first visit was in season 1987/88, a 4-2 win, our first in many away games.

over the ground, and we watched on as Bradford went ahead. News came through of closest rivals Palace winning, with a City fan going on the pitch telling the boys to "get a move on", then Trevor Morley scored the equaliser and at the end of the game they opened the gates and allowed us onto the pitch to celebrate. The relief was tangible.

March 1998, we had a decent run, arrived nice and early, and parked on the road near the ground. We went for a stroll but when we arrived back at the car, I realised that I'd locked the keys inside! There followed frantic phone calls to the RAC. The engineer, who was brilliant, arrived shortly afterwards, and managed to retrieve the keys in time for us to make the kick off. Sadly, it was a 2-1 loss despite going a goal ahead and relegation loomed. We repaired to the Whopping Spring post-match, then took in a Ray Davies gig back in Manc.

Awayday Zines City Gent, Bernard of The Bantams.

GRIMSBY TOWN

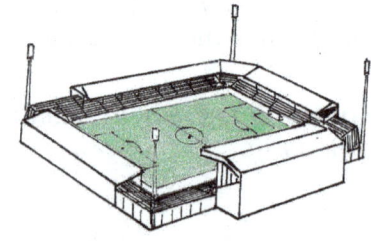

First KK visit was in season 1996/97, a 1-1 draw. On the way there we stopped at Birch services and bumped into David White who now played for Sheff, United, and was waiting for his dad to give him a lift

■ Blundell Park, my first visit was in season 1958/59, a 2-2 draw in the F.A. Cup 3rd round, on a snowbound pitch. We lost the much-postponed replay 2-1.

to Bramall Lane. At the ground it was interesting watching the cars rolling up to the official car park. Franny was told to park near the wall, Ian Niven, then Colin Barlow picked a prime spot, whilst Bernard Halford and Miike Turner were turned away and went to find a side street, just like the rest of us.

We played them a further couple of times, 1999/2000 1-1, when tickets were scarce with City fans ringing the Grimsby ticket office who'd devised a quiz and Don Price (P &W branch chairman) was asked "do Grimsby play in Grimsby or Cleethorpes" and Don replied - "You've got me there pal, can I go 50/50?" No ticket for Don!

In 2001/02 the route was over the M62 and the new Humber Bridge to Cleethorpes. We were generally housed behind the goal, or in the adjacent temporary 'Gene Kelly' type stand where the local kids threw stones at us at the end of the game. Sales were awful, despite winning 2-0. The fish and chips weren't much better at Barney's Cafe, especially considering it was a seaside town. In the programme Stewart Rawson (a closet rag?) reckoned "City have looked on in jealousy and rage at United's success". I did of course, write to the club to complain.

Awayday Zines Sing When We're Fishing, Feast In The Garden.

HUDDERSFIELD TOWN

First KK visit was in season 1996/97 a 0-0 draw. It was usually a fairly decent run over the M62, and down to the ground where we parked right outside the away end and the stewards were friendly and helpful. In 2000 the car park was reserved for permit holders only, so we found a local car park, where there were reports of pubs being trashed by Blues? Slubbers Arms was a popular drinking hole where 'Dickovs Delight' beer was sold. Strangely, catering outlets were outside in the open air/rain, behind the stand. Memorable match was the 1998 game which we won 3-1 to boost our hopes of avoiding the drop, to no avail, and it was the Terriers, who stayed up. We played them in the F.A. Cup 5th round in 2016/17 (0-0), and in the Prem for two seasons, 2017/18 (2-1), and 2018/19 (3-1). We'd also played a friendly there in 2001/02, 2-0 win, Dyson testimonial

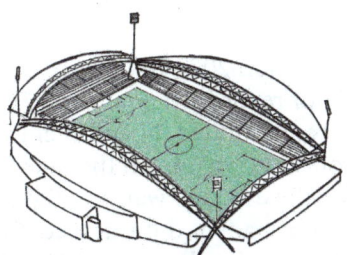

■ Leeds Road, and my first visit was in season 1983/84 a 3-1 win, but we never played there in the KK years. MacAlpine/John Smith/Kirklees Stadium, opened in August 20th 1994 and my first visit was with youngest daughter Kaye in 1995, for the REM gig. It was a hot summer's day, Michael Stipe donned a Terriers shirt, and they were supported by The Beautiful South.

Awayday Zines Hanging on the Telephone, A Slice of Kinder Pie. Those Were the Days.

HULL CITY

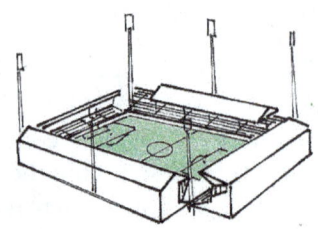

It was the first game of the 1988/89 season, Tony G and I drove over on the M62, which was gridlocked so we diverted onto the A roads then rejoined later, eventually arriving in Kingston upon Hull, well in time for kick off. Sadly, there was no City fanzine on sale, as we listened to Phil Collins reworking of and destroying 'A Groovy Kind of Love' being played on the Tannoy.

■ Boothferry Park, my first visit was for a friendly in 1985/96 with daughter Marnie, a 2-1 loss.

Tony advised that if I fancied doing my own fanzine, which we'd previously discussed, he could arrange for printing at a reasonable price, leaving me to ponder.

City dominated, missing chances, then let a soft one in, Dibs missing the cross, to lose the game 1-0, but looking good enough for promotion.

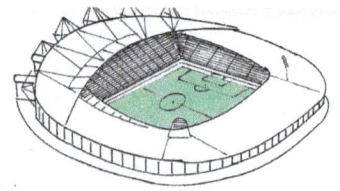

■ KC (now KMM) stadium opened in 2002 (share with Hull FC).

The new ground was built in Hull's West Park which included a massive car park plus the bonus of a leisure centre with a cafe. First KK visit was for a friendly in 2005, resulting in a 4-0 City win. We played them five times there in the Prem, between 2008 and 2016, winning three, drawing one and losing one. Season 2008/09, we drove over the M62, in Tom P's car. The programme had our record attendance as 73,295 (not 84,569) as our 'no history' narrative was compounded. No problem from officials for selling but sales were low, plus we once suffered from the fake £20 note scam. On the way back from the 2016 game the dreaded warning lights came on in the car, which, after limping home, the garage advised it was a costly repair. We swiftly visited Arnold Clark's and traded it in for the current Vauxhall Corsa.

Awayaday Zines - *Hull, Hell and Happiness, To Hull and Back, Amber Nectar.*

LEEDS UNITED

First KK visit was in season 1988/89, a 1-1 draw, no KKs on sale yet (match report in KK1). It was usually a decent trip over the M62 and parking up in the large car park just off the motorway. Selling was always OK, City fans being housed in the South stand, where the cops once came into the crowd with a photocopy of a hoolie, and arrested a Blue I knew as a really good lad, who'd stood near us for years on the Kippax. He came back in later, innocence proved, and whether they nicked the real thug we never found out. We were then housed in the corner next to the new Lowfield Road stand, now covered, as opposed to the old days when Leeds fans used to come out early and lob bricks over on to City fans. We were once allocated the end of the new stand with a spacious concourse then finally at one end of the main stand. Many highs, including the 1-0 win in 1995/96, Gerry Creaney's rare goal in the fog helped elevate Alan Ball to Manager of the Month, and gave us the front cover of KK49. Low was the 3-0 loss in 2002/03 first game of the season when City fans were sarcastically serenaded with "City are back". "You're just a small town in Kippax" was the response! They eventually made it back to the Prem, and we played them over there in 2020/21 (1-1, Ruben Dias' debut)), 2021/22 (4-0) and 2022/23 (3-1), without a KK presence

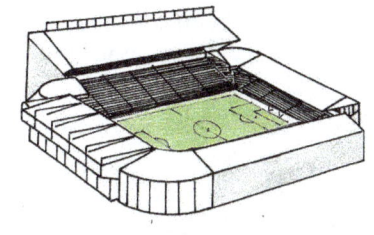

■ Elland Road. My first visit was in season 1958/59 Division One and a 4-0 win

Awayday Zines *The Hanging Sheep, Just A Quick Word Lads Please, The Square Ball, The Peacock, Crossbar, Till the World Stops, Marching Together, We Are Leeds.*

LINCOLN CITY

First KK visit was in season 1996/97, a 4-1 loss in the League Cup 2nd round 1st leg, City in Division 1 with Lincoln in Division 3. City went ahead after one minute through Rosler but Lincoln, impishly, knocked in four against an appalling Manchester City team performance. For the first time in my entire City supporting career, I'm afraid I booed the boys off. To compound the situation, we lost the return leg 1-0 with an even worse performance, after I was on the radio claiming we'd win 3-0!. "Surely this has got to be the lowest point we can ever reach?" I penned in my KK 55 editorial, but of course it wasn't!

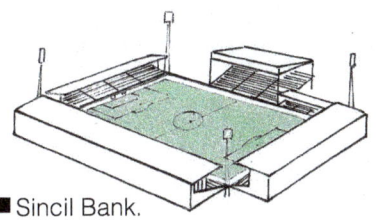

■ Sincil Bank.

We then had a 2-1 loss in 1998/99 on a Tuesday night in Division 2. Sean R: "Contra flow roadworks on Dunham swing bridge in the middle of nowhere and delays on the A1, meant a horrendous journey yet again for many Blues. The K.O. was delayed until 8pm but actually it was 8.15pm. Lincoln went 2-0 up with the strong wind behind them. City eventually pulled one back in the

83rd minute with an own goal, which was marred by a special cop wading into a celebrating City fan, on another night to forget. How many more do we have to endure?" The weather and the result ruined KK sales.

We also played a friendly there in 2003/04, a 2-1 win, which Ged maybe went to?

Awayday Zines Yellow Belly, The Deranged Ferret, The Banker Magazine.

SCUNTHORPE UNITED

Just the one visit in season 2009/10, with a 4-2 win in the 4th round of the F.A. Cup. (Ironically, we'd also played them at home in the 3rd round of the League Cup, a 5-1 home win.)

Needless to say, it was a treacherous snow bound drive over the M62 with grandson Joe, Tom and Steve as we safely parked up in a car park for £2, next to the ground. I remember seeing Tommy Muir's coach arrive with a replica F A Cup in the front window, and Blues singing "United debt" songs plus a couple of "One Kevin Keegan's". It could have been a banana skin, on a frozen pitch, but we safely cruised our way into the next round with the dreams of Wembley still in our thoughts, until we came a cropper in the 5th round at Stoke 3-1 in a replay.

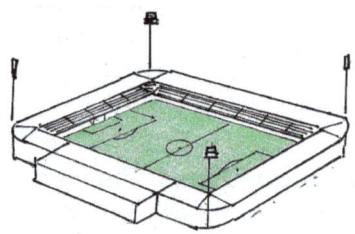
■ Glanford Park, opened August 1988.

We'd also played a friendly in 2001/02 of which I have no recollection!

Awayday Zines Son of a Ref, Get a Grip Ref, Big Thing, Lip Service.

YORK CITY

Just the one disastrous visit. December 1998. Sue and I parked in the street local to the ground, sold a few KKs then made our way round the back of their Kop to our seats in the adjacent stand. As we went round, they scored and the stand 'went up'! City equalised but couldn't manage a winner, so just before the end we made our way round the back of their Kop again to sell a few more zines at the City end. Unfortunately, they got the winner, and the stand 'went up' again, so we didn't bother selling. City dropped to 12th in the third tier, our lowest in our history, but we recovered, winning at Wrexham, then at home to Stoke and eventually promotion via the play offs v Gillingham. In the return last game of the season, City won 4-0 to relegate the Minstermen, and our fans sadly stoned their coaches.

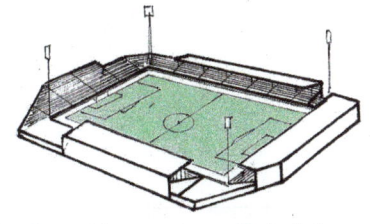

■ Bootham Crescent, my first visit was for the League Cup 4th round 0-0 draw in 1974.

Awayday Zines What A Shambles, Terrace Talk, New Frontiers, The Y Front.

7. MERSEYSIDE

Short trips to Everton, Liverpool and Tranmere.

EVERTON

First KK visit was in season 1989/90, December 17th, a 0-0 draw for Howard Kendall's first game in charge. A bit different to when we played there in season 1990/91 when he'd gone back to 'his wife'

We usually parked in the car park near Anfield and walked through Stanley Park, with eyes in the back of our head, to Goodison. Later in Steve's car, arriving early enough to park next to the ground, which was more expensive but enabled a quick getaway. Pre match we'd grab a coffee, cheeseburger and have a nap. We were usually housed at one end of the wooden Bullens Road stand with restricted views. Stewards were OK outside, but a pain inside the cramped concourse, and sales weren't usually too good.

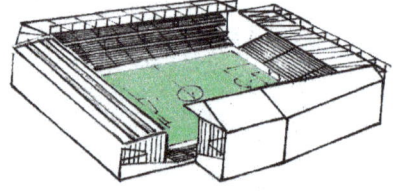

■ Goodison Park, my first visit was in April 1958, a 5-2 win, and I was impressed with Goodison's four double decker stands, but not the fight when a scouse Ted knocked seven bells out of a City fan.

Results were dreadful and after the 2003/04 game 0-0, on the way back to the Stanley Park car park in frustration I projected my chewing gum and kicked it as far as I could. A young scouser driving past, wound the window down and shouted "eh mate, you showed more skill deh dan Robbie Fowler!" Everyone in Liverpool is a comedian? I was on Talksport later and one Blue thought I was harsh, but another thought I was fair!

There was much banter and arguing between Blues in 2005/06, re the Joey Barton late transfer request. Did he do a moony at the end of the game? Season 2009/10, we had a pleasant walk through Stanley Park, watching the kids playing football, one wearing a rag shirt! We were not allowed inside the stewards' cordon to sell, then housed in the lower tier two rows from the front

so a poor view of play, which was delayed for nine minutes, as a fan handcuffed himself onto a post, protesting that his daughter couldn't get a job, baffling Joe.

Season 2011/12, after the 1-0 loss Fergie said it was "all part of the plan" after ex rag Gibson scored, but Evertonians, on the way back to the car park were telling us to "go on and win the title". Which we did!

The turning point came in the 3-2 win in 2014. Evertonians were unimpressed with our Stevie Gerrard chants initially, until they realised the meaning and were happy to sing along! Barkley's early wonder goal was a worry, but we went on to win euphorically 3-2 to set us up for the title. We lost 2-1 in the 1st leg of the S/F of the League cup, in season 2015/16, but we went through winning 3-1 at the Etihad, preventing an all scouse final.

In Pep's first season 2016/17, their 4-0 win exposed our ageing lightweight team, when his tenure looked decidedly dodgy. Since then, we've won 3-0 in the F.A. Cup 6th round and all seven league games including the 3-0 in 2023 when we found out the next day, after Arsenal's loss at Forest, that we'd won the title for the third year running, before going on to complete the Treble. Finally, the 3-1 win in December 2023, on our return from winning the Club World Cup, sparked off the run to the end of the season, when we clinched the title for the fourth time in a row.

Generally, their fans were pretty decent, indeed we became bosom buddies when we continually prevented Liverpool from winning Cups and Titles.

We did play a few friendlies there, in 1991/92 4-1 A. King T/M, 1999/2000 0-1, Ebrell T/M, 2000/01 1-3 J. Parkinson T/M.

Awayday Zines When Skies Are Grey, Speke from The Harbour, Sati, Blue Wail, Gwladys Sings the Blues, Singing The Blues, The Blue Watch, Blue Blood.

LIVERPOOL

First KK visit was the opening game of season 1989/90, a 3-1 loss. £7.50 a ticket, a reduced allocation of only 3,000, but with an improved segregated area for away fans, seating, programmes, toilets and refreshments. No fences but heavy police and stewards' presence. Game was noticeable for the first airing of the "One banana, two banana, three banana four", Blue Moon song, which killed off the banana craze.

We'd drive down the East Lancs Road, A580, appropriately referred to as the ASBO! Initially we were able to park in the Stanley Park car park adjacent to Anfield, before it became season ticket holders only, when their gates increased. It was then the garage at the bottom of the car park, eventually local car parks and courtesy of Blue Vicar Steve Parish who used his not inconsiderable influence, once or twice on a local Vicar's driveway.

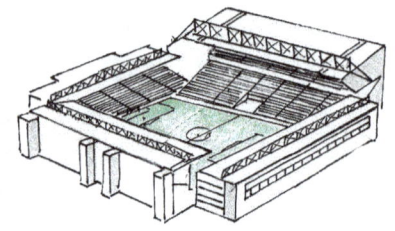

■ Anfield, my first visit was in 1971/72 season with brother Frank, a 3-0 loss, which virtually cost us the title

We generally sold on Anfield Road before kick-off, and outside the away end turnstiles post-match, where Liverpool fans deliberately and aggressively walked through the City fans exiting. Blues were housed in part of the Anfield Road stand with an appalling view if you had a seat at the back, finally resolved when it was rebuilt in 2024, but too late for us I'm afraid.

Worst KK moment was in December 1991, when I insisted Danny carried on selling inside Anfield, as the other zine sellers were still selling, even though the cops had told him he'd be arrested if he continued. Unsurprisingly he ended up in the cage during the game, almost made worse by his dad's bad tempered 'intervention', for which I was in the doghouse from Sue when we arrived back home!

Results were dreadful, including a 4-0 League Cup, and 6-0 League loss in the same week of season 1995/96 (giving us the front cover of KK48) We were once treated by Tony Grayson's printer company to seats in the Executive stand for the 2000/01 season. It was a 3-2 loss when we were actually awarded and scored not one but two penalties. The stadium announcer kindly gave our 33rd wedding anniversary a mention at half time.

We picked up a few draws and an actual win in 2002/03 with a late Anelka goal, his 2nd of the game, which I missed of course as I popped out early to sell KK.113. City fans exited the ground chanting "where's your European place gone".

Walking back to Stanley park car park post-match, (2006/07) we were astonished to see Norah Mercer 87 years young striding past. A few minutes earlier she'd have been caught up in the bottles raining over on City fans, by the young scouse scallies.

Things came to a head in 2014 when Liverpool were odds on to win the title for the first time since 1990, with the media going overboard and Kopites lining the route to Anfield at every home game. It was the 25th anniversary of Hillsborough, well respected by the City club and fans who were then rewarded by the 'sporting' scouse crowd, who booed every touch of the ball by City players and cheered when injured Yaya Toure was stretchered off. Liverpool won the game 3-2, but failed to win the title assisted by Steve Gerrard's slip at home to Chelsea, although scouse 'journalist' David Maddocks insisted that

Liverpool were the best team. Less points, less wins, less goals scored and less conceded by City! Of course they were!

The hatred continued when City had the audacity to sign Raheem Sterling, and reached an all-time high when the City coach was attacked prior to the Champions league Q/F match in 2016, a 3-0 loss with appalling refereeing decisions, in Liverpool's favour, compounded similarly at the Etihad in the return leg, a 2-1 loss.

Liverpool escaped a lengthy ban for the coach attack, which was predicted and caused £20K worth of coach damage with not a single arrest. They were let off by the ineffectual UEFA with just a 'slap on the wrist' fine.

For the 2018 game, Marnie drove, we were on the 2nd back row of the stand, crouching down to watch the match, so I put the bag of zines behind us and it was nicked, bafflingly, presumably by a Blue. We left early at 1-4, to check if it had been dumped on the concourse, but no sign so we went back to the car park for a quick getaway, but were blocked in so an even worse Anfield day than normal, even though we pulled it back to 4-3! Later, at the home West Brom game, the empty bag was handed over to me by City fan Keith Bolton who'd found it at the Bristol City away game. We came closest to a win in 2018/19 when Mahrez missed a late penalty at 0-0.

Generally, it was a story of total bias for Liverpool regarding refereeing decisions, and abuse - on and off the pitch with coin throwing at Pep and his back-room staff amongst other incidents. We finally managed another win in season 2020/21 4-1 with no fans present, celebrated on the cover of KK275, which marked the end of our KK Anfield visits, though Steve P still managed a few more.

We generally had good relationships with Liverpool fans in the early years, mainly through the FSA contacts, but lost touch once we became successful, though we always have good banter with Anthony our boiler man, and Matt the chap who collects our Leigh lottery ticket money every week.

Awayday Zines *Through The Wind And The* (deleted when they realised it spelt TWAT!) *Rain, When Sunday Comes, One Minute To Go, Red All Over The Land* (Nice letter in KK 119 re new stadium), *Another Wasted Corner, Our Days Are Numbered, All Day and All Of The Night, The Liverpool Way, Another Vintage Liverpool Performance.*

WEMBLEY MARCH 2016, CARABAO CUP FINAL, 1-1, WON 3-1 ON PENS

We saw The Cult at the Albert Halls on the Friday night, drove down on the Saturday, stayed at a hotel in Uxbridge. Took the train to Wembley, sold a few zines in the bitter cold wind, sat with Tom and Steve P who travelled separately. We missed a host of chances, wondering if Sterling had been given the Gerrard 'scouse mafia' treatment, but drew 1-1 and won on pens.

Then it was the 2019 Community Shield 1-1 aet, 3-1 on pens. On the Friday we were delivering KK 261 to the kiosk in Manchester, and bumped into

Bernardo Silva (with his missus) who was most impressed with the zine asking incredulously "you do this?" We travelled down on the Saturday, watched Jesus Christ Superstar at the Barbican with friends R and C. Selling was tricky, trying to find a good spot, so we made our way up to the top tier. Scousers booed the National Anthem, and we felt sorry for the girl singers, they also booed the Bee vocal mental health choir singing Blue Moon, disgraceful. Sterling (12) opened, Matip (77) equalised, their flags came out in our end - annoyingly, but we won 5-4 on pens. Daughter Marnie and hubby Andy in the bottom tier were pelted with food thrown down on them. Good run home.

It was the F.A. Cup semi-final in 2021/22, 3-0 down early doors, pulled it back to 3-2, then in 2022/23 it was the Community Shield again, at the King Power as Wembley was unavailable 3-2 loss, Nunez got their 3rd, Haaland missed a late sitter, and they gloated that Erling would be outscored by Nunez in the new season! Oops!

TRANMERE ROVERS

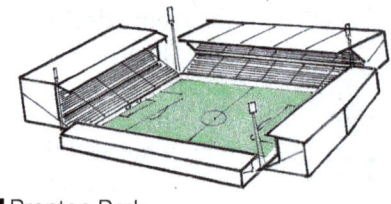
■ Prenton Park.

First KK visit was in season 1997/98, in the 2nd tier. John Bainbridge, from the Merseyside branch (City fans with scouse accents) arranged that City fans in cars and coaches could meet at a pub just four miles from the ground between 11.30 am and 2pm for a few drinks, meal if required, and a sing song, then travel to the game. Steve P and myself attended but then partook of the Executive bit, thanks to Tony Grayson.

It was a nice run over the motorways to the Wirral to face the 'plastic scousers'. We played them four times in the 2nd and 3rd tiers. On another occasion, Tony G. wangled us into the Executive suite which we enjoyed, though we managed to fix his car which had broken down on the way! KK sales were poor, as is often the case for fairly close away games, despite massive away attendances.

Friendlies - 1998/99 2-2, Bill Shankly Tournament at Preston, lost on pens. For the Eric Nixon testimonial game in 2002/03 I was interviewed by Radio Manchester at the Little Chef in Bromborough as we were about to sell Georgi Kinkladze, which I disagreed with. After the game's 7-1 win we went to a local cafe for a Pizza, and were inadvertently 'entertained' by comedian Stan Boardman, who we, (Louise in particular) didn't find at all funny, if he ever was? Finally in the 2005/06 friendly, it was a 0-1 defeat.

Awayday Zines *Gives Us An R,* (We gave editor Dave Goat permission to use the KK ground diagrams!)

8. LANCASHIRE

Those were the days, when we travelled the short distance, to Blackburn, Blackpool, Burnley, Preston and later Oldham and Wigan.

BLACKBURN ROVERS

First KK visit was in season 1988/89, a 3-2 loss in the Simod Cup round one. Later in the season, it was a 4-0 defeat on April 15th, with left footed Ged Taggart picked at right back. The game became insignificant though, as news filtered through of the events at Hillsborough, in the Forest v Liverpool F.A. Cup semi-final, when 97 Liverpool fans lost their lives due to incompetent organisation by the authorities. Eventually, after 25 years being proved unlawful.

Then in September 1990 it was the Noel Brotherston testimonial, a 2-0 win and a decent drive from the M61 to Blackburn via Darwen. It was always a pleasant run through the Lancashire countryside, and parking on the street or later in the big car park close to the ground, but selling was always a hassle, as we were made to stand on the street opposite the ground, and not allowed to sell inside. Indeed, on one occasion they were so awkward that we were refunded our money, and watched the game, a 2-0 loss, firstly from the notorious hill which was decidedly dodgy, frequented by druggies, then through a gap in between the stands. I arranged to meet with their stadium manager on the following Monday and we had a cordial chat to no avail.

■ Blackburn Rovers, Ewood Park, my first visit was in 1958/59 season, a 2-1 loss.

One high was the 3-2 win in 1995 which helped stave off relegation for us, but looked to have gifted United the title, which actually went to Rovers. Obviously the biggest high was the 4-1 win in 2000, when we were promoted back to the Prem. In the week before the game Eddie Humphreys and I went to the pub at dinnertime, in Hale Barns and who should walk in but Bish and Dicky, who we chatted to advising that "we should be alright". After the 4-1 win, Rovers hitting the post on numerous occasions, we celebrated at Maine Road, Albert Square and outside the Midland Hotel.

On one occasion we parked up next to Paul Hince who was having a nap, when a car pulled up next to us and Tommy Docherty jumped out. He banged on the roof of Paul's car who woke with a start exclaiming "Bloody hell Doc, you nearly gave me a heart attack". To which the Doc replied "It's the only attack you'll have all game!" One Christmas I did attend as the Sky Blue Santa!

FA Cup 6th round, 2006/07, we had a coffee at McDonalds, plus a moan about the Blues, "What we need is a Happy Meal" John Rowan said! This time the Safety Officer and stewards co-operated and allowed us to leave our bags with KK143s in their room until after the game. Blackburn were down to ten men but won 2-0. At the end of the match the players came over to the fans and the abuse they received was off the scale from the majority of the 7,000 strong City support. I went out early to sell KK's (not because "I'm not a loyal fan" according to a Blue on the GMR phone in, which gave passing Blues a much-needed laugh on a bad day).

Away Day Zines: 4,000 Holes, Many Miles from Home, Loadsa Money, Colin's Cheeky Bits.

BLACKPOOL

My first KK visit was in season 1997/98, a 1-0 loss in the League Cup 1st round 1st leg, (2nd leg won 1-0 but lost 4-2 on pens at M/R) then later that season in the 3rd tier it was a 0-0 draw. Season 98/99 City fans disgracefully, smashed up several local hostelries after the game

Originally, we stood on the Kop. In the Prem in 2010/11 we were housed down the side in the new temporary stand. I was offered £120 for my ticket, and at half time I almost wished I'd taken it.

We were at the home of the 'Maestro, The Wizard of Dribble' Sir Stanley Matthews, and we needed such a rarity, a player of that ilk, to change the game. Roberto didn't disappoint, on came David Silva, and despite the bugger of a pitch, he turned the game round, with a scintillating performance, mesmerising the Seasiders' defence, and scoring a

■ Blackpool, Bloomfield Road. My first visit was in season 57/58 a 5-2 win.

goal of rare beauty, going this way and that, notching the third goal, his first in the Prem, to clinch the win. Blackpool scored at the death to make it 3-2, Ian Holloway ("City have no 'istree" to whom I sent a letter, putting him right) was not happy. Good!

Parking and food was never a problem, with local car parks and welcoming cafes. Selling was OK outside the ground but very cramped inside so a bit tricky.

Away Day Zines A View from the Tower, Tangerine Dream, Another View from The Tower, Do I Like Tangerine? Now That's What I Call Progress.

BURNLEY

First KK visit was for the FA Cup 3rd round, a 1-0 win in season 1990/91, Burnley 4th in the 4th division. M62, M66 down to the ground. We parked up in one of the side streets right by the ground. Lingered on the tree lined avenue by the cricket ground as 7,000 Blues filed past, so sales were good.

We've played them in the F.A. Cup, League Cup, 3rd tier, 2nd tier, friendlies (including Lee Bradbury's two goal debut) and Prem, generally winning comfortably. Probably the most important was the 1-0 win in 18/19 which was crucial to us going on to win the title. City fans usually took up the whole of the stand behind the goal, then when they became successful, after promotion to the Prem, we were just allocated half the stand. Selling was OK outside, inside and after the game, though sales weren't that good.

We once went in Marnie's car which sported City stickers, parked on the street, and when we arrived back, found it had been bricked by a little scrote who was chased off but not caught by Blues who'd disturbed him in action. After swapping with their *When The Ball Moves* fanzine in 2009/10, we went 3-0 ahead inside the first seven minutes, and it was 5-0 at half time, a Premier League record. The rains came down, but the full 90 minutes were played out, for a 6-0 win.

■ Burnley, Turf Moor. My first visit was the first game of the 1958/59 season, 4-3-win 3 nil down at half time.

Away Day zines The Claret Flag, Bob Lord's Sausage, Kicker Conspiracy, The Claret flag, When the Ball Moves, Marlon's Gloves.

OLDHAM ATHLETIC

First KK visit was in season 1988/89, a 1-0 win. (The previous season, on a boiling hot August day in 1988, the weather changed to icy rain, and caught T-shirt wearing Blues out in the 1-1 draw).

Obviously, it was a short drive, car park next to the ground, so it was easy to nip back to the car if sales exceeded expectations. We always had big away support. What could be better (maybe results?) and we were often moved on by the stewards and had to duck and dive whilst selling inside or outside the ground, so it wasn't hats off to Oldham (I told 'em!)

Ice station Oldham which, surprisingly, isn't the highest ground in the country, did give us some interesting visits. Probably the highlight was the 5-2 win on the last day of season 1991/92, when United had just lost the title to Leeds, as we chanted "We beat the Champions 4-0". Certainly, the low point was the 1-0 loss in the 3rd round of the FA Cup in 2005. Lowly Division One club Oldham's win causing City manager Kevin Keegan to slump in his seat (front cover of KK 130) in the dug out, shortly before his departure. City fans were housed behind the goal in the newish covered seated stand but were everywhere inside the ground, and just for a change it was perishing and a horrible windy day. I was interviewed by Ian Cheeseman, for Radio Manc., after the game with Paul Tyrell, City's PR guy, lurking, and chipping in with such remarks as "I thought we'd agreed not to discuss that?" Which were ignored!

■ Oldham Athletic, Boundary Park, my first visit was in season 1983/84 a 2-2 draw.

We played plenty of welcome pre-season friendlies at Boundary Park, before we hit the big time, last in 2012/13 a 2-1 loss!

Away day Zines Beyond the Boundary, The Exploding Latics, Inevitable, Mouldy Old Dough.

PRESTON NORTH END

First KK visit was in season 1998/99, pre-season. It was the Bill Shankly testimonial game for Ryan Kidd, when we beat Preston 3-2 but lost to Tranmere on pens in the final, after 2-2.

Then in the League, April 5th, it was a 1-1 draw. Tony G. travelled separately, enjoying breakfast at 'The Tickled Trout', just off the M6 on a corporate freebie, and quite a few Blues had the same idea. TG - "Mid-day kick-offs will take some getting used to though, with everyone asking what the other (non-existent) half time scores were at 12.45pm and other games kicking off as you arrived back home". After a tribute to the legendary Sir Tom Finney, on his birthday, and a bizarre opera performance, the game kicked off and we were caught cold within a minute, Basham scoring, but Michael Brown (22) equalised.

Next visit was in season 2001/02, a 2-1 loss, when Jon Macken scored their winner from the half way line, prompting us to buy him later that season. In 2006/07 it was a 3-1 win in the F.A.Cup 5th rd, Pre-match we visited the National Football Museum, housed at the stadium, now transferred to Manchester. They originally banned inflatables for health and

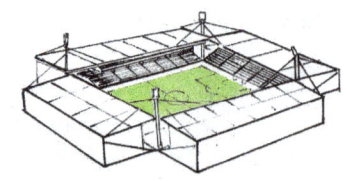

■ Preston North End, Deepdale, my first visit was in season 1958/59, a 2-0 loss.

safety reasons but saw sense and relented.

It was another short drive, parking up in the muddy car park on Sir Tom Finney Way opposite the ground. Sales were usually poor. We finally played them in the League Cup in 2019 winning 3-0, when the final ground developments were complete, in what is the most impressive rebuild of a once old fashioned stadium.

In 2021 I was in Preston hospital in the next bed to a prisoner (United fan) chained to two prison guards, waiting to have my big toe amputated. I could see the Deepdale floodlights in the distance as I gazed out of the window from my bed, every cloud..!

Away Day Zines *Raising the Coffin, Silence of the Lambs, The PNE View, Pie Muncher, Who's That Jumping Off The Pier?*

WIGAN ATHLETIC

First KK visits were in 1998/99 season in the wind and rain on an open terrace in atrocious conditions, with a 1-0 win, which was as good as it got. Several isolated incidents before the game were advised by a local Wigan fan who also told us "City fans had ripped the Wigan town apart". Fairly local for us but always a tortuous route to Wigan, parking was on the street, and selling was OK.

Later that season it was, of course the 3rd tier play off semi-final 1st leg, when tickets were in scarce supply and we were lucky to obtain a couple with the help of Rochdale Blue Tony Dempsey (RIP) (Later called "a splitter" by a Blue) in their main stand.

Both sets of fans mixed amicably in the pubs pre match we were advised. Just prior to KO, it was amusing to see a group of City fans scaling a fence behind the goal and dispersing onto the terrace with accompanied cheers all round! We were soon a goal down when Wiekens and Weaver left our throw in to each other but Paul Dickov saved our bacon. As we sold after the game there was much scurrying about, and, apparently, running battles in the local streets. We gave P. and W. supporters club Chairman and Blue legend Don Price a lift home, but he wasn't confident about the 2nd leg, which we won 1-0 with a disputed (by Wigan fans) Shaun Goater goal.

After the 4-3 loss in December 2005, at the new ground, I was selling in the car park when a prominent member of the 'Forward with Franny' campaign, (whose name I won't mention), and his sons walked past.

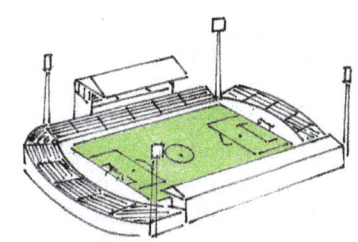
■ Wigan Athletic, Springfield Park. My first visit was in season 1982/83, a 1-1 draw in the League Cup 2nd round 1st leg. 2nd leg 2-0.

He'd attended supporters club meetings advising "don't worry about money, we've got more money than you can imagine", which turned out to be false. He was up against me as 'Fan on the Board' in 1994, and lost. However, I did think that he was a top bloke, but was disappointed when he was amused as he condoned his sons chanting "Wallace is a w*****" as they walked past.

Prior to this was a similar chant, from them in the summer of 1998, which they started at a Junior Blues function I attended in the Kippax stand top tier, when I stepped up to win a raffle prize. Six bottles of Champagne were clutched to my chest, as I walked off head held high! They'd also put an envelope with my name on it, but with no money enclosed, to try and get me into trouble. What a hoot, from the blokes who were obviously delighted we'd sunk to the third tier of English football?

Sue and I had a week away in Spain when we played Oxford at home and Portsmouth away. It was reported to me that the same fella was on the radio after the Oxford game, advising that myself and Elliot Rashman, who was at the MTV awards, orchestrated the after-match demos!

New issue KK173, was out in 2009/10 and the Sky cameras filmed the front cover whilst we sold. but didn't show it as it was probably too controversial. Smart bloke in a grey suit approached and said hello, who turned out to be David Moyes. We were a goal down just on half time. "F*** off Hughes," shouted some Blues. Steve Parish got ejected for complaining to the stewards and police that Wigan fans were singing offensive and racist songs about Adebayor, despite a three-page spread in the programme on racism. Kick it out.

Final KK visit was in 2017/18 FA Cup 5th round it was a 1-0 loss to third tier Wigan, due to a mistake by Kyle Walker which allowed 'Will Grigg's on fire", to score. City were down to ten men after Delph was sent off. Pitch invasion by Wigan fans post-match.

■ Wigan Athletic, DW/JJB/Brick Community Stadium opened in 1999. First KK visit to the JJB in season 2002/03 when we lost 1-0 in the League Cup 3rd round, prior to beating United 3-1 at home.

Away Day Zines The Latic Fanatic, Cockney Latic.

WEMBLEY FA CUP FINAL 2013, LOST 1-0.

Must go down as one of our more recent lows. Rumour had it that Mancini was about to be sacked. It was a horrible drizzly day, which affected sales. The coach we (Me, Sue, Frank, Alex, Joe) travelled down on with the Swinton branch was clapped out and at one point we didn't think it would make it to the game. After Zaba was sent off, Watson scored the late winner and his name is etched in my mind along with Jamie Mackie, from the QPR game. Wigan were later relegated, as City finished runners up in Cup and League. It was disappointing that our players wouldn't play for their manager, but even worse, they couldn't play for us, the fans.

9. GREATER MANCHESTER

Short trips to Stretford, Bolton, and Bury

BOLTON WANDERERS

First KK visit was in season 1989/90 Nat Lofthouse Testimonial 2-0 win, then in 1990/91 Freddie Hill T/M 1-2, 1992/93 Frank Worthington T/M 2-4, which we attended with Bolton fans Brian, Larraine and son Danny Wilson, but competitively it was in the 1995/96 season, and a 1-1 forgettable draw.

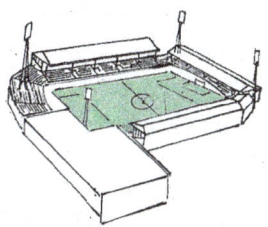

■ Burnden Park. My first ever City away game was at Christmas 1955, and a 3-1 win.

We were usually located on the Embankment behind the goal and could park virtually next to it, so selling was quite handy. An incident stands out particularly in one game. Bolton's most vociferous fans were located to our left, and jeered City players as we took a throw in right in front of them. 'Kinky' received the ball and did an outrageous body swerve, which silenced the crowd and put the whole of the Bolton defence on their backsides. Surely the worst ground redevelopment in the country, but at least it kept the club afloat? (Pink Floyd's Nick Mason later reported as a benefactor)

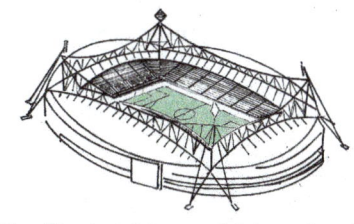

■ The Reebok/Macron/University of Bolton/Toughsheet Stadium, opened 1997.

First KK visit to their new home was in season 1999/00. Parking was good as the dedicated away car park was right next to the ground, which is set in one of the most picturesque parts of the country on the Middlebrook Estate. City fans were located behind the goal.

In the 09/10 December game, I was

standing right behind the goal, when Craig Bellamy was scythed down for a blatant penalty. He'd already been booked for mouthing off at referee Mark Clattenburg, who then booked Craig and farcically carded him for diving. Clattenberg later admitted in his book that he wrongly sent him off as he was such a pain! Gary Cahill scored for Bolton in that game, and I could never understand why City didn't sign him?

We generally met up with Bolton supporting friends, the Wilson's for a meal after the games, win, lose or draw at a pub opposite the ground where we blagged our way in as it was designated for home fans only.

January 2006, 2-0 loss - Sue and eldest daughter Marnie were doing the Executive bit, so it was down to grandson Joe (8) and myself to do the KOTK honours. We went in early though and watched the lads limbering up, plus admiring the cheerleaders. Their goal celebrations comprised of two fat blokes running up and down the touchline with flags to the tune of Amarillo! Stewards were evicting Blues for next to nothing, causing a half time fracas. We hung around after the game waiting for the girls to appear, without a burger van or coffee kiosk in sight. Needless to say, as soon as they arrived, a bit worse for wear (it has to be said), Joe shopped me for shouting and swearing during the game.

It was cold and windy in 2006/07, hence the nickname 'the Horwich wind tunnel'. A fire alarm caused the hotel at the ground to be evacuated. I signed the memorial book for the 46 who died on the Embankment in the 1946 F.A. Cup game v Stoke, when my Dad, a Bolton fan, was luckily in the opposite, Lever Street end. A Testimonial game was later played at Maine Road.

Season 2007/08, there were one or two scuffles, quickly squashed after the League Cup 1-0 win, and there was an altercation between an older and younger Blue in the seats near us which required police intervention. Season 2010/11, after our F..A. Cup final win over Stoke who'd beaten Bolton 5-0 in the S/F, City won 2-0 to clinch 3rd on goal difference to Chelsea. We again met up with Brian, Larraine and Cassie Wilson after the game for a meal at the Meadowbrook. Bolton were relegated in 2012, in a draw at Stoke, on the day we clinched the title v QPR.

Awayday Zines Tripe n Trotters, White Love, The Normid Nomad, The Wanderer, The Trotter, Wanderers Worldwide.

BURY

First KK visit was in season 1997/98, in the 2nd tier, a 1-1 draw. KK62 on sale. Almost a home game. Parked on the street, and sold inside and outside. Many pre-season friendlies were played with big away support to help swell the Shakers' coffers, and we always sold very well. "I wouldn't wipe my arse on that", a Blue shouted at me after one game, "Thousands buy it" I replied, and other Blues smiled as they walked past. On another occasion, season 2002/03 I sent a £20 donation, with an accompanying letter advising I'd be selling KK and would donate any sales monies to the club. The stewards however, stopped me from selling at half time saying "They're going mad up there, watching you on CCTV". So, we moved out of range and carried on selling, but I didn't donate those sales!

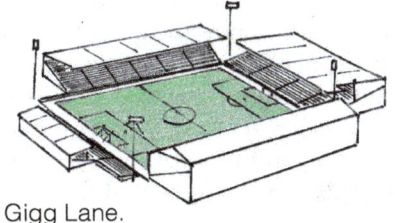
■ Gigg Lane.

Awayday Zines The Hatchet, Where Were You at the Shay? Robbie The Bobby.

MANCHESTER UNITED

First KK visit was for the 1989/90 friendly, Mike Duxbury T/M 2-0 win. Later, in February, it was a 1-1 draw when 'Bob' Brightwell 'wellied' in the equaliser. We parked up in Alexander House car park on Talbot Road where I was working at the time, then took the short walk to the ground. The City team bus passed us on the way, with rags banging on the sides, and giving our boys the (American?) one finger, which gave Reddo in particular a laugh. We had tickets in the Family stand as members of the Junior Blues and I managed not to lose my temper! The 1-1 draw in 1992 with 'Dissa' Pointon sent off, and Curly's penalty (last one until Haaland 2023) celebrated by a pitch invading City fan with Keith, was a particular memory, as youngest son Alex was taken there with his friends Sam and Ben, courtesy of their dad Gwyn, all reds. Obviously, he remains a staunch Blue.

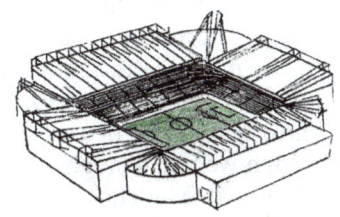
■ Old Trafford, my first visit was in 1957, a 4-1 loss

Parking was always OK in car parks fairly close to the ground, just off Talbot

Road, and we were often asked the way to the ground by red-bedecked strange people with non Manc accents, as we walked past the tackiness. We didn't sell outside, needing "hands free on Derby day", usually arriving early to avoid the insults, mayhem, bricks, bottles, spit etc, but often took a few KK's in, tucked inside the jacket to sell, generally unimpeded. There were many lows at the swamp, including the 0-5 in 1994/95, but the 2008, 50th anniversary of Munich, was particularly sweet, and the minute's silence was impeccably observed, despite the provocation of objects thrown down on City fans. One Blue got the timing just right just right before its end with his "C'mon City" shout.

The 4-3 loss, in 2009/10 was hard to take, with Mike Summerbee having a rant on TV, but we were "getting closer".

Then the Rooney shinned effort in the 1-2 loss in 2010/11, marked the end of their dominance. A Neil Young tribute night was held that year on the same night that United had a function with ex City fan and rag David May saying it was "to celebrate 35 trophyless years of City failure". United class? No, never, and don't get me started on Patrice Evra, or Goldbridge. The likeable Alan Keegan, who was a Junior Blues compere and Maine Road announcer, (though always a red), became particularly annoying as "The Voice of Old Trafford" with his "Glory, Glory, Theatre of Dreams, C*untry Roads, Greatest club in the world" shite, plus the naff gloating song he played after their League Cup semi-final win in 2010. I spoke to him before an O/T game later about it, telling him he should know better, and he replied "I'll always be professional David" Good answer, which we had a laugh about, as by then City were by far the most dominant force in Manchester, England, and Europe.

Not sure when THAT banner went up, but instead of annoying us, we just thought what sort of club would allow, indeed condone such a thing, ridiculing their neighbours inside their own ground? A big club? A massive club? The World's greatest club? Or a small minded, bitter club with no class? No brainer. Then when the cheeky Tevez poster went up, in town, they went apoplectic, and have tried to emulate it ever since featuring every new (failed) manager or player. If ever a club deserved the Glazers, it's them, but deep down we all know they were shafted, and some of their fans commendably formed F.C. United.

Of course, in recent years we have had a good number of successes. My favourite quote after the 6-1 was from Neil Shaw, who boarded the tram which was full of early leaver reds, one of whom was even more dismayed when he exclaimed "Oh no, they didn't get a 5th did they?"

The ground exit and walk back to the car park was generally incident free if you weren't daft, but there were always stories of City coaches getting attacked. Frankly

I don't like myself on Derby days, the whole place, area and their fans bring out unhealthy feelings, which I struggle to keep under control. There is a saying "the worst kind of Man United fan", which needs little further explanation, compounded by their legendary selective memory syndrome, Considering I went to school in Salford, and had my bob hat pinched in 1960, mainly through the FSA, I have met the occasional decent Red, including Martin and Clair, our local Dentist and Hygienist!

We always managed a decent getaway, driving back into town and out again down the East Lancs Road, as United fans were usually heading 'darn sarf'. or for ferries to Ireland, or Manchester Airport. (Just my little joke! Or Is It?

Awayday Zines Red Issue, Red News, United We Stand (who we swap with), Walking Down The Warwick Road, Our Day Will Come (United/Celtic), Shankhill (wrongly spelt!) Skinhead, Joe Royle's Head, K Stand, In League With The Red Devils, Blackburn Reds, Northern Exposure.

WEMBLEY

First visit was for the 2011 F.A, Cup S/F, City massive underdogs. We travelled down on the Friday, only saw Blues, no rags, stayed at Boston Manor hotel in Ealing. On the Saturday we drove over to R and C's in Regent Park, spotted a City car with a sky-blue scarf in the back window and suddenly felt more confident. Had a stroll, to settle the nerves, then off to a London restaurant but was horrified to find our party included a couple of reds, who were actually OK. We boarded the train at Marylebone to Wembley, rags singing "Stockport, Stockport give us a song". Infuriating, but I managed to keep my temper with just a "f*ck off back to Norwich" response. We were at the West end, with seats on the upper tier near the back. Berbatov missed two early chances. Half time 0-0. Yaya's goal came on 52 minutes, Joe tipped a free kick over the bar, and Mike Dean sent Scholes off for a foul on Zabba ("Scholes can't tackle"), as we hung on, enjoying incredible emotion at full time. Mario's wink upset Rio especially, who years later apologised for his behaviour.

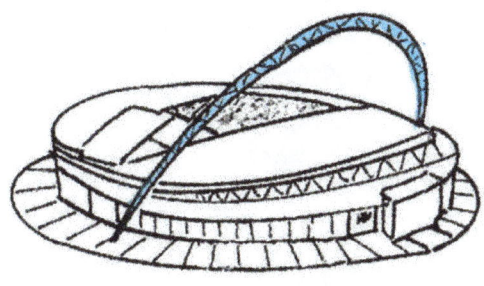

We'd taken many years of abuse, now they just couldn't handle it. A City fan shouted "nothing else matters now" I corrected him. Sunday breakfast in St Johns Wood, before driving home, past London pubs full of Stokies singing Delilah.

For the 2011 Community Shield we headed down to the Smoke and Steve P. and I attended the third tier Brentford v

Yeovil game, Uwe's first match in charge of the Bees, 3-1 win.

Sunday morning and brekky at the Landmark hotel opposite Marylebone station. We had our City shirts and colours on and enjoyed marching out with the smartly dressed United players, resisting a playful kick at the bastards, as they walked the few yards to their coach, so we cocked up all the sycophants' photos. Train to Wembley, flogged a few zines, went up to our seats on the front row of the 2nd tier. Two goals up at half time, then 2-2, Steve P. went off to the loo, despite my protests, "before extra time", so I (unfairly) blamed him for the 3-2 loss! Sombre drive home, mainly Blues at the services, and I was surprised to see a few rags as far North as Oxford!

2023 F.A. Cup Final 2-1, sadly we had to give it a miss (first since 1956). We were, however, well represented by the family. Eldest daughter Marnie, Andy, plus youngest son Alex, Granddaughter Heather was sitting with her partner Adam, a red, in the lower tier, brave boy in this family, but fairly quiet and reserved. thought it could have been a 7-0 when the early goal went in and he left immediately after the final whistle, to be found later, sat on a bench, looking forlorn, as our Treble loomed!

Apparently, Wembley got the car parks the wrong way round, causing problems mainly from reds, but overall, I'm told, City and United fans were drinking together, though there was trouble reported at service stations on the way home, rags lying in wait for City coaches to arrive, and attack. Finally, it was the 2024 F. A. Cup Final, ridiculous 1-2 loss, then the 2024 Community Shield game 1-1 aet with City winning the shootout 7-6 on pens.

10. CHESHIRE, STAFFS & N WALES

Fairly local trips to Chester, Crewe, Macclesfield, Port Vale, Shrewsbury, Stoke, and Wrexham, even including THAT Wembley outing

CHESTER CITY

First KK visit was in season 1991/92, in the League Cup 2nd round. 1st Division City won the 1st leg against 3rd Division Chester 3-1 at Maine Road. The return leg resulted in a 3-0 win which was played at Edgeley Park, not sure why, but very handy, as most Blues, allegedly, live in Stockport? Parking on a fine September night was good, and whilst selling we clocked the Chester manager Harry McNally walking past who seemed like a decent chap.

Wayne Norris and I sat on the front row of the main stand and enjoyed encouraging the City subs as they warmed up along the touchline within touching distance. Needless to say, the win, assisted sales.

Deva Stadium, opened 24th August 1992 and first KK visit was in season 1999/2000, City (Div 1) v Chester (Div 3) and a 4-1 win in the 3rd round of the F.A. Cup.

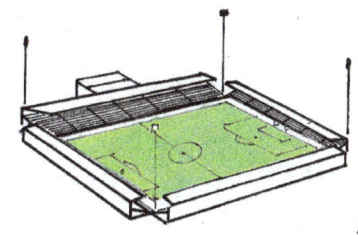

■ Deva Stadium.

KK Contributor Brian Duffy attended one friendly, where he was faced with a picket line as Chester fans were protesting against their American owners. Most City fans were baffled, and having made the journey, entered the ground to watch the match.

Awayday Zines *Hello Albert, The Onion Bag.*

CREWE ALEXANDER

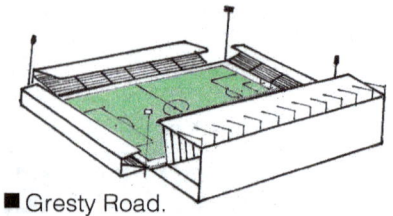
■ Gresty Road.

First KK visit, against another team we never expected to play in the League, happened in Div. 1 (2nd tier) in 1997/98, Boxing Day. We opted for a trip down to The Wheatsheaf in Onneley, meeting with the Droylsden supporters' club, entertained by mine host Mark Bittner (RIP), for an excellent Christmas lunch. then a coach trip to the ground, with high expectations? Needless to say, we lost 1-0 to a 19th minute Holsgrove goal. Never mind, it was back to the Wheatsheaf in silence for a few bevvies and City chat. We then drove down to South Wales to visit daughter Kaye, where we watched Oasis unplugged on the telly, Noel performing magnificently, whilst Liam was sulking off stage with Patsy.

In 1998/99 they were actually in a higher division than City. In 1999/2000, it was a 1-1 draw, and our next visit was in December 2001/02. The original match was postponed due to a frozen pitch, which we found out about as we travelled to the game. It was eventually played in March, a 3-1 win, though we'd run out of fanzines, which foxed some Blues who used my selling place as a meeting point! Nosh at an Italian restaurant on the way, the owner, a Juventus fan, hated United, always worth a tip! We were joined by Nick Spencer who was doing the Telegraph match report of the game.

Awayday Zines Super Dario Land, He's Not Danny Grady.

MACCLESFIELD TOWN

The Macc Lads v Manchester City, surely a physical impossibility, but rub your eyes, it actually DID happen in season 1998/99. Tickets were like gold and were collected after a long, time-consuming queue at Maine Road. We finished up somehow with four tickets and Tony G, John Keohane and myself travelled. I therefore had a spare ticket which I attempted to sell at face value, and was threatened with arrest by the police. Luckily my charm prevailed with the use of the magic words "you gotta be joking" and "you cannot be serious", right out of the John McEnroe phrasebook which stood me in good stead. Naturally I escaped a jail term, and

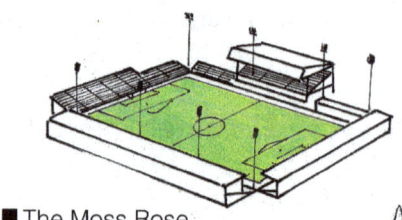
■ The Moss Rose.

indeed sold the ticket! City scraped to a 1-0 win with a late Shaun Goater goal but promotion looked as far away as ever. We also played a friendly there in 2005/06 (1-1) on the day the news broke that SWP was to be transferred to Chelsea which upset everyone except Ishmael Miller's mum, who advised us not to worry as her son would save us. The other good/bad news, advised by MEN reporter Chris Bailey, was that the ageing Andy Cole would replace him.

Awayday Zines Wraggs To Riches, Pyramid.

PORT VALE

First KK visit was in the F.A. Cup 4th round in season 1990/91, a 2-1 City win, Clive Allen celebrating his goal kissing the badge.

Then it was the night match in 1996, 2-0 win, when 'Lucky' from the Levenshulme branch's 'City till I die' song was first aired, later adopted by most clubs in the country, including supporters of the English National team, but City fans don't sing it these days. In 1997/98 it was a 2-1 loss, the game in which 'Kinky' decided to down tools.

Season 1999/2000 it was another 2-1 win, when, on the way to pick up Steve P in Warrington, we passed the Ian Botham crew charity walk and put some money in the bucket, with a rousing City chant.

■ Vale Park. My first visit was actually in season 1989/90, Vale, with Alex Williams in goal v Bolton with the Wilsons (City away).

For the friendly in 2001, the Martin Foyle Testimonial, in which Robbie Williams was rumoured to be appearing. Steve P and I drove down and there were big queues, causing the K.O. to be delayed. Robbie did actually appear but it turned out to be a comic cuts game with Robbie scoring a twice taken penalty and Martin's kids putting in an appearance, with Nicky W, allowing one of them to score. Commendable that Robbie supports Port Vale, but disappointing when he was interviewed on T.V. at a United cup final when he confessed that "If you support Port Vale, you have to have a fantasy club, Manu". Hmm.

A further friendly was played in 2006/07, with a 3-0 win. It was always a decent trip and we could park close to the ground. Sales far exceeded expectations on one occasion with around 400.

Awayday Zines The Memoirs of Seth Bottomly, The Vale Park Beano.

SHREWSBURY TOWN

First KK visit was in season 1988/89. Sue and I travelled over by car for the April evening game, hoping for a boost to our promotion hopes. We parked up opposite the ground, and sold KK4, outside and inside. Neil McNab was in our crowd and unimpressed when I shouted "read about Roy Paul's views on penalties" which was an article included inside. (Neil had missed a late penalty in a previous visit) but I didn't mean to sound insensitive, sorry Neil). The game finished 1-0 to City, but I missed Trevor Morley's headed goal, as I exited the ground on 85 minutes to sell KK, and Sue missed it, as everyone jumped up in front of her!

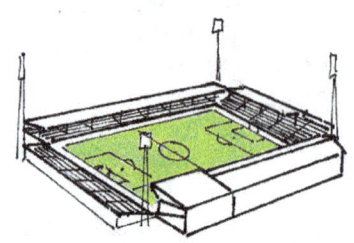
■ Gay Meadow, my first visit was in season 1983/84 a 3-1 win.

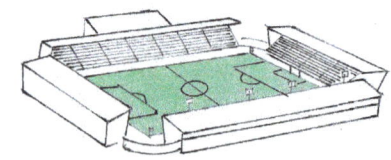
■ New (Croud) Meadow, opened July 2007

Just the one visit with Sue and Steve P. for the pre-season friendly at the new ground in 2007/08. A 2-0 City win when we had a bit of culture with a visit round the Hawkstone Park Follies pre match. Roland Foster wasn't so lucky as he got a dose of food poisoning from one of the outlets!

Awayday Zine *A Large Scotch.*

STOCKPORT COUNTY

First KK visit was in season 1997/98, a 3-1 loss. Sean R - "On the night before the game Blues were queuing in the freezing cold and driving rain at Maine Road to get one of the handful of tickets for the away game at Crewe. Many of us had lost pay/overtime and made other sacrifices, but typically, spirits were high, as the hours passed by. If the players had that kind of commitment then we would have a team of world beaters."

Corrie's Les Battersby was getting mobbed by Blues, pre match, Junior Blues helper Michelle was wafted in the face by a Police horse's tail, necessitating a hospital visit. We were 3-0 down within the first half an hour, the game finishing 3-1.

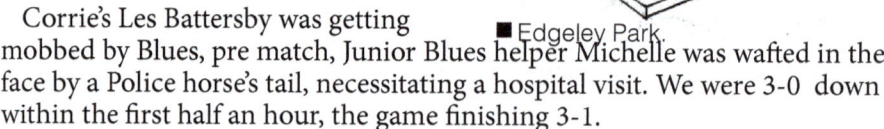
■ Edgeley Park.

Further games were played in 1999/2000, 2-2, and 2001/02 1-2. We also played a number of pre-season friendlies, including 2000 when there was chaos at the turnstiles, where separate tickets and pay gates were unmarked.

Local pubs and car parks were always available, and City generally took massive support, so sales were always good, especially for pre-season friendlies, as it was usually the first KK of the season, and we didn't have any problems selling. I once received an apology from a Blue who'd slated me on the radio, but now accepted I was right regarding the running of the club at the time, as we headed for the third tier.

Awayday Zine The Tea Party, I-O County.

STOKE CITY

The first KK visit was on Boxing day 1988, when 12,000 Blues made the trip in a 24,056 crowd, the majority being in fancy dress as suggested by Blueprint fanzine and with the banana craze in full flow. However, in 'Typical City' fashion, after the team ran out with inflatable bananas issued to Blues in the crowd, and going a goal up, it was a 3-1 win for the Potters. For some unfathomable reason pre-match I decided to ring their club secretary to ask permission to sell and I actually drove down to meet him, table the zine KK2, but he was unimpressed, and refused permission. Obviously, we still sold, with Danny dressed as a Beefeater and yours truly as Henry 8th. amongst others, which gave us the back cover for KK3.

■ Victoria Ground, my first visit was in season 1971/72, a 3-1 win.

Many further visits were made, up until 1996/97, when they vacated the ground. for the Britannia stadium. The final game was at the start of that season when Alan Ball was given grief by both sets of fans, and the 2-1 defeat contributed to his sacking, and

Franny's subsequent managerial merry go round.

First KK visit to the Britannia was in season 1997/98. There was a large car park next to the ground in its own compound for away fans' coaches but we usually parked in local car parks. However, for the 1998 showdown we decided to travel on a supporters' club coach which, surprisingly to us, had a stop off on the way, so we arrived too late to sell. Unfortunately, the 5-2 win didn't save us (both) from relegation to the 3rd tier, as Port Vale and Portsmouth (ironically managed by Alan Ball), both also won, but at least it gave us hope for a swift return.

After the game I foolishly decided to try and sell, as I'd a load of unsold zines to get rid of, whilst the rest of the KK team left me to it. Obviously, our relegation was all down to me and a Blue, full of vitriol, squared up to me. I dropped my bag in anticipation but for some reason he decided not to take a swing. I think that goes down as probably my lowest point as a KK editor and seller. Bricks and bottles then rained down on us from Stokies who'd taken up the high ground, prime position, after furiously exiting their stands.

Season 2007/08 and despite Rory Delap being sent off for a foul on SWP on a bitterly cold day, we lost 1-0. At half time

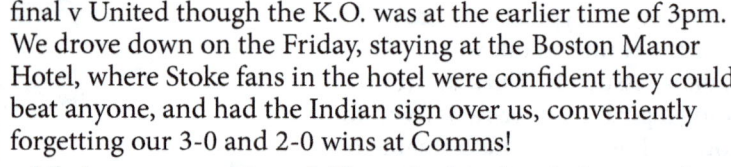
■ Britannia Stadium/Bet 365 Stadium, opened 30th August 1997, renamed in 2016.

City fans thought, further to United fans who'd done it recently, that it would be entertaining to throw plastic bottles at each other spraying all with beer, injuring some youngsters, then emptying bins, causing the cops to move in with dogs.

WEMBLEY F.A. CUP FINAL 2011, WON 1-0

Some 13 years after relegation for both teams to the 3rd tier, we faced each other in the F.A. Cup final, We adopted more or less the same routine as for the semi-final v United though the K.O. was at the earlier time of 3pm. We drove down on the Friday, staying at the Boston Manor Hotel, where Stoke fans in the hotel were confident they could beat anyone, and had the Indian sign over us, conveniently forgetting our 3-0 and 2-0 wins at Comms!

We drove over to R. and C.'s, parked and took the train from Marylebone. We met KK subscriber Gene Laschuk, over from Australia specially, chatted to fellow Blues and sold KKs. We held our breath as Joe saved point blank from Kemlyn Jones, went mad when Yaya scored the winner, and cried with joy at the end. Our 35-year trophy drought was over.

On the Sunday we went into Regents Park, breakfasted and reflected on events with Steve P. and youngest son Alex. The season had been a long, cold one, and after selling the zine in the snow, wind and rain, we all deserved our day in the sun. To see all those long-suffering Blues friends, family, colleagues, KOTK subscribers, sellers and contributors, finally enjoying success was a real joy. I was invited onto Granada TV on the Monday in Albert Square, when Lucy Meacock quizzed me on my thoughts, before spotting, grabbing, and asking Mike Summerbee, all the same questions on air, which stole my thunder!

Awayday Zine *The Oatcake, The Victoria Voice, A View To A Kiln.*

WREXHAM

Just the one visit, but a very significant one, on an awful rainy day in December 1998, 12 noon KO, with City languishing in 12th place in the 3rd tier after the loss at York. A Gerard Wiekens goal gave us the 1-0 win. Ian Rush (who we were once given first dibs to sign, but declined, before he went to Liverpool) for the first time ever, didn't score against us. The game was a blur, the weather was dreadful, hurricane like conditions, and the rain made selling outside the stand behind the goal, where the 3,000 City fans were housed virtually impossible. The fightback was on, followed closely by the 2-1 home win over table topping Stoke City, then promotion in the play off final v Gillingham, marking the start of our rise from the third tier to eventually become the Club World Cup Champions. Pinch me!

We'd previously played a friendly there in 1995/96 a 6-1 loss, ex Blue Cliff Sear's testimonial, which we missed. We also visited on a red-hot August night, an early game for Joe Hart, and a 3-3 draw, when we chatted to Steve Harrison, 'The Charlatans' manager. After which we stayed in eldest son Danny's caravan in Ruthin.

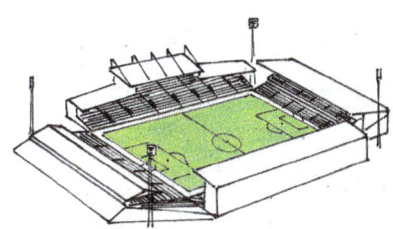
■ The Racecourse Ground.

Awayday Zine *The Sheeping Giant, Red Passion.*

11. SOUTH YORKSHIRE & DERBYSHIRE

Over to Chesterfield, Derby, Doncaster, Rotherham, Sheff United, and Sheffield Wednesday.

CHESTERFIELD

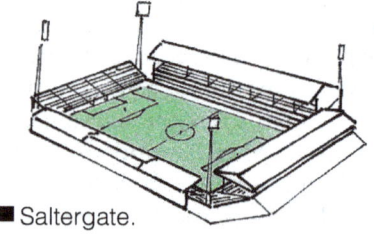
■ Saltergate.

First KK visit was in season 1998/99 in the third tier. On the Friday before the game, I received a phone call from the Beeb at 8.15pm, asking if I would go on the 24-hour news programme at 8.20am on the Saturday morning to talk about City, I agreed despite fancying a lie in and was joined by Ged, but forgot that Reading tickets were going on sale at Maine Road! Then it was off to Chesterfield, we parked in a car park close to the ground and sold some KK75's.

Some Blues sitting behind us took exception to the interview and chanted a few obscenities at me, water off a duck's back, but nevertheless, not very nice. The game finished up as a 1-1 draw, as our stuttering campaign continued, Lee Crooks (51) scoring our equaliser, leaving my detractors in a sate of delirium, no doubt. We also played the League One club in the League Cup 2nd round in 2006/07, on a Wednesday night, with Mick Curtis * on driving duty, in his Rover, so we exhausted our knowledge of the Rover songs we knew - The Irish Rover, The Gypsy Rover, The Wild Rover plus the classic He Called He Rover, she was a showgirl (!?), and parked a reasonable distance from the ground. We sold out of zines before the game, criminal! It was too far to go back to the car to replenish and get back to the ground before kick-off, so we had to suck it up. Had a chat with Nicky Weaver's dad at half-time. The pathetic 2-1 loss wouldn't have enhanced sales after the game anyway! They were also relegated at the end of the season.

Awayday Zines *The Crooked Spireite, Tora, Tora, Tora, What Happened to the Crooked Spireite.*

DERBY COUNTY

First KK visit was in season 1989/90, a 6-0 loss. Drove over the M62, through the roadworks, M1, A52, then looked out for the floodlights. Parked up, sat in the stand behind the goal and watched the debacle unfold. The loss put paid to Mel Machin's tenure as manager, only a few weeks after one of our greatest ever results, beating United 5-1 at Maine Road.

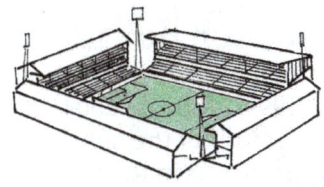

■ The Baseball Ground. My first visit was with daughter Marnie in season 1983/84, a 1-0 loss, to finish 4th in Div 2.

■ Pride Park - Opened 18 July 1997

First KK visit to Pride Park was in the 1998/99 season, in the League Cup 1st leg, round one, with City in the 3rd Tier, Derby 4th in the Prem, and we managed a creditable 1-1 draw (lost 1-0 2nd leg.) Parking wasn't handy but selling was OK. We travelled over from Centre Parks in Nottingham, where we were spending a few days and bumped into Stuart White, David's dad, then a Director at Sheffield United, after falling out with City completely a few years previously, though he was now welcomed whenever he could make it to watch the Blues. Sue and I spent half the holiday figuring out the format for KK71, our tenth anniversary issue, but avoided divorce proceedings somehow, whilst youngest son Alex and his mate Kyle disappeared each day to enjoy the swimming, and escape the arguments. We also played them in 2000/01 drawing 1-1, in the Prem. I was working at Manchester Airport and an engineer working for one of the sub-contractors and also a Derby season ticket holder, had a car park pass, which he photocopied. We used it in the official car park, as parking spaces, (cleverly) weren't numbered or allocated. At the end of the game, we said hello to Derby's Gio Kinkladze, who'd parked nearby, (car reg K1 NKY) and I serenaded him with a brief rendition of Boz Scaggs' Lido Shuffle - "Gio, oh-oh-oh- ohio, one more goal ought to do it, one more goal should do it, Gio……" which I once tried at City, but unsurprisingly, it never caught on?

On another occasion 2007/08, a bitterly cold night, I went with Dave Woodhouse, Andy and Steve. We parked in a side street, but needed a quick getaway after the 1-1 draw, so no post-match sales. Driving back from Dave's in Mosley Common to Leigh, I was stopped by a Copper for doing over 30 mph. He asked where I'd been and I told him Derby for the match with City. He must have taken pity as he didn't book me!

Awayday Zines Shilton Saves, Mutton Mutineer , Hey Big Spender, The Sheep.

Mick has had a very tough time in the last few years but is now hopefully on the road to recovery.

DONCASTER ROVERS

Friendlies were played in 1999/2000 and 2004/05, both 1-1 draws, but the only competitive game was in the League Cup 3rd round of 2005, which resulted in a 3-0 loss on pens after 1-1 aet, Nedum Onuoha having been sent off, which was later rescinded. Ged drove over, we parked up next to the ground, sold a few KK's and it was all looking good, as we stood up behind the goal, but sadly watched the debacle, another one, unfold. I was just glad I wasn't still working in Doncaster at the time!

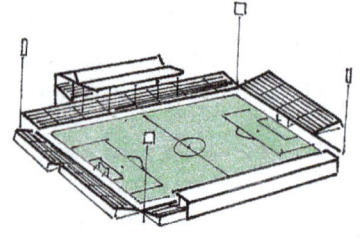
■ Belle Vue.

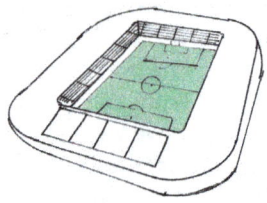
■ Keepmoat Stadium, opened in August 2007.

We played a friendly there in 2007/08, just after it opened, in an early game for Sven resulting in a 3-1 win. The media claimed he was given a hostile reception, which was nonsense, as his name was chanted throughout by City fans. KK 151 was the only City fanzine left, on sale.

Awayday Zines Keegan Was Crap Really, Raise The Roof, No Smoking In The Main Stand, Popular STAND.

ROTHERHAM UNITED

Just the one KK visit, in season 2001/02 a 1-1 draw. Kevin Keegan was advised by a Millers' punter that he couldn't manage a team like Rotherham, "why would I want to" he replied. Why indeed! City fans were kept in at Yates' wine lodge pre match by the police until ten minutes before KO. The game was a bit tense as we seemed to struggle, but eventually, after going a goal down, equalised for 1-1.

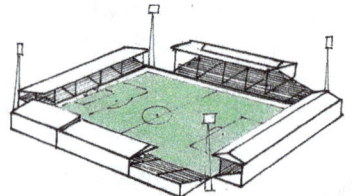
■ Millmoor. My first visits were in the 60s with a Millers supporting work colleague, when we lived in nearby Conisbrough.

Awayday Zines Moulin Rouge, Windy and Dusty, Mr Whippet's Dead, Two Up, Two Down, The Scrap book.

SHEFFIELD UNITED

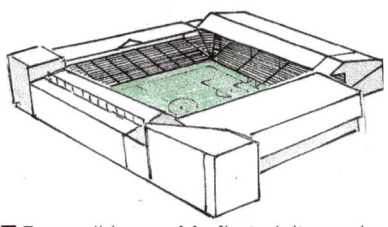

■ Bramall Lane. My first visit was in 1961/62 season, a 3-1 loss.

First KK visit was in season 1990/91, a 1-1 draw, and it was the short drive over the Pennines. At the ground I was confronted by a policeman on a horse asking if I had permission to sell 'that thing', as I was causing an obstruction, even though I was standing next to the programme sellers, who obviously weren't causing one!!

We'd usually park up on the street, but selling was always a pain as we were moved on by the stewards to the opposite side of the street where no City fans walked past, although on one occasion in 2000 they relented, We had tickets in their main stand, away allocation sold out, when Michael Brown scored their winner and we were the only ones not celebrating.

Season 2006/07 we stopped at Woodley services on the M1, bumping into media moguls, Fred Eyre, Cheesy, Chris Bailey, and Charlie Hadfield, Ian partaking of an all-day brekky. "Are you watching Alan Menzies" they chanted to me (Alan was critical of them in his KK column!).

The climbing centre on Bramall Lane was closed so we had no food, and we were housed in the lower tier, underneath the extended roof on the new terrace with no pillars to block the view.

The most memorable game for all the wrong reasons was the 2008 4th round F.A. Cup clash, when some of the turnstiles were broken so we had to dash to the ones that were OK. It was a 2-1 loss, nicknamed Balloongate, as their first goal was scored after the ball and City's defence became bamboozled with the sea of balloons in the penalty area.

We also met twelve years after Balloon gate, in the 4th round of the F.A. Cup in January 2020, a 1-0 City win. Aguero (73) scored, with Henderson saving Jesus' weak penalty, diving to his right. (Just as he did in the 2025 F.A. Cup final for Palace, though he should've been sent off previously in that game) We visited our friends Dave and Kay Pugh in Conisbrough, before setting off to the Lane where we parked up in a side street. Mike Pickering was standing in front of us. After the game, we stayed overnight in Conisbrough.

WEMBLEY 2023 S/F 3-0 We left this one to our kids.

Awayday Zines *The Flashing Blade, Greasy Chip Butty, The Cutting Edge, Red and white Wizaaard.*

SHEFFIELD WEDNESDAY

First KK visit was in season 1989/90, New Year's Day K.O. at 12 noon, and a 2-0 loss. We'd usually park in Marsden's (a subsidiary of the firm, Robson's, I once worked at) car park and take the short walk to the ground. We played them in the F.M. Cup in 1991/92, a 3-2 loss. After collecting KK20's from the printers I drove over with Louise, but arrived late, as I took a few wrong turns, but sold well at half time and full time. Next visits were in the 2007 F.A. Cup 3rd round 1-1, (2-1 home)

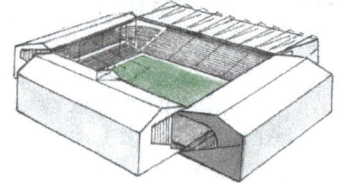

■ Sheffield Wednesday, Hillsborough. My first visit was in season 1957/58, a 5-4 win.

We sold outside the away end, the infamous Leppings Lane, where we said hello to Wednesdayite subscriber Mick Grayson (see KK 267) ("Wednesday won't improve until we get out of debt.") Mark Herbert, producer of 'Dead Man's Shoes, This is England' etc, and 'Just Another Wednesday' fanzine editors and sellers Judith, Martin and Daniel Gordon (who also produced films on the 1966 North Korean World Cup team and The Orgreave scandal.) We Blues usually took up our allocation in the whole stand.

On the Tuesday night after the Villa Carabao Cup final, we met in the F.A. Cup 5th round in 2020, a 1-0 (Aguero 53) City win. We drove over to our old neighbourhood Conisbrough to stay with friends Dave and Kay again. Arrived in good time, parking up for a fiver. Sainsbury's beckoned for a snack, where we met up with Chris a long-term KK purchaser, who told me to check the facts in the Villa final programme, which I did, noticing they'd omitted our Cup Winners' Cup win in 1970, the latest in the 'anti City, no history' campaign and I sent a letter to that effect to the FL. I received an utter bollocks reply about how they go to a lot of trouble to get things right, but no apology for omitting our European achievement! We sold at the end of Lepping Lane again, taking up our seats in the lower tier. It was a cold night, and a poor display but we got through, and had a good drive home.

Awayday Zines *Just Another Wednesday, War of the Monster Trucks, Cheat! Boddle, A View from the East Bank, The Blue and White Wizard, Out of the Blue, Spitting Feathers, Taking Wednesday into Insanity.*

12. WEST MIDLANDS

Down to Villa, Birmingham, Cheltenham, Walsall, West Brom and Wolves.

ASTON VILLA

First KK visit was in the April of season 1989/90, which was most memorable for the 2-1 win which secured our place in Division One, though we were infiltrated by Poll tax protesters. It was our first win in 51 First Division away games, and our first win on Live TV since the 1969 FA Cup final.

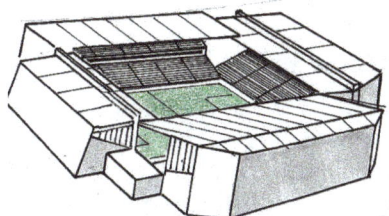

■ Villa Park. My first visit was in December 1957, a 2-1 win. I was very impressed with the ground and the massive Holte End.

It was generally a good place to visit with only the occasional loss. The 5-1 win in April 1991 was particularly enjoyable, David White scoring four. We used to park on the local streets and later in Morrison's car park not too far from the ground. It was always awkward selling as their stewards took delight in moving us on outside, and it was ducking and diving inside. Penultimate game of the season in 1996, and a vital 1-0 win kept our survival hopes alive, before we dashed home to watch the emotional Oasis gig at Maine Road. Sadly.......

At the F.A. Cup tie in 2006 North stand upper, the stewards, who were concentrating on stopping us selling, took their eye off the ball, and left the board room unlocked allowing City fans to pop in and help themselves to beer and food plus wrecking the joint! Micah scored the equaliser in the last minute, and we heard the roar from inside, as we'd left early to sell. Post match Micah swore live on TV, which he's never been allowed to forget, but the 1-1 draw boosted sales. (2-1 win in the replay).

Once, when Tom drove, we parked on the other side of the park. A bloke came out to mind the car, but the cops arrived and he swiftly disappeared back inside his house. After the game he re-appeared and asked for his money, so we told him that the cops had advised us not to pay if he asked. Tom drove off, just missing his foot!

We usually met up with Dave Woodhall, editor of the Villa zine Heroes and Villains, and enjoyed good banter until Dennis Mortimer, captain of the Villa European Cup winning team of 1982, which we applauded at the time, walked past and Dave said "There's a man who's lifted a Cup that you'll never win", so I walked away.

A Villa fan brought KK 145 back as he thought it was a programme! Another said "King of the Kippax, you're having a laugh". "Yes, we are actually!" 1999/00 a Villa fan said "I hope you stay up; this division needs you". So not all bad!

We went out early in 2016 after Iheanacho's hat trick in the F.A. Cup 3rd round to beat the traffic as we were heading down to S. Wales. We followed the sat. nav. which sent us to the M5 via West Brom. whose game had just finished and we were stuck in traffic for ages.

Awayday Zines Heroes and Villains, Witton Wisdom, Never Loved Ellis, The Holy Trinity, The Villa Bugle, Deadly Doug.

WEMBLEY MARCH 1ST 2020 CARABAO CUP FINAL, 2-1 WIN

Fine dry day, but encountered a couple of blizzards driving down on the M6. We stayed over in Uxbridge and enjoyed a leisurely morning before catching the train to Wembley. Bumped into Cheesy and from a distance watched the City coach outside their hotel, which was serenaded/bombarded by Villa fans

singing a song about 1982. We popped into our usual Cafe Nero then entered the ground without the usual hassle from stewards, but with low sales. Tom and Steve did a bit better despite abuse from Villa fans. Close game, highlight being the wonder save from the much-maligned Claudio Bravo to maintain the 2-1 win.

We boarded our train at 8.40pm to Uxbridge, so home in the early hours after delays on the M6, and I got a speeding ticket, doing 50 not 40 mph in the roadworks. Overall, Villa fans were a disgrace with their chants, in the ground, and in the queues for the trains post-match. Losers.

BIRMINGHAM CITY

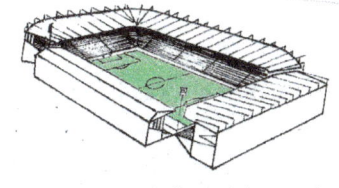

First KK visit was in season 1988/89 and a 2-0 win which I related on request for their 'Tired and Weary' fanzine.

Fairly short journey to the city centre location in Small Heath, home of the Peaky Blinders. There were car parks close to the ground, and it was an enclosed area for City fans to access the away stand, behind the goal, without much hassle from the stewards, or away fans. It was amusing to buy a 'Kipper tie' or cup of tea from the kiosk!

■ St Andrews, my first visit was in December 1958, a 6-1 loss (but we beat them 4-1 at home the day after) Another impressive ground with steep terraces behind the goal and the Kop along the side of the pitch.

Carin drove, circumnavigating road works in 2002/03 on the M6 taking the outside lane with standstill jams on the two inside lanes. It was always amusing to observe jams north bound from Brum to Manc full of rags. Banter from home fans included "you can stick that up your arse, Kippax that's a long way up North, shit of the Kippax, we're gonna stuff you", Response was "You're just a town full of roadworks". Then at night we saw Ian McNabb at the Academy 2 with Sue, and Colin Nicholls, absolutely brilliant.

In 2003/04 season we took John James Claxton, who was released from HMP Springhill, to his first game since the 70s. John's story was related in KK's 54 and 55, he loved the craic despite the 1-2 result. We scored in the 88th minute, then in the 92nd and 97th minute conceded two goals. Tommy Muir's coach was bricked on the way in. John sadly took his own life a few years later, for personal reasons, unrelated to football, and we were devastated.

Awayday Zines *Wake Up Blue, Blues News, Tired and Weary, The Small Heathen, The Zulu, The Penguin.*

CHELTENHAM TOWN

Much to the disappointment of Pat Higgins and Bill Cronshaw of the local City Supporters club, who'd waited many years for this, the 3rd round Cup tie in season 2020/21 was played behind closed doors, due to the pandemic. City, playing a weakened team (why?), went behind through May in the 59th minute and things looked dodgy. The inevitable changes were made and Foden (81), Jesus (84), then Torres (90+4) saved our blushes for the 3-1 win, thus avoiding one of our (less frequent these days), legendary banana skins.

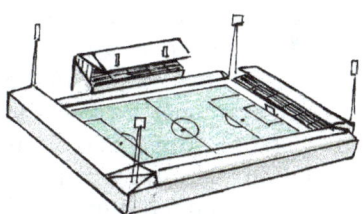

■ Jonny Rocks Stadium.

Awayday Zines *Murphy's Frog.*

WALSALL

First KK visit was in season 1988/89 March 25th, when KK 3 was still on sale. We parked in a local car park and it was a memorable game towards the end of the season with Dibs. off injured, Gleghorn in goal and 2-1 down, recovering to go 3-2 ahead before a rush of blood from David Oldfield gifted them an equaliser for 3-3.

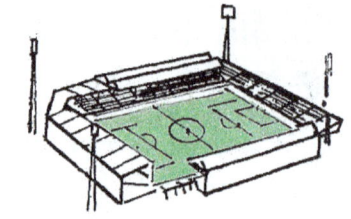
■ Fellows Park.

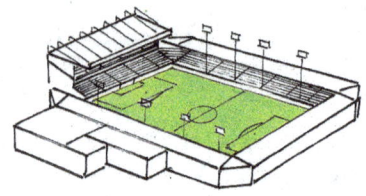
■ The Poundland Bescot Stadium, opened in August 1989.

The Poundland Bescot Stadium is the most viewed ground in Europe as seen from the M6 motorway. We parked on the industrial estate next to the ground, which was a bugger to exit, and watched a 0-0 draw in 1999, suffering sleet, rain and hail. Our tickets were sorted by F.S.A. mates Tony Jesson and Dave Woodhall, in the home seats. However, we did go top of the First division (2nd tier) in season 2001/02, after a 0-0 draw.

Awayday Zines Blazing Saddles, Moving Swiftly On, Chasing The Dream.

WEST BROMWICH ALBION

First KK visit was in season 1988/89. It was a mid-week game so I drove down after work with Mark and Stuart, M6, M5 then the A41, and eventually parked on the street some distance from the stadium. Consequently, I didn't take in many KKs, and we entered the ground ten minutes after kick off so I couldn't even sell. The highlight of the game, (a 1-0 loss) was the entertainment provided by City fans, involving confrontations between inflatables. The players on the pitch wondered what on earth was happening on the terraces. Humour not hooliganism! Needless to say, it was a 1-0 loss, but nevertheless a memorable evening.

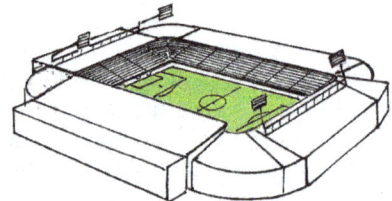
■ The Hawthorns. My first visit was in January 1958, and a 5-1 loss in the FA Cup 3rd round on a foggy Brummie afternoon.

In season 2001/02 the 4-0 loss put a dent in our promotion prospects, and after the game Steve P. bumped into Frank Skinner, who was surprised as he thought all the City fans had left early. Eventually we were able to park up in one of the many car parks close to the ground.

West Midlands police, in 2005/06, were carting off Baggies, including one who bought KK as he liked Ricky Hatton. The gates to the away end were closed before K.O. so we had to be quick to get through and after the match we had to walk all the way round the ground to get back to the car park, unless you hung on and waited for the gates to be opened. We sometimes chatted to Gary Owen and often saw Adrian Chiles and once saw Mick McCarthy. Sue was once prevented entry with her umbrella.

■ John Cleaver and the Ed on way to WBA in 1958

City fans were housed in the new stand behind the goal taking up the whole stand, but later occupied just half when Albion fans turned out in greater numbers, after they reached the Prem. We often met up and swapped zines with Simon Wright and his missus Glenys, (they once, kindly, gave us a mention in the programme) who produced Grorty Dick, the Albion zine. Selling was a pain as we were moved on by the stewards outside the ground and they made it difficult inside and outside post match. Indeed, I was once escorted off the premises by a grumpy steward. Eventually I wrote to the club and they instructed the stewards to be kind. Needless to say, the instruction did not register and we were required to produce the necessary documentation to assist our case, after which all was well. The stewards even agreed on one occasion to hang on to the tickets we had for our friends Dave and Barbara Moreton, who were stuck in traffic, travelling up from S. Wales, and handed them over when they finally arrived.

I'd often wait for an Albion fan who'd bought every issue. but one City fan told me "It's shite as some of the contributors don't go to games" adding "I only buy it cos I buy all things City"

Awayday Zines *Grorty Dick, Last Train to Rolfe Street, Albion Till We Die, Fingerpost*

WOLVERHAMPTON WANDERERS

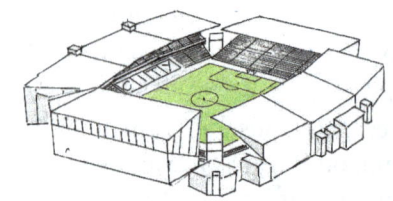

First KK visit was in season 1996/97, a 3-0 loss. There is a pub near the ground with a car park where they allow away fans to park for a small fee. It was a short walk to Morrison's, where famously in 2012, we listened to United's game at home to Everton. After they went 4-2 ahead and hit the bar, Everton made it 4-3, then equalised as the cafe, full

■ Molineux. My first visit was in 1958/59 season, a 2-0 loss, when I remember entering the ground at the back of the South bank, to view probably the most breathtaking terrace in the country, and the most characteristic ground

of City fans went up, startling the shoppers. That meant as Hadge Johnson (RIP) told me with a smile, "if we won our last four games v Wolves A (2-0), United H (1-0), Newcastle A (2-0) and QPR H (3-2) we'd become Champions". Impossible(?) but achieved, "I'll swear you'll never see anything like this ever again" …..Agueroooo.

Selling was OK, actually undercover outside the Steve Bull stand and out of the rain. Inside, the concourse was cramped and on the terrace, we were subjected to missiles and worse from the upper tier. Wolves' fans bought KK and once told us we were the best fans in the country. August 2018, I sold to a Wolves fan from Salisbury who joked about the Russians trying to kill them with Novocheck, black humour in the Black country! The 3-2 loss in 2019/20 season, after Ederson was sent off and we went two goals up was a choker, but we recovered winning three of the next four visits including a 5-1 in 2021/22 with four memorable goals from KDB.

Awayday Zines *A Load of Bull, Wandering Star, Manchester Wolves, The Tatter*

13. EAST MIDLANDS

Not the easiest places to get to, Burton, Coventry, Leicester, Notts County, and Forest, after leaving the motorways, but better than going to London!

BURTON ALBION

Just the one visit, in the second leg of the League Cup S/F in season 2018/19. We travelled in Tom's car, on an extremely cold night. Parked in a car park close to the ground, visited Mackies for food and to keep warm, braving the elements with consequently poor sales, like about a dozen!! The 1-0 win made it ten nil on aggregate and we were off to Wembley again to lift the Carabao Cup.

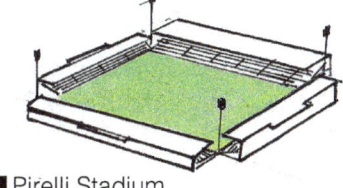
■ Pirelli Stadium.

Awayday Zines Up Front, Clough The Magic Dragon.

COVENTRY CITY

First KK visit was in season 1989/90 a 2-1 loss. But in season 1992/93, Saturday November 21st, I was working on the new T2 Terminal project on site at Manchester Airport, and was listed on the rota for working on the Saturday but advised them I couldn't do

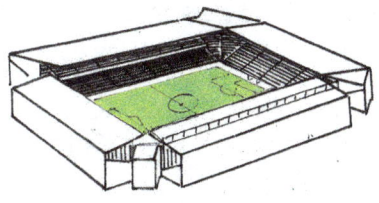
■ Highfield Road, my first visit was in season 1968/69, a 1-1 draw, at the home of the Sky Blue Imitators.

it. Me, Danny, Louise and Richard (who'd come from Blackpool) set off a little later than intended. Bombing down the M6, rainy conditions and roadworks there was a traffic jam ahead, so I slammed on the brakes, stopping just ahead of the car in front. Unfortunately, the car behind hit me, forcing me into the car in front, so damage was done to the front and rear end. After exchanging details, we limped into a layby to examine the damage. Turning back was never an option, daft to continue, yes, but our priorities were right. However, a piece of string would be required to provide a temporary repair to the front bonnet and lo and behold we found a length of rope by the side of the slip road, and carried out emergency repairs, which enabled us to proceed, park up and sell some zines. Unfortunately, City were soon two goals down but recovered to win 3-2. We drove home in the dark with full beam, but it looked like dipped headlights, as the front end was damaged. On the Monday morning, I took the car into the firm's garage for repairs and to pick up a squad car. When I arrived back on site I was greeted with a written warning, from my arsehole of a boss.

There were plenty of other visits, parking was generally fine, as were sales. One of the more memorable games was the F.A. Cup 4th round tie in 1996, 2-2, City fans hurling snowballs and sheets of ice at the pitch during play. In the re-play it was a 2-1 win, when Coventry fans in the North stand, stormed the main stand, scaring City families. Then an early game for Ali Benarbia, but a 3-4 loss, in 2001/02.

Awayday Zines Westender, Sky Blue Army, Peeping Tom, Twist n Shout, Gary Mabutt's Knee, Lady Godiva Rides Again., In Dublin's Fair City.

LEICESTER CITY

First KK game was in season 1988/89, a 0-0 draw, Andy Dibble saving a penalty, his second for City. After leaving the motorway it was the drive through the Leicester suburbs, to park up in the local streets or car parks. After our 5-0 loss at United in 1994/95 we faced The Foxes away in the next game, winning 2-1. Typically, as I was selling KK pre-KO, a United fan walked past, at a safe distance, shouting "KK, you must mean Kanchelskis" Rags dontcha just love em?

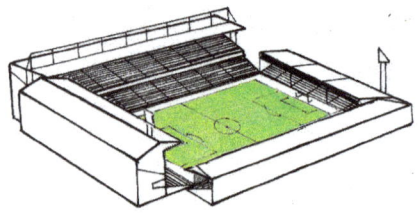

■ Filbert Street, my first visit was in season 1959/60, a 5-0 loss.

In the 2000/01 game, pre-KO, an Owlish looking City fan shouted "don't buy KOTK it's biased", then stood in front of our sellers shouting abuse, which they'd not really signed up for. After the game, a 1-0 win. Wayne X conned us both into the players' lounge, which wasn't too impressive.

The Walker Stadium/King Power was built fairly close to Filbert Street, so it was the same route, and we usually parked in a Polish fella's drive for a tenner. 2003/04 1-1, home fans allowed to walk straight past the away exits, subjecting us to some abuse. One Leicester fan with his daughter (presumably) spat on the fanzine I was selling, as a few expletives were exchanged, then after wiping it clean, the complete opposite happened when a Leicester fan bought the slightly soiled zine.

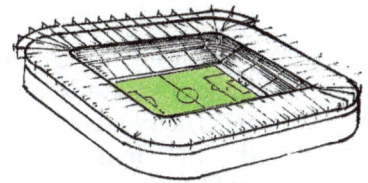

■ The Walker Stadium/King Power, opened 2002 as the Walker stadium, then renamed The King Power

In the draw for the F.A Cup 3rd round tie in season 2010/11, Serge Pizzono, of Kasabian, pulled out the Leicester City ball number 21, followed by Noel Gallagher who extracted the City ball number 23.

Tom drove and parked up. The game started badly with an early Leicester goal, but City fought back to earn a 2-2 draw, celebrated with a Neil Young tribute. We won the replay 4-2, which set us off on our rise to the very top of World football. All down to Noel, but don't tell him!

Awayday Zines *The Fox, Filbo Forever, Where's The Money Gone? When You're Smiling*

WEMBLEY, 2021 COMMUNITY SHIELD 0-1, MISSED THIS ONE.

NOTTS COUNTY

First KK visit was for the 5th round Cup tie in 1991, a 1-0 loss, We parked up close to the ground, and KK 15 was on sale at 80p. Unfortunately, I'd forgotten the bags of 20p coins which was a bit embarrassing, but we managed to get some change at a local garage, though sales were inevitably poor, compounded by the massively disappointing 1-0 loss,. We'd hit the woodwork on numerous occasions, which gave us the front cover for KK16.

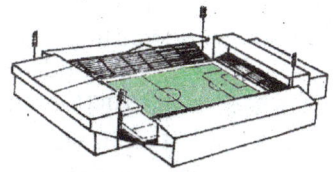

■ Meadow Lane, my first visit was not for the F.A. Cup 3rd round tie in 1962, 1-0 win, as I had flu, and my mum wouldn't let me go, but in 1982 a 1-0 loss.

On September 11th 2001 League cup 2nd round, it was the day of the World Trade Centre attack in New York, which we learned of on the radio as we drove down. City won 4-2 aet in a game of subdued atmosphere for a match which really shouldn't have been played. City fans were housed in the new stand behind the goal. After the game we spoke to Nicky Weaver's mum and dad, "back to his best "I told them. "Written things are crucifying him, so I don't read anything now" his dad said. Got flashed on the M60 on the way home, despite being the only car on the road, and was duly fined.

For the 2010/11 F.A. Cup 4th round tie, they'd just sold their star player and a disgusted County fan wanted to sell us his ticket in the home end. I was interviewed before the game by Sully (RIP), saying that City were a different team these days, than 'Typical City' of old. However Bob played a weakened team, a philosophy that didn't work, as they went ahead, before Dzeko equalised and we escaped a late scare.

We arrived back in Manc in time to see The Cult at the Academy with budding guitarist grandson Joe, who'd been invited to the sound check by Billy Duffy earlier on, and was thrilled when he was allowed to hold Billy's guitar. We won the replay 5-0.

Awayday Zines The Pie, Thin Yellow Stripe, Flickin'n'Kickin', No More Pie In the Sky.

NOTTINGHAM FOREST

First KK visit was in season 1989/90, the Zenith Data Cup 2nd round, a 3-2 loss, which I attended with FSA friend and Saints fan Ged O'Brien. Later in the season it was, of course, the infamous Gary Crosby goal, when he headed the ball out of Andy Dibble's hand and tapped it into the empty net. It should have been disallowed, the ref later admitted, and Dibs took the ribbing in good spirit, later auctioning his gloves off for charity.

■ The City Ground, my first visit was in season 1958/59 a 4-0 loss, after which I wrote a letter to the Pink complaining about the entrance prices, for which I received the princely sum of 7/6d for my trouble.

It wasn't an easy place to get to. Once we had a chat with Colin Todd at Woodall services, also met and chatted to Blues', Simon Hill from 5 live and Miles Barter from Brummie radio. Then we drove through the City centre to Trent Bridge, where once in a traffic jam on the bridge a car driving in the opposite direction, somehow got through at speed, very scary. If you were lucky you could park on the car park next to the away end. We were generally located in half the Bridgeford stand behind the goal. I don't remember us being hassled for selling.

Awayday Zines The Tricky Tree, The Almighty Brian, Trent Times, Garibaldi, Forest Forever.

14. ANGLIA & SUFFOLK

Turn left at Birmingham for Colchester, Ipswich, Norwich and Peterborough.

COLCHESTER UNITED

First KK visit was in season 1998/99 for the first ever Saturday night TV K.O. in Div. 2 (3rd tier) and a 1-0 City win, with a Shaun Goater goal. We travelled down in my 'new second hand car' with Ged and Carin,

■ Layer Road.

We parked up in a local car park and walked to the ground, where a Blue had a pop calling me "Mr. Critical". However, after convincing him that EVERY article in KK is not written by me under a nom de plume, he seemed appeased! The Sky TV cameras were lurking about and I was interviewed, telling them that I thought we'd get promoted via the play offs. but South Yorkshire Blue, Gary Brough reckoned we weren't good enough!

After the game I was also told by a Colchester fan (?) that we wouldn't go up because "You're not good enough". adding "I'm a Man. United fan actually". Hackles rose, but a little voice in my head told me not to rise to the bait. Well, we're never more than six feet away from one, like rats, proven right once again. Sometimes selling the zine on the street even after a win can be a right pain. Return fixture was a 2-1 win.

Awayday Zines *The Blue Eagle, Out of the Blue, Popular Stand.*

IPSWICH TOWN

First KK visit was in season 1988/89, a 1-0 loss, Vinny Tovey, the KK representative on this occasion. Not the easiest ground to get too but certainly better than Norwich as you didn't get stuck behind tractors and the roads are better. We were tipped off by one of the cops, Jimmy, a red, who attended Maine Road on duty, and travelled with Blues, that there was a great B & B near to the ground which we booked on a couple of occasions. He was a bit miffed that it was full up when he tried to book it! Turns out later, it was located in the red-light district, where the five prostitutes were murdered by Stephen Wright.

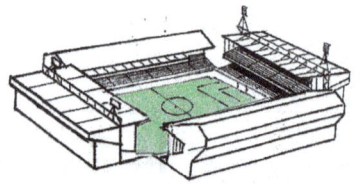

■ Portman Road, my first visit was in season 1982/83, a 1-0 loss, City 2nd in the table, eventually relegated. I'd attended the match after wangling an expediting visit to a firm who were producing equipment for a project I was working on. They were based in a little town called Soham, which became infamous later for the murder of the two little girls photographed wearing United shirts, by Ian Huntley.

Blues would often take advantage of the seaside amenities in nearby Great Yarmouth, and I managed a bit of Karaoke. Results were never good, including a 2-1 loss in 2001 which relegated City, after United deliberately and pathetically lost at home to Derby, and Ipswich fans held up a banner stating "You are the Weakest Link, Goodbye".

Ironically, Joe Royle later became their manager! We spent a few hours at Felixstowe on the Sunday, at the veteran car rally, then enjoyed a trip round Cobbold's brewery before the game on Monday 7th May. Post match, I was approached threateningly by one of their 'top boys' presumably, so thanks to 'Jimmy the Plod' for stepping in. However, we did manage a win in 1994/95 season, 2-1 our first in 23 visits and then the 4-1 F.A. Cup 4th round win in season 2001/02, so quick revenge for THAT banner. Liverpool knocked us out in the next round though.

Awayday Zines
Dribble, A Load of Cobbolds, Those Were the Days (available from a stall behind the North stand) Blue, Without A Care In The World, Score.

NORWICH CITY

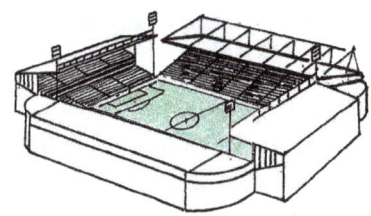

First KK visit was in April 1990, with Danny, Louise, and Richard, the 1-0 win securing our First Division place, with a 4th minute Adrian Heath goal. We travelled down on the special and sold well (I was next to my favourite tree!). We nipped into the home seats before the end of the game and exited swiftly, beating Blues who were kept in, so managed to get good seats on the train home.

■ Carrow Road. My first visit was the first game of the 1982/83 season and a 2-1 win, but we were relegated at the end of the season.

We later drove, a tortuous journey, getting stuck behind tractors. We sometimes stayed over at the Cavalier hotel. fairly close to the ground, with the Chadderton Blues, including the Bernard Buckley road show, which involved an after-match Karaoke/disco. Once at The Artful Dodger pub we witnessed a local lad sing on Karaoke, a phenomenal and memorable version of Bon Jovi's 'Bed of Roses.' We'd often park in a car park a good way from the ground, so estimating how many KK's to take to sell was always a challenge, as it was criminal to run out, which we sometimes did, and it was too far to go back to the car to replenish. I always had my special tree to lean against and sell!

We had many memorable visits, April 1997, four days after the Tuesday night trip to Ipswich, and a visit to the docs, (given the all clear?) so we didn't set off from rainy Manc until 11 am. Reports of chaos on the roads due to IRA bomb threats, meant we finally arrived at 5.30 pm, The game finished 0-0, and the journey home was less traumatic, with a little detour to Moss Side to drop Debbie Derbyshire off. It was the last away game of the season, KK attending every single one. We finished KK60, and sent it to the printers but I was too ill to attend the final game at home to Reading (see Sunderland).

Then in season 2004/05, we sang "there's only one City" and "sing when you're cooking". We stayed at freezing cold Comer. Blues made a fuss of Joey Barton's brother spotted entering the ground. 2-0 down then 2-2 at half time, but we missed Delia's rant as we were selling at the back of the stand. City won 3-2 and we sold in the snow post-match. In 2012 Steve P.. and myself travelled, and we went to the White Horse Inn in Trowse at night, where we took part in the Karaoke, when the locals were very friendly. We won 6-1, including the Tevez golf swing celebration. Norwich fans stayed until the end, being quite gracious, as they didn't want the rags to win the title!

Eventually the Hotel at the ground would allow us in for drinks, food, and to watch TV. Final KK visit was in September 2019. Steve P.. sorted an Air B & B right next to the ground. It was a disappointing 3-2 loss, when we realised even at that early stage we'd lose the title to Liverpool.

Awayday Zines *Never Mind the Danger, The Citizen, Sing When We're Ploughing, Liverpool Are on the Telly Again, Spud International, Attack, A Fine City, Ferry Across The Wensum, I Can Drive A Tractor, Cheap Shot. Man Utd Are on The Telly Again, On The Ball, A Tint of Yellow, Attack.*

PETERBOROUGH UNITED

Just the one visit in the FA Cup 5th round, in 2022, City winning 2-0, with goals from Mahrez (60) and Grealish (67).

KK were represented by Sean Riley, he left work at 2pm, Wilkie and Ozz caught the train over from Manchester to meet up with him in Sheffield and they drove down, parking up by 4pm. A couple of the local hostels were visited including the rather charming Charters Bar, a decent sized boat moored up on the banks of the River Nene. Outside they were showing support for Ukraine in the form of scarves and flags, Zinchenko was captain for the day. No skinhead mob to deal with this time around, unlike in 1981! An A4 size souvenir programme was produced, and the mixture of the two old stands which still remain from the 1981 game and the solitary floodlight pylon blended in well with the much more modern stands. The game was generally uneventful, settled by two late City goals. The journey home was interrupted by the Highways Agency, (no announcement) and a 40-mile detour plus road closures added an extra hour for most travelling Blues.

Amazingly, as we, and they, went up and down the divisions, we managed to avoid each other completely over the KK selling years.

Awayday Zines The Peterborough Effect.

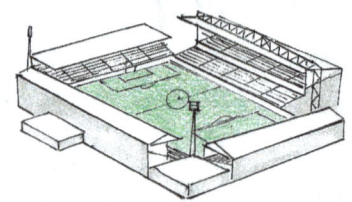

■ London Road, my first visit was for the 1981 5th round F.A. Cup tie which City won 1-0.

GILLINGHAM

First KK visit was in May, season 1998/99. We travelled by coach with Ged and Carin, for the 2-0 win, with no idea of the play off final to come. I sold outside the ground and was called a Munich c*nt by a Blue, from a safe distance.

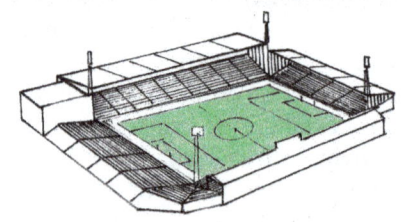

■ The Priestfield Stadium.

WEMBLEY, 3RD TIER PLAY OFF FINAL, 2-2 AET, WON ON PENS

The game became notorious for the distribution of tickets with massive queues outside Maine Road and fans waiting for hours to collect..

Tickets were like gold. We, Tony G. and myself. collected ours from Alex Channon of the Swinton supporters club, on the night United fluked their Champions League win over Bayern Munich, clinching a never to be repeated

(?) treble. We drove home giving the V's to armchair rags, dancing on the pavements and in the road. We also obtained further tickets which we were able to provide at face value to genuine Blues, one of whom said we were on his list, if and when he won the lottery. Still waiting!

We drove down, meeting up with Steve and Cath Knott and their son, staying over at a Travelodge then taking the train into Wembley. It was our first visit to the stadium since the Full Members Cup Final in 1986 and it was a horrible drizzly day. We were warned off selling, so decided that producing a KK special for the occasion would be futile. Pre match we chatted to Billy Duffy (with his dad) who advised that whilst we'd won Cups at Wembley this was the most important final in our history.

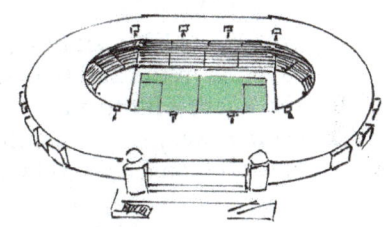

■ The old Wembley Stadium

Before K.O. Russell Watson (a decent red) sang Nesum Dorma (when I could still hit the Vincero high note!) and we settled down to watch the formality of a comfortable City win. The game is well documented. When you watch the recording of the game at 2-0 down you could not see a way back as we missed opportunities. Blues were streaming out, programmes were being flung down from the top tier and then suddenly Kevin Horlock scored what looked like a consolation goal, but as the 'five minutes' sign came up we had renewed hope and when Paul Dickov scored there was only going to be one winner in extra time. However, it didn't happen, and it took the nail-biting penalty shoot out to see us home and start the most remarkable recovery to the very peak of World football. We made our way back to the train station exhausted, drained, and could not muster a cheer, when Blues on the opposite platform expected us to join in with rousing City songs. The relief was tangible and the drive home uneventful, as we prepared for life in the First Division and beyond. As it happened. I was proud of young Blues at the services singing "You can stick your effing treble up your arse!"

Our next visit was in the 2000/2001 League Cup 2nd round 2nd leg after the first leg had resulted in a 1-1 draw. It was a long drive down necessitating an overnight stay in a Travelodge. We bumped into Gary Owen in reception who was on the phone to GMR presumably. We sold KK 88 and won 4-2 aet. Driving back, we broke up the journey, taking in the NEC Birmingham Conveyorex exhibition, which enabled me to claim some petrol money on expenses from work (Manchester Airport).

Awayday Zines *Brian Moore's Head Looks Uncannily Like The London Planetarium.*

SOUTHEND UNITED

Just the one KK visit in season 1996/97, in the 2nd tier. Sue and I gave a lift to a Blue, and we were very lucky that the game was played on a cold wet October Tuesday night, as the day before the whole of Essex was gridlocked, and we'd never have made it to the game. As it happens it was a 3-2 City win, Georgi Kinkladze having one of those games as we went three goals up, Kinky scoring 2 and assisting the other. Southend pulled two goals back after he was clogged, injured, then substituted to leave us hanging on in 'Typical City' style! We sold well as the only City zine present, and stayed overnight, our passenger finding his own way back home.

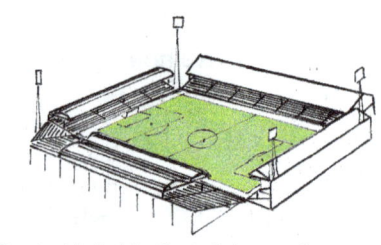

■ Roots Hall. My first visit was for the League cup 2nd round 1st leg in 1986/87, a 0-0 draw the day after Billy McNeill left to join (and relegate) Aston Villa. A 'Swales out' petition was provided on the special which I didn't sign as no alternative was offered.

Sean R: "We left Manchester at 1.15pm and the M6, M1 & M25 were relatively kind to us allowing time for a couple of jars before kick-off. A group of drunken Blues caused damage in the pub close to the ground, thanks lads, City don't need you. There were about 1.600 Blues in attendance, sitting/standing in the cramped 'International bicycles' stand opposite the old Kop, which is now a minute two tier stand with flats built behind."

Ed's note *What a friendly and co-operative club Southend is. No problems selling zines, good grub, pleasant and helpful police and stewards, Ta folks.*

Awayday Zines *Roots Hall Roar, What's The Story Southend Glory? The Seasider, Roots Hall Rambling, Shrimp Season.*

15. SOUTH WEST & SOUTH WALES

Youngest daughter Kaye, Everton-supporting (?) hubby Brian, with kids, Isaac and Laura live in Newport, so a handy base for South West and South Wales' games. Down the M6 and M5 to Bristol and Bath, plus M4 to Cardiff, Newport, Swansea, and TNS.

BRISTOL CITY

First KK visit was for the friendly in 1999/2000, a 1-0 loss. We played there in the League Cup 2nd round in 2007 winning 2-1, and we visited Blaise castle on the way down. Then it was the Gerry Gow's testimonial game in 2014, a 1-0 win. We were advised by Derek Partridge, who was managing the former City players team that there was room on the coach if we fancied it. Grandson Joe and myself duly boarded, with team players, and some of Arnie's Bredbury branch members on board, but we set off much later than we would normally have done for this game in the holiday season. We stopped off at Knutsford services, waited for Eric Nixon and his son to arrive, by which time the Bredbury branch jumped ship, as they'd "had enough!". We were stuck in traffic for ages, we finally arrived in Bristol a couple of hours late, after they'd agreed to wait and put the K.O. time back. The game went as expected, with the winning goal coming from Shaun Goater, who played for Bristol first half, and City in the second. Young Joe confided, "I know it's only a friendly, but you still want City to win!" Afterwards we enjoyed drinks and sandwiches in the Executive lounge, and chatted to Kevin Bond, Shaun, Big Joe and Gerry himself, which was very pleasant, finishing off a day in the sunshine enjoyed by everyone in attendance. KK216 sales of about tewnty were donated to Gerry's Testimonial fund.

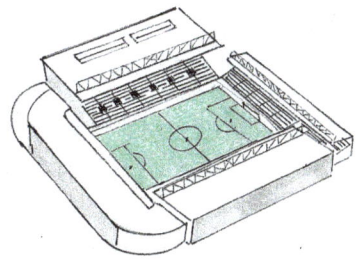

■ Ashton Gate. I first visited Bristol in 1980 with Sue (who read a book in the car park) whilst I inspected the Silos being manufactured by the Braby company for a BXL Bromborough Project I was managing. I was surprised to find that their factory was based right next door to Ashton Gate, so I couldn't resist a peek.

The big games were the League Cup semi-finals in season 2017/18, after they'd knocked out United in a previous round. First leg finished 2-1 to City, after a scare, when substitute Sergio's stoppage time goal rescued the Blues.

For the return leg we set off early, stopped off at Strensham services, bumping into Blues and arrived in Bristol in plenty of time, and parked up. We were collared by Radio Bristol and did a little interview. City fans were later labelled jokingly as 'cardboard cut outs" by a presenter, but there was a real buzz of excitement and anticipation around the place. We popped into KFC for a snack where we had a nice chat with a Bristol fan and his grandson, then picked up a souvenir programme and made our way to the away end, past all the stalls and razzamatazz. We were on the front row for the game which they pulled back to 2-2 after we'd been 2-0 ahead, but we went on to win 3-2. On the way back to the car we were stopped by some of their fans who were delighted with the game, and wished us well for Wembley, saying we should have no trouble with Arsenal! We reciprocated by wishing them good luck for promotion, which they sadly didn't achieve.

We listened to Bristol radio on the way back to Wales, where we stayed at our daughter's home, before attending the next match, Cardiff City in the F.A. Cup. Bristol fans were proud of their team's performance and gushing in their praise and admiration of the Blues, the best team they'd ever seen at Ashton Gate. All in all, I cannot remember many better away days. Full marks to Bristol City, our boys and Pep, for putting out a strong team and performance.

Finally. in season 2022/23, it was a 3-0 away win in the F.A. Cup 5th round which we watched on TV.

Awayday Zines The Cider ed, Come In Number 7, You're Time Is Up, Stand Up, City Gent, One Team In Bristol.

BRISTOL ROVERS

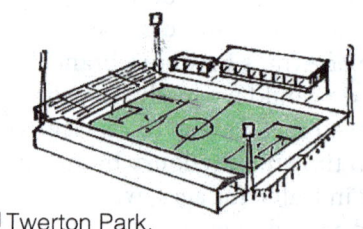

■ Twerton Park.

First KK visit was in the League Cup 2nd round 2nd leg of 1992/93, a 2-1 win which compensated for the 0-0 draw at Maine Road in the 1st leg. It meant a few hours off work and a pleasant three-hour drive, arriving in Bath in plenty of time on a cool October evening. Decent parking and selling. City zines were mentioned in the programme, including my working colleague at Cottam Power Station in 1970, Pete Abrams, who used to drive me daft with his oft repeated "Shipshape and Bristol Fashion" phrase, plus his Adge Cutler stuff, ooh aarh!!

0-0 at half time, Gary Flitcroft announced as 'Flip Flop' on the Tannoy, replaced Mike Sheron. City went a goal up via Maddison's og. Rovers equalised, but in the final minute Rick Holden screwed in a shot which their goalie helped onto the post and over the line. Rick celebrated as though he'd won the Cup, and

T.C. turned to the Blues behind the goal and expressed his delight.

We also met in season 1998/99, after they'd switched grounds. Pre match it was a one-minute silence for Sir Alf Ramsey and a disappointing 2-2 draw after being two goals ahead. We'd made it into the play offs, having missed out on 2nd place which Walsall had already secured. We enjoyed an overnight stay and the next day we had an ice cream (wow!) by the Clifton Suspension bridge, before driving back up to Manchester to watch the brilliant Bruce Springsteen at the MEN Arena.

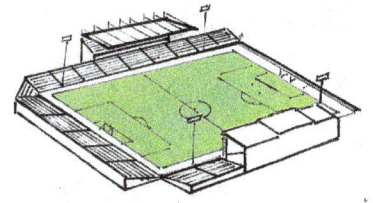
■ The Memorial Ground, opened 1996.

Awayday Zines The Gashead, Black Arab, The 2nd of May,

CARDIFF CITY

First KK visit was in season 1993/94, for the F.A. Cup 4th round tie. Drove down, parked up, dodging puddles in the car park. We sold KK36 outside the away open-end entrance, watched the team walk past as they had to abandon the coach within walking distance of the changing rooms as news came through of the Franny Lee takeover. It was time to enter the ground as the atmosphere turned nasty. Second Division Cardiff won 1-0 with Keith Curle missing a late penalty. Lots of off field aggro. reported, which completely passed us by.

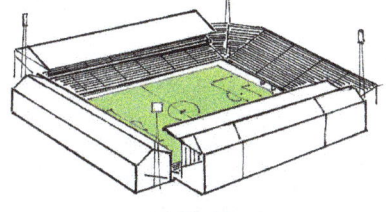
■ Ninian Park, my first visit was in 1961 for the FA Cup 3rd round tie, a 1-1 draw.

■ Cardiff City Stadium, opened 22nd July 2009.

First KK visit to Cardiff City Stadium was at the start of season 2013/14 in the Premier League. We naturally stayed in Newport, at youngest daughter Kaye's, whose hubby Brian, dropped grandson Joe and myself off, to witness the 3-2 defeat. Waiting to be picked up after the game we were engaged in mild banter like "now you know how Swansea fans feel". "Trophy winners" changed their mood (Swansea won the League Cup in the previous season!) Our friend Dolly, who travelled separately with Joe advised "congratulations, you've just beaten the Champions". Bold words which ultimately proved to be true.

Further games were played for the 2018 F..A. Cup 4th round tie in season 2017/18, after the Bristol City S/F 2nd leg. I was given a lift by Kaye's friend and Cardiff fan Suzanne, with her friend and boys who were very excited at the prospect of City being in town. They also disliked United and were miffed at the signs on the motorway advertising the rugby match in a week's time instead of today's match. "That's how much they think of football in Cardiff", Suzanne said. Arrived there early as they like to see the team coach roll up, but were unsuccessful with autograph collecting. I sat outside Costa for a while, chatting to a young Cardiff fan, who was surprised that Ryan Giggs (the new Welsh

manager) and I went to the same school in Swinton. I had a chat with another bloke; a member of the Cardiff City Trust and we exchanged stories of supporters' reactions to Trusts and Fan on the Board type stuff. The game ended 2-0 to City, but with some controversy over a foul on Sane, which their manager Neil Warnock dismissed. I know he's not everyone's Cup of tea but I quite like him and he's said nice things about City recently after he was invited to our training ground.

Final visit was in November 2018, in the Prem. This time, again, Suzanne and son Anakin, gave me a lift, but car parking at the ground was now just for permit holders only, and so we parked on the street. It was too wet to sell KK253 our 30th anniversary issue, but I was compensated with a nice mention in the programme, and a chat with Marc Riley at half time, plus a 5-0 win.

Awayday Zines Bobbing Along, Oh Bluebird of Happiness, Watch the Bluebirds Fly, Bluebird Jones, Cover the Grange, In The Ada, The Thin Blue Line, I'll Be There, Intifada 12.

NEWPORT COUNTY

Only KK visit was in the F.A. Cup 4th round in season 2017/18, which was a bit special, (and I had a letter published in the local paper to that effect), considering the family connections.

■ Newport Stadium, also known as Spytty Park.

We were able to have a pleasant weekend, being dropped off in the town centre, have a snack and walk over the bridge to the ground. Sales were poor, and the queues to get in were hectic. However, we won 4-1 and eventually made it to Wembley, winning the F.A. Cup.

Awayday Zines County Connection.

SWANSEA CITY

My first visit was in season 1983.84 to The Vetch Field and a 2-0 win, but never visited in the KK years.

First KK visit to the Liberty Stadium was in season 2011/12, March 11th, and the bitterly disappointing 1-0 loss, which seemed to have blown our title chances. We always travelled across from Newport, parking up either in local streets or more often in the Pizza Hut car park when, before and after the game, we'd take in the food and drink, chatting to fellow Blues. On one occasion however, it was pouring down, we'd arrived late, it was closed, but we parked up, and ultimately received a parking ticket, which we disputed, and the manager came to our rescue and managed to get it rescinded which was very much appreciated. We had our own fenced off area where the coaches parked, and were . able to sell without any hassle, plus the stewards were particularly friendly. In the May 2013 pre-Cup final game, the bars were closed as City fans let off flares on the concourse. Before the September 2016 game we decided to try and get a photograph at the Pete Ham of 'Badfinger', blue plaque at Swansea station, but ran out of time.

■ The Liberty Stadium, opened 10th July 2005.

For the F.A. Cup 6th round tie on March 16th 2019, we couldn't make the trip due to a request from a German TV company who wanted to film my Bert Trautmann memorabilia collection, then to be filmed watching the game with City supporters. We ensured my fanzine/memorabilia room was presentable for filming, and sorted out books, programmes, scrap books and anything relevant on Bert. Their philosophy was to produce a documentary of a week-long investigation into what City supporters thought of Bert as a German joining City and how Manchester, Blues and Reds, took him to their hearts and helped improve Anglo/German relations so soon after the war.

We then drove up to the Astley and Tyldesley supporters 'Subby club' where they filmed Blues watching the game. Down and out, two down at half time, Raheem and Sergio came on to change the game and provide a fantastic film experience as we won 3-2, and the place rocked. The video has been shown in Germany, prior to the opening of the film 'The Keeper', which starred actor John Henshaw (John and his missus Margaret are big City fans, subscribed to KK and always have time for a chat) as Jack Friar, Bert's-father-in-law, and has proved to be a great success.

Awayday Zines Jackmail, Jackanory, Jackplug, Jack's Eye, Swansea Oh Swansea, The Dud, Jack Swan, South of Morfa, Mouthful of Lead, The Jack, Black Swan, Jackanory, A Lot To Answer For, Love. Peace and Swansea City, Better than Sex, And Raynor Must Fall., Nobody Will Ever Know, Swimming In Swansea Bay Voice of the Vetch, London Swans.

TOTAL NETWORK SYSTEMS

One and only visit was in the UEFA Cup Qual/Rd 2nd leg in season 2003/04. Traffic around Brum was horrendous, but we arrived in plenty of time to stop off at our youngest daughter Kaye's. Son-in-law Brian thought it might be useful having someone with a Welsh Dragon tattoo on his arm clearly on view, to accompany us (?). We caught the train to Cardiff, armed with bags of fanzines, and were amazed that we took so many fans, estimated at over 9,000. Many struggled to cope with the traffic, including Ged and Sean. Tom and Steve did OK, but plenty City fans had been there for the day, as all the pubs within the vicinity of the ground were packed to the rafters.

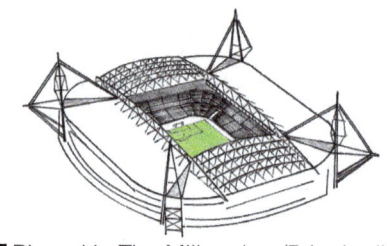

■ Played in The Millennium/Principality Stadium, as their own ground was too small and the Racecourse Ground in Wrexham was unavailable.

The decision to play the game with the roof closed made for an eerie atmosphere, and a good number of Blues sported flags and bananas. Trying to get served with drinks in the ground was a nightmare, bottles of coke being painstakingly poured into cartons, but I do kid my daughter (but not my son-in-law!), that Wales is a Third World country (as advised to us by the owner of a hotel we once stopped at on the outskirts!) The game was virtually a dead rubber, as we were five nil up from the 1st leg, so there was little to shout about with virtually a second team fielded for the 2-0 win. As we exited the ground it was raining but we sold quite well under the circumstances. We then overheard a Welsh voice ask "big crowd, is it late night shopping?" We then boarded the train back to Newport. Third World country indeed!

I also saw my first ever England game there. I'd fallen down stairs at Kaye's, in the morning, sober, and broke two toes, so attended the match on crutches. It was a 1-0 England win which I found quite emotional. I mention this as I bumped into 'Halifax Steve' on the train, then 'Hadge' Johnson outside a pub, both big City and England fans, who have since sadly passed away.

TNS are now renamed The New Saints.

16. SOUTH MIDLANDS

Moving further down South to Luton, Northampton, Oxford, Reading, Swindon and Watford

LUTON TOWN

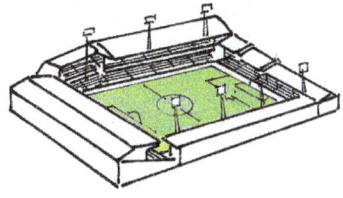

First KK visit was for the League Cup 4th round in 1988. Tony G. and I travelled on the 'special' and were then bussed to the ground. We sold KK2 on the train, which received a good response. At the time Luton were a better run club than City, a division above us and won 3-1, on the bouncy, bouncy, plastic bloody pitch.

■ Kenilworth Road, My first visit was for the F.A. Cup 4th round tie in 1961, a 6-2 win, 2-0 down then Denis scored all six, postponed after 69 minutes, due to a waterlogged pitch. We lost the-arranged game 3-1!

Further visits were by car, with Steve P, Danny, and Gideon. We usually stopped off at Corley services, then parked up in a local car park, as the ground was quite close to the M1. It was a challenge when away fans were banned but plenty of Luton fans, those involved in the F.S.A, disagreed with the ban and helped Blues obtain tickets. I once spotted England fast bowler and City fan Bob Willis on their main stand concourse.

At first, we were housed behind the goal in their newly covered Kop, mingling incognito with home fans, then in the main stand, where we took a low profile when we scored. However, half the stand went up, as we realised, we were amongst a large contingent of Blues! Final score that day 2-2.

Finally, for the 3rd tier visit in 1998/99 with the normal ticket allocation, we were situated in the Oak stand. Blues are still housed in there, but with half the allocation, as Luton managed promotion in season 2022/23 back to the top flight, though we didn't take in that one as it was post KK300. The 2-1 win helped us to get back on track in the Prem, and it was followed later by a 6-2 win in the FA Cup 5th round.

Awayday Zines *Mad As A Hatter, Half Time Orange.*

NORTHAMPTON TOWN

Just the one visit, in season 1998/99. We went in Ged's car which inexplicably wouldn't start after the Corley services pit stop, but a set of jump leads and friendly motorist, despite clocking Ged's City shirt, saw us on our way to Sixfields. Free parking, nice sunny day, KK71, our tenth anniversary special sold, and we were given a nice mention in the programme.

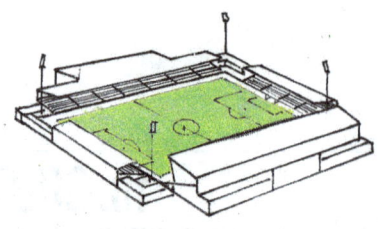

■ Sixfields, opened in 1994.

We expected a win but had to settle for a 2-2 draw, as we continued to fail to set the Division (3rd tier) alight. 7,653 record crowd.

Awayday Zines What A Load of Cobblers.

OXFORD UNITED

First KK visit was in April, 1989. After two defeats, at Blackburn (0-4) and Barnsley, home (1-2,) City were in need of a win to keep our promotion hopes alive with four games to go. I travelled down on the supporters club coach, and things looked bleak as we were two down at half time. I sat on a barrier with Kevin Cummins as City rallied to win 4-2. The game was marked by the surprising presence of riot police in the park behind the away end.

■ Manor Ground. My first visit was with daughter Marnie in season 1984/85 a 3-0 loss.

February 1997, we had a magnificent 4-1 win, live on TV, when Kinky turned on the magic. Parking and sales were usually OK. In November 1997, I was invited to be on TV, Channel 5's Turnstyle programme, in Southampton on the morning of the game. I was in the 'Green room' with Paul Walsh (who told me that after we beat Blackburn 3-2 away in 1995, Chairman Franny Lee came into the dressing room and said "Why did you do that, I can't sack the manager

now!" (though he may have been joking?) and Micky Quinn. Franny did sack Brian Horton at the end of the season, nuff said about that!.

I was asked by the presenter if City would go up or down, and replied "Up, but not this season." (We were relegated!) I then bombed up the motorway and made it before kick off in time to sell a few KK's. It was KK63 with Colin Bell on the front cover and I was astounded by the negative unprintable reaction from some Blues to the front cover. It was, however, a 0-0 draw.

For the League Cup 3rd round in season 2018/19 we stayed at daughter Kaye's in Newport then travelled over, parking up early at the leisure centre, and actually went to the pics to see 'The House with the Clock in the Wall' film starring my favourite actor, the brilliant Jack Black. We were joined at the turnstiles by Tom and Steve, for a bit of token selling of KK254. After the game, a 3-0 win, we returned back to the Leisure centre and watched on TV, amongst Oxford reds, ha-ha, United get knocked out on pens at home to Frank Lampard's Derby County. We then had a nice drive home on the Wednesday.

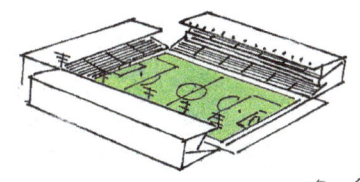

■ Kassam Stadium, opened 2001, a strange three-sided ground, with some fans watching the game at the open end on top of various vehicles, in the adjoining car park!

The following season 2019/20 we met in the 5th round of the League Cup, a 3-1 City win, which we watched on TV. Jamie Mackie, the former QPR player who gave us palpitations in the 2012 game when he made it 2-1 to QPR, was now playing for Oxford, and has moved on to become a TV pundit, and I still quake every time I see or hear his name.

Awayday Zines The Raging Bull, Rage On, Yellow Fever.

READING

First KK visit was in season 1992/93, five time a 4-0 win in the F.A. Cup replay after 1-1 at Maine Road. I'd booked a week off work so Gideon, myself and comedian (and City fan) Wayne 'Check' Allen travelled down in my car. We set off at 2.45 pm in the rain, aiming to arrive at six, but were stuck in a traffic jam on the M6 for a couple of hours

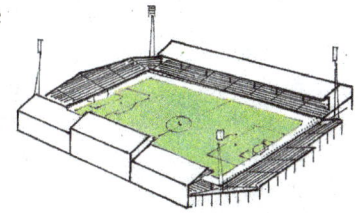

■ Elm Park, my first visit was in season 1987/88 a 2-0 win.

due to an accident. Wayne had one of these new-fangled mobile phones and rang the radio to give a traffic update, consoling us by saying we just had to be grateful we weren't involved in the crash.

So, we arrived in Reading, parked on a double yellow, and entered the ground just as we scored the first goal. Selling KK 28 was restricted to half time and we sold out. Amazingly we didn't get a parking ticket and it was a much shorter and happier drive home. Later when I was selling KK, outside Maine Road, Wayne advised me "not to get involved" in the 'Swales out' campaign, which fell on deaf ears. Last visit was in season 1993/94 League cup 2nd leg, and a 2-1 win, when news came through, I'd been appointed as 'Fan on the Board'.

First KK visit to the Madejshi was in season 1998/99, March 27th, and a 3-1 win. Sean R - "Ours was only one of just 15 league games not to be re-arranged due to Internationals and my England v Poland ticket became surplus to requirements., as I'd originally planned to get there for half time. Two hours before kick-off with heavy traffic, mainly Blues, queuing a mile back on the M4, the inevitable happened and the kick off was duly delayed until 1.30pm.

■ The Madejski Stadium, opened in August 1998.

It was a scorching hot day (for March) and as always, the Blue Army was out in force, approximately 4,500 of us present. The new stadium gets the thumbs up from me. Post match the traffic jams didn't seem to matter as we listened on the radio, to England beating Poland for a perfect day."

As for selling, we found a perfect spot where the fans from the train station had to pass by and we sold loads. Next visits were in 2004/05 a friendly, and 4-1 win. Then in 2006/07 September 11th, the game was moved to a Monday night. I was invited for a phone chat with Reading radio, and predicted a 2-1 win! (We lost 1-0) Good run, so arrived early enough to park at the ground. I smiled at Noel Gallagher but received no response. Steve Mingle advised "Another night of misery!" Raymond Ashton said hello.

Bumped into the media fellas at Warwick services, Fred Eyre, Chris Bailey, Andy Hinchcliffe, and Cheesy about to eat a massive fish on a barm cake. "looks like that f*cker who killed Steve Irwin last week" Chris said. Surprisingly, Ian couldn't finish it.

The next season, on the drive down, Eamonn 'rag' Holmes (remember him?) on the radio, couldn't resist advising Portsmouth they'd have a long journey back from Old Trafford after a fruitless F. A. Cup visit. Luckily Pompey knocked them out! Sadly, we lost 2-0 and were out sung and out-shouted by the home fans. Fair do's.

Awayday Zines *Taking The Biscuit, Heaven Eleven, The Whiff.*

SWINDON TOWN

First KK visit was in season 1988/89, it was a 2-1 win on New Years Eve. I travelled down on the coach, and was sitting opposite my cousin Denise's 'son, Clark Daley, with his mate. Clark was to celebrate his 19th birthday on January 5th, my 45th.

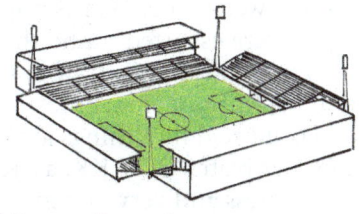
■ County Ground

He switched from United to City as a youngster, after Harry Godwin took him under his wing. Smooth journey there and back plus a few zines sold.

Next visit was for the 1993/94 Premier league game, a 3-1 win and Brian Horton's first game. Then it was a 2-0 loss in 1996/97. Season 1997/98, it was an early game under Joe Royle, which saw us win 3-1 and take a step towards safety, or so we thought? Sales were generally very good even after, on one occasion, selling mid-week after a game at

■ Pic shows top, Ian Niven, Clarke, with Denise and Alex.

nearby Reading, where we'd also sold well. Finally in season 2021/22 in the F.A. Cup 3rd round it was a 4-1 win, which we watched on TV.

Awayday Zines TBring The Noise, Five to Three, The 69er, Randy Robin, The Magic Roundabout.

WATFORD

First KK visit was in season 1988/89, a 1-0 loss. Luckily, I opted for the coach on this one, as apparently on the way home the engine on the Football special burned out and there was a two-and-a-half-hour delay! I sold KK 3 on my own. Later, we travelled by car, parking near the

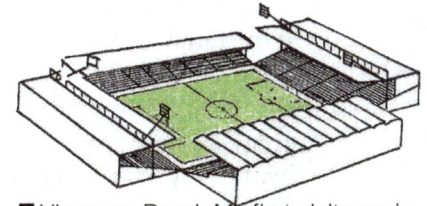
■ Vicarage Road. My first visit was in season 1882/83, a 3-2 loss.

allotments, sometimes in a local resident's drive, and eventually in a local school playground. We often called in at Arsenal fans Rog. and Mo's in Letchmore Heath, Mo kindly laying on food and drink. For one night game it was pouring with rain. We arrived late, and it was a bugger to park. Second half was boring so I nipped back to the car for more zines, then heard a roar and thought "oh shit" but the cries of "City, City" rang out as we went on to win 2-1. Selling outside was usually OK but inside the concourse was very narrow.

For the 2007 end of season match, we once more took in the hospitality, on the way down, from Rog and Mo, who have since become firm friends. We sold KKs outside, watched the Oasis boys being serenaded with "who are ya, who are ya!".as they were escorted round the pitch (from hospitality?), and into our end, It was a disappointing 1-1 draw to relegated Watford. After the game we were invited to Susan Bookbinder's lovely cottage in Chorleywood, where son Zac and dad David said nice things about the mag. and Susan gave us a personalised set of number plates CI7Y KK, as 'KK was her favourite City fanzine', which left us speechless and very grateful. Susan had laid on a splendid spread of sandwiches and cakes, which were very welcome. Ian Cheeseman was supposed to join us but was delayed interviewing Joey Barton who had a rant about the state of the club, expressing surprise that fans were renewing season tickets. It virtually determined the fate of manager Stuart Pearce, even though we were safe from relegation, but Joey didn't last much longer after his physical attack on Ousmane Dabo.

For the 2016 game Ged, Steve P, Mick and myself, travelled down in the Ged mobile, braving the traffic, rain and 50 mph speed limits. We parked up in the Watford High School for Girls car park for £8. A particularly memorable visit was in season 2017/18 when we travelled down with Steve P, took in the brilliant Johnny Cash show, stayed overnight and watched City win 6-0 the next day. I was impressed with Watford goalie Hueralho Gomes who, after half time with City three goals ahead, came over to have a kind word with some cheeky young City fans.

Awayday Zines *Clap Your Hands, Stamp Your Feet, The Ham, Blind, Stupid and Desperate, Mud, Sweat and Beers, Big Watford Love, Golden Pages, The Hornet Express.*

WEMBLEY, F.A. CUP FINAL, 2019 WON 6-0

Before the game, Troy Deeney, a Brummie, who I quite like, never one for mincing his words, advised that Watford would be roughing City up in the Final. City had won the Community Shield, the Carabao Cup, and the Premier League, so we were looking to become the first ever team to complete the domestic Quadruple.

On the Saturday we took advantage of the Thomas Cook coaches, laid on and paid for by the players, a much-appreciated gesture. We were on coach number six, dedicated to Eliaquim Mangala. Hmm! Nice and fine at Wembley, Annie Mac was the pre match DJ, and with a record equalling 6-0 win, City took the Cup in fine style after an early scare and John Stones nearly made it seven. Watford fans were great considering their team's performance, receiving a standing ovation from Blues at one point. The abiding memory though for me was Vinny Kompany giving Troy Deeney 'the look' after one of our goals, not quite Mario's wink at Rio, but right up there, as we completed the historic Domestic Quadruple, much to the bitter media's disgust.

17. NORTH LONDON

Down to Arsenal, Barnet, Spurs, and Wycombe Wanderers

ARSENAL

First KK visit should have been in October 1989, but I was re-tiling the shower room so gave it a miss, John Rowan filed the KK match report. It was the infamous game when City came out in the all-yellow kit for the one and only time, and lost 4-0!

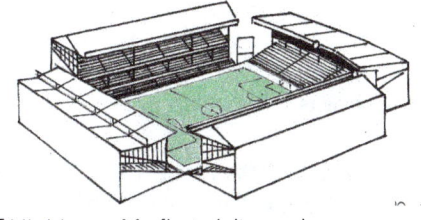

■ Highbury. My first visit was in September 1960, a 3-1 loss. My favourite ground, and classic 50s programme.

First KK visit was in 1990/91. We always found good parking on the streets, often on the road near to the Drayton Park pub. We were tipped off where to park by Arsenal fans Roger and Maureen Hewlett, who lived in Letchmore Heath near Watford where we were invited to call in pre match in 1991. After a bit of umm-ing and ah-ing we, Danny, Louise and Gideon did oblige, and we were greeted with a pile of sandwiches and drinks straight out of an Enid Blyton novel, before the rare 2-2 draw that night!

We would often have a chat with "the Gooner" guys, who we always swapped with before games and sometimes later, David Bernstein's lads would give us a wave.

Away fans were located behind the goal in a corner, entrance was through a row of terraced houses, but a couple of times I watched from the North stand, going round to the City end pre- and post-match to sell. We lost 5-0 when down to ten men in 1999/2000, when a regular KK hater advised me afterwards "something else for you to whinge about".

We also once (2004/05), parked on the Ashburton Grove site thanks to Steve P, courtesy of the friendly and enterprising night watchman, for a small fee. We were always hassled inside the ground by stewards, particularly on our last visit in 2005/06, after 17 years of selling, when I said to one of them "does that make you feel good", and he replied NO!

We'd sometimes stay over with friends Raymond and Chrissie, taking in a show, or sometimes being treated to meals at various posh restaurants, including The Ivy, where one time, Bruce Welch of the Shadows was on the next table. He'd also strutted about hoping to be recognised, which, needless to say, I fell for, and had a chat, talking bollocks, and he signed his autograph. Sue said I was cringeingly embarrassing. Who me?

■ The Emirates, opened 22nd July 2006.

First KK visit was in season 2006/07. Parking was very tricky, so we used to drive to Cockfosters tube station, park up and then catch the tube in. Never got much hassle selling, but sales were nowhere near as good as at Highbury. The turnaround in results finally came in the League Cup 5th round in 2011/12 season with a 1-0 win, (the same day my 'Us and Them' book came out) I travelled with Ged, Mick, Carin and Jason, who showed no interest in it whatsoever! Later in the same season we lost 1-0 to a late Arteta goal, when Mario was sent off, infuriating pundits, leaving us an impossible eight points behind United with only six games to go! Since then, we've hardly looked back, winning seven, drawing three and losing only twice including season 2023/24, 1-0. One time we were given a parking permit by a City fan who lived locally, which was very welcome.

Awayday Zines The Gooner, An Imperfect Match, Arsenal Echo, Echo, On The Box, One Nil Down, 2-1 Up, Highbury High, Up The Arse, Arsenal Mania, The North Bank, Boring, Boring Arsenal.

WEMBLEY

Visits included F.A. Cup semi-finals in 2016/17 1-2 aet, and 2019/20 0-2, played behind closed doors due to Covid. League Cup 2017/18 Final 3-0, Community Shield 2014/15 0-3, and 2023/24 1-1 aet 1-4 on pens.

We made it to most of them, sometimes with family, but the best one we had was for the League Cup final in 2018. We travelled down on the Saturday, had a good run, stayed over and on the Sunday morning, we caught the train to Marylebone station and met up with friends Raymond and Chrissie for lunch at the Landmark hotel, where the team were staying. We observed Al Mubarak with his minders, said hello to Danny Wilson. Pep was hovering about, Leroy looked bewildered, and I got Fernandinho's autograph on his pic in Bryan Duffy's article in KK 249, whilst wishing him good luck. Very cold at Wembley but our Brent council letter didn't aid us to sell as we were on Wembley stadium property apparently. We won the game comfortably 3-0, and for good measure went on to beat them at the Emirates 3-0 again on the following Thursday.

BARNET

■ Underhill

First and only KK visit was in season 1994/95 in the League Cup second round first leg, losing 1-0. on a rainy night. The game had a bad-tempered finish with Tony Coton kicking the ball at City fans behind the goal who were giving the team abuse .after the appallingly poor performance. The tie was remedied though when City won the second leg 4-1.

Sean Riley adds - A small crowd of 3,120 with just over 1,000 City fans present. The slight incline on the small pitch resembled a ski slope, and assisted their early goal. Woeful finishing by their team meant we were saved from an even bigger humiliation. In fairness City did have two goals disallowed and hit the post, but generally, it was a dreadful performance. Unfortunately, the team coach driver also took the brunt of the fans' anger, after the game.

Awayday Zines Buzztalk, What's The Number On Your Back?

TOTTENHAM HOTSPUR

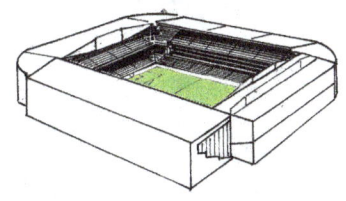

■ White Hart Lane. My first visit was in season 1985/86, 2-0 win, 17,009 crowd. The Shelf was a sight to behold.

First KK visit was in the January of season 1989/90. Danny and I travelled down on the Football special to Euston then took the tube to Northumberland Park station, with a police escort, continuing down the Seven Sisters Road. There was some sort of fracas, resulting in a police horse going over and Spurs fans running out of a local pub, dispersing City fans with mayhem ensuing. Danny and I stood back with the bags of fanzines at our feet and we continued on our way to the ground, selling out, in the 1-1 draw.

Later, I usually parked up in a school playground car park, opposite the ground, which was quite expensive, but very handy. On one occasion, however, they refused to give us a refund when the game was postponed. John Burridge was particularly annoyed that day, as he was to make his debut as the oldest ever player in the league! Spurs fans were generally the most aggressive. I was often spat at and confronted before and after games, whilst stewards were strict on selling inside. Once, we were outside chatting to Susan Bookbinder with her son Zac, Colin Savage and Ged Isaacs, all Jewish, with Spurs fans going past shouting abusively "Yid Army" at us, which I found a bit ironic. "Will you ever beat the Spurs" was another chant from them.

After the 2003/04 Coca Cola Cup game, a 1-3 loss, I walked out with an impressively coated Liam Gallagher, who was surprisingly smaller than me and had his hands in his pockets. He was well behind his brother and his mates, so they'd probably, god forbid, been involved in some sort of argument? "That was shit Liam" I was going to say but I stopped to sell KK and he walked on. I thought he was taking a bit of a risk as any Spurs nutter, of which there were many, could have taken a swing, but there were no reports of any such incident. Usual 'mare getting away but Steve P. often manoeuvred us back to the motorway with slick navigation.

Later that season it was the memorable F.A. Cup 4th round replay, 3-0 down at half time, Anelka off injured, Barton sent off, and a 4-3 win. We missed it of course, City laying on a TV relay in the Kippax top tier suite. I took up a table for ten of us, with wild scenes ensuing at the final whistle. It was Kevin Keegan's finest hour (after promotion in 2002). Other visits included chatting with Sir Howard Davies with his son George, Tilly Vosburgh, Nick Conway and once spotting ex-Chairman John Wardle going up to the top tier with City fans. Some Spurs fans did have a nasty streak so it was difficult to have any banter with them, apart from Paul Mckenzie who I'd been on Sky TV with a few times. "You've got a fanzine, you're having a laugh", spouted a middle-aged moron. Once, after a City winning goal, an object chucked at City fans missed and hit one of their disabled fans.

Further visits; In 2009/10, I went down with Fred, Charlie, and Ian who drove. The 0-3 loss marked the end of Hughes' reign on the following Saturday v Sunderland, despite a 4-3 win. In 2010/11 it was 0-0. Friday night stayed with R. and C, one Spurs fan bought KK, with a Scottish fiver, another chanted "Champions League, you're having a laugh". It was David Silva's debut, a pundit told us he had no pace! Joe Hart was outstanding. 2011/12, I watched it in the pub and a 5-1 win to "the team of individuals!" Generally results were good, but a particular low was the 4-1 loss in 2015/16, after which Spurs fans were gloating on the radio how their young team would go on to great things!

They played at Wembley Stadium for two seasons, 2018/19 & 2019/20, whilst the new ground was constructed, and the League Cup final in 2021.

First visit we boarded our coach, one of three, setting off at about 12.45, from the North car park. Good run down stopping off at the Norton 'Harry' Kane services on the M6 Toll Road. Parked up at Wembley at 6pm just time for a snack at Costa and chat with a couple of decent Spurs fans. One minute's silence held for the centenary end of WW1, impeccably observed. Sold a few KK's before and at the end of the game. "It's ages since I bought one of these" was a familiar theme from a Blue, then I was asked to move on by a female steward! We won 1-0 thanks to an early Mahrez penalty. Back on the coach with one Blue missing arriving back at 3am, to a frosty car. Thanks to Thomas Cook for the free travel. Then in 2019 it was a 3-1 win, which we attended with Marnie and Andy, finding out the next day, after staying over, that United had lost at home to West Brom, and we were Champions again! Finally, we got some sort of revenge for 1981, with the 2021, 1-0 Carabao Cup final win, Laporte's late goal winning the cup in front of a few thousand spectators due to the Pandemic restrictions.

Our first KK visit was for the Champions league quarter final tie in season 2018/19. We travelled down on the Mostonian coach from City, which parked up in the nearby streets. Now WHL was always a problem to and from the ground so building the new stadium with an increased capacity on the same site was surely a mistake? The ground itself was magnificent as we took up our places in the safe standing area, watching Sergio miss an early penalty, Spurs went ahead, Pep's (too late) subs didn't help, though Kane was injured, and out for the 2nd leg. Sales were poor. We were accompanied by Spurs fans, who were very helpful and friendly as we walked back to where the coaches were parked. We lost the 2nd leg cruelly, winning 4-3 but going out on away goals, despite scoring a late goal, with Spurs players lying on the pitch devastated, until VAR reversed the decision, as it was marginally offside.

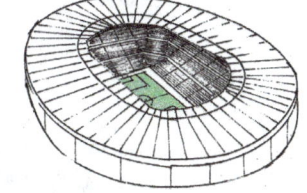
■ New WHL, opened April 3rd 2019.

We didn't win at the new WHL until the F.A Cup tie in 2024 1-0 then again in the League game 2-0 with THAT save from Ortega from Son, when Spurs fans were happy for us, as it looked to have denied Arsenal the title, which it did. No complaints anywhere for United deliberately losing at home to Arsenal in the hope it would prevent City winning the title!

Awayday Zines *The Spur, My Eyes have Seen the Glory, On The Shelf, Off the Shelf, The Spurs Screws (Sugar Me!) Spur of the Moment, Cock-A-Doodle Doo.*

WYCOMBE WANDERERS

First KK visit was in season 1995/96, in the League Cup 2nd round 1st leg, resulting in a 0-0 draw, return leg a 4-0 home win. Then it was a 1-0 loss in the 3rd tier, in season 1998/99, Ged and I had seats in their main stand, compounded by a 2-1 loss at Maine Road.

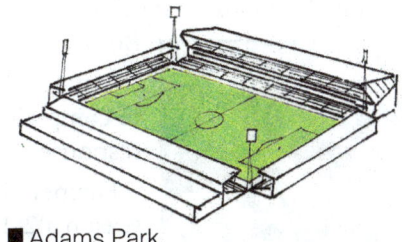
■ Adams Park.

We travelled down giving a lift to Dante Friend, parked close to the ground, but found it difficult to get away as it was only the one road in and out. We later played them at home in the League Cup 4th round? in season 2021/22 resulting in a 6-1 win.

Awayday Zines *The Wanderer, Chairboys Gas, The Adams Family.*

18. EAST & WEST LONDON

Continuing the London tedium, it's Brentford, Chelsea, Fulham, QPR and West Ham.

BRENTFORD

First KK visit was for the F.A. Cup 4th round tie in 1989, a 3-1 loss. I travelled down on the special, on my own, and sold out of KK3's before reaching the end of the train. It was a tortuous walk from the station to the ground, narrow entries, yuppy estates, with no police escort despite the possible menace of Chelsea and Millwall fans, but without incident.

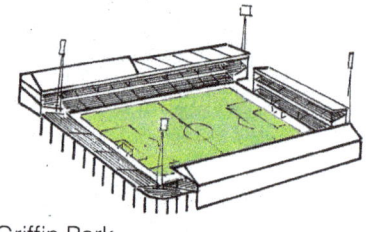
■ Griffin Park.

I spotted Billy (Nick Conway) from Bread on the terrace, where it was all going off, with fans being chased by the police for some reason, and my mate Bill Dawson commenting on their presence.

City fan, Sheila Bradley later wrote to the police to complain, but not sure if she got a satisfactory response.

Further visit was in the League Cup in 1989/90 season a 2-1 loss in the 2nd round 1st leg, when the train was delayed outside the capital, meaning we didn't get in until half time, so received a refund! Return leg was a 4-1 City win.

The F.A. Cup 1997 3rd round tie was much postponed, indeed on the second occasion we found out just as we arrived at the ground, the pitch was frozen, the game was off and I had to recycle 300 KK58's I'd saved for the game as KK59 was at the printers and would be out for the next match. When it was finally played, we parked up on a seedy looking croft, next to a mattress, and noticed Stan Bowles lurking about in the back streets, with a blonde floozie, so he didn't turn up at the match for a presentation. Wonder why? It was a 1-0 win under Frank Clark who looked the biz. "I never felt more like Singing the Blues, under Frank Clark we never lose, oh City…" It was also the occasion when a (presumably) Brentford fan bought a KK and asked me where the Braemar Road stand was. "I dunno" I said and as he walked away, he shouted back at me "well you should do, as after all you're selling the programme".

After their promotion we played there twice, in seasons 2022/23 a 1-0 loss after we'd won the League, and in 2023/24 which resulted in a 3-1 win. Tom and Steve Parish held the fort in the 2022/23 game as Tom wanted to tick the new ground off his list, but we were unrepresented in the 2023/24 season.

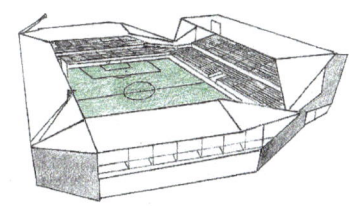
■ The G Tech Community Stadium. opened 1st September 2020.

I was chuffed to see my "Thomas The Frank Engine" quote was utilised by The Mirror at a later date!

Awayday Zines *Voice of the Beehive, Beesotted, Hey Jude, Thorne in the Side.*

CHELSEA

First KK visit was in September 1990, a 1-1 draw. We took the special to Euston, had a brisk walk to the tube, taking us to Fulham Broadway, then the short walk to the ground. The Copper on the video camera told us that we were being filmed "just in case there were any incidents."

■ Stamford bridge. My first visit was in April 1960, Peter Bonetti's debut, and a 3-0 loss

We then travelled by car, down the monotonous tedious route M6, M1 and through London. Usually managing to park in local car parks, which became more and more difficult. We sold at the back of the West stand on the pathway leading to the open away terrace behind the goal. Later selling became more tricky as City fans were moved around as the ground was redeveloped. We were housed at one end of the lower tier of the East stand and eventually in the upper and lower tiers at the end of the Shed end.

For the 1992/93 game on January 9th, it looked like rain so Gideon and I opted for seats in their West stand, having to keep quiet when we scored although there were other Blues in there, including one brave chap wearing his City scarf. and reading KK at half time. It didn't rain, and we won 4-2!

We finished up selling on the road outside the away end, which was unsatisfactory, but at least we were able to meet up with fellow Blues, including Sir Howard Davies, after he'd lunched with David Mellor. We'd chat about various things including having a chuckle about Boris Johnson's latest misdemeanours (who later,somehow became PM?).

Other visits, we'd stop at Warwick services, bumping into Simmo, Stuart Brennan, Charlie Hadfield, and Cheesy. One time, Tom drove and we parked in a school playground for £12.Tickets were expensive, so Sue fancied shopping, but she was given a ticket off a kindly club official. Lou Macari walked past. My final visit was in season 2018/19, a 2-0 loss, with Ian Cheeseman, Fred Eyre and Chris Bailey in Ian's car, parking in Cockfosters and taking the tube into Fulham Broadway. I was moved from the turnstiles by stewards to the road some distance away, so it was slow selling, but at least some Chelsea fans bought it. Also sold at half time dodging CCTV. Then I hung about after the game watching autograph hunters who spotted Peter Bonetti, then Petr Czech carrying his kid, plus his bag, with two women following, so he refused to sign. to sign. Ged drove on another occasion, and after a heavy loss, his car broke down, which was lifted onto a truck, in which were driven hope.

Awayday Zines *They had a stall on the Road and I'd deliver a few KKs for them to sell. The Chelsea Independent, The Westander, Cockney Rebel, Curious Blue, The Red Card, SW6, Blues Bros (Chelsea, Linfield, Rangers), Mathew Harding's Blue and White Army and much later, Carefree. The editor decided to give me an unsolicited fanzine lecture in 2006, and reckoned Chelsea's Boot boys took the Kippax in the 1971 European Cup Winners' Cup semi-final and out-sang us. As I remember it, City fans vacated the terrace well before kick-off, and went over to occupy the newly opened North Stand.*

WEMBLEY/VILLA PARK

We've played them in the Community Shield in 2012, won 3-2 at Villa Park, when it poured down thus affecting sales, Then in the F..A. Cup S/F in 2013, won 2-1, 2018 Community Shield won 2-0, Carabao Cup Final 2019, 0-0, won 4-3 on pens, F.A. Cup S/F 2021 0-1, 2024 F.A. Cup S/F won 1-0.

Season 2012/13, we drove down on the Saturday, Stayed with R. and C, full of nerves on Sunday, train to Wembley, walked up with Paul Dickov, did our meet and greet act selling zines listening to "you're only famous cos of Oasis" chants, escalators packed in. After the 2-1 win we drove home, stopped off at Teddington services, didn't see 'Two Ton Ted' again, but did say hello to Noel Bayley.

We varied our visits, staying with R. and C, or going on the train with Marnie and Andy. I once had to write to the F.A. re the programme which included pics of Klopp and Salah, obviously inserted by a mischievous scouser employed by the printers, but no response.

For the 2019 Carabao Cup final, we opted for the official supporters club trip, so we were up at 5am, to get sorted, and be at the North car park for about 7am. Quick stop at Warwick, then arrived at the Green Man at about 12 ish. Nice day, especially for February. We took the zines out of the bags as instructed by the Stewards. Sue then took the bag to a drop off point miles away and was charged £10 for the privilege, as did many other Blues, mainly families with kids who'd brought changes of clothes as they'd no idea what the weather would be like in London. Meanwhile tough looking guys, who joked with the steward, were allowed in with rucksacks. Steve and Tom, obviously more streetwise than we were, got in with no trouble. The game finished 0-0, we left early in order to collect our bags and get back to the coach in time, with the news coming through that we'd won the shoot-out 4-3, "top bins boss" according to Raheem.

FULHAM

First KK visit was in season 1998/99, and a 3-0 loss on a Friday night. A nightmare scenario, pulled off the M6, drove around Willenhall, Steve and Ged assisted directions but we finished up in

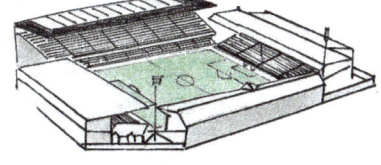
■ Craven Cottage. My first visit was in season 1960/61, a 1-0 loss.

a scrap yard (Steve's 1950's version Ordnance survey maps, way out of date!), before having a good run, even though the London rush hour traffic, listening to and laughing at Marc and Lard on the radio. A Copper said to me with a smirk "not selling many of those Sir?", I replied "we've already sold 3,000 and are at the end of the run of games". Off he trotted.

Good run down in 1999/2000 with Steve, Tom (taking Sue's place as long as he sold KK 78) and Ged. No probs at Birmingham, arrived at 12 noon, able to have a stroll in the park, bumped into media moguls Chris Bailey, Mike Barnett, and chauffeuse, plus Carin Bowman and brother Spencer. London based 'rogue trader' Nick Leeson said hello whilst we were chatting to Kevin Cummins and indeed sold one to Tony Dempsey, but the cops were being stroppy, which, as an ex prisoner, Nick found both hilarious and ironic.

It was always one of the most picturesque settings, next to the Thames and the park, with the friendliest home fans. We were usually housed in the left hand side of the Putney End stand behind the goal. Parking was great at first, on the street parallel to the ground but restrictions were introduced, and we diverted to a local Vicar's (friend of Steve P's) back garden. Selling outside the ground was always good, whilst spotting celebrities, including John Stapleton and ex footballers, Trevor Francis, Stan Horne etc. Stewards tried and failed to stop us selling on the pretext of causing an obstruction, one of whom actually bought the zine on one occasion. Inside we took a low profile selling and at the end of games sold on either side of the exit alleyway, but were often moved on.

Season 2008/09 we went to Banbury late on the Friday night, then on the Saturday morning drove to London. We parked in the local Vicar's driveway. Nice cafe on Fulham Palace Road, Sir H. and son George stopped for chat, they were in the Directors box with Alistair MacIntosh. We were asked by a steward if we had permission to sell KK. "Yes, off A.M., give him a ring to confirm", so he wandered off, then my favourite female steward bought one for her friend who lives in Portsmouth and is a City fan. That night after the match, we dashed up the motorway to attend the Merseyside branch Xmas do, thanks to Chairman Tony Rawls, with special guest Norah Mercer.

After the 2010/11 4-1 win, selling KK183, we were told by a Fulham fan it was "the best team performance he'd ever seen here". We drove down Fulham Palace Road behind Helios, the *Blue Moon Rising* documentary boys' mini bus.

For the 2011/12 2-2 draw, the steward on his megaphone welcomed us to the "oldest club in London", I had a word in his ear so he added "and you can buy your fanzines and programmes here". We sold out pre-match. City went 2-0 ahead but took our foot off the gas to draw 2-2. A tough looking Fulham fan said to us after the game "you'll win the title next year and good luck for the rest of the season". Nice!

2012/13 season in September, we refreshed in the Magic cafe on Fulham Palace Road, then parked on the street next to the media boys Cheesy etc waiting for the Vicar to arrive and let us in to park, but they couldn't risk waiting for him and drove off to find a parking spot elsewhere, Sold KK 200, spotted a fox in the street, and stayed with R and C. Since then they've been up and down but we've won every game home and away.

*Loftus Road, they played here for two seasons from 2002 to 2004, whilst Craven Cottage was being upgraded.

First KK visit was in season 2002/03 KK110 on sale. Steve P's finest moment was refusing Al Fayed a copy as he refused to pay, "That's how you became a millionaire" Steve told him! We saw Susan Bookbinder, John Stapleton, Tilly Vosburgh, and Mike Pickering, whilst Fulham fans sang "We've only got two grounds!" For the 2003/04 game Ged drove. We arrived there after 12.00 and had a stroll through the park, but the Leisure centre had disappeared, so we went to a local cafe. Took up our selling positions, Gallaghers were present, Liam wearing his daft hat, I told him that their music stands up to anything from the 60s, onwards, Cheers he said!

Awayday Zines *There's Only One F in Fulham, Where Were We.., Where Else We.*

QUEENS PARK RANGERS

First KK visit was in season 1989/90, April. Spotted Martin Tyler at Piccadilly station and gave him a KK, took the special to Euston, was escorted to the tube station, on a lovely spring evening. Arrived at Shepherds Bush at 6pm but we were held for twenty minutes before making our way to the ground. Outside, we chatted to ex-Blues David Oldfield and Clive Allen, City won 3-1, with Parker and Megson sent off, but it was our first Division One double since Spurs in 1985/86. Sadly, the news came through that United had beaten Oldham and were through to the F.A. Cup final, though the strains of Blue Moon filled the air.

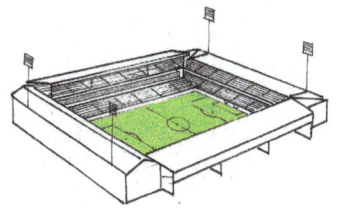

■ Loftus Road. Mmy first visit was in season 1986/87 a 1-0 loss.

It was usually a good run, sometimes having the time to visit Sportspages in London, or the Leisure centre in the local park (later demolished) pre-match with street parking locally, and a short walk to the ground.

We always took up both tiers. Selling for the upper was on one side of the ground, and lower the other side, and it was quite a walk round the houses from one to the other. It was usually an interesting selling spot for the upper tier where the Oasis boys would arrive early, and I could watch the police forcibly arresting the burger bloke which was a bit unfair. We were never moved on from selling outside, but sometimes inside the stewards were a bit officious.

After the 2-2 draw in November 2014, we stayed over with friends R. and C. and on the Sunday morning had breakfast at ahem, The Landmark hotel where, as it happens, we were on a table next to Willy Caballero and his family. Zab and Martin D. were also there as Argentina were playing a match at Wembley in the week. Needless to say, I failed to congratulate him on his near penalty save at Dundee, but I did chat to Joe Hart whilst he was eating a boiled egg, and he told me we were gonna be alright.

I did therefore miss an opportunity to remind him of when I was on Cheesy's TV Christmas radio Manc show with Arny's (Ian Arnfield) Bredbury branch, and we all had to pull a player's name out of the hat. Mine was Shay Given and I said he was a good 'on the line keeper' but we should get Joe Hart back from loan at Birmingham. I was shouted down by the rest of the Branch, plus Lakey and Gleghorn! In 2011/12 we drove down to QPR for the 5.30 KO, parking up nicely and City won 3-2. In the upper tier, an intimidating steward told me to sit down as the woman behind me couldn't see. "That's my wife" I said and he walked away, without a word to the hundreds of Blues standing up in front of everybody.

Awayday Zines *A Kick up the R's, In the Loft, Ooh I Think it's My Groin, Beat About the Bush.*

WEST HAM UNITED

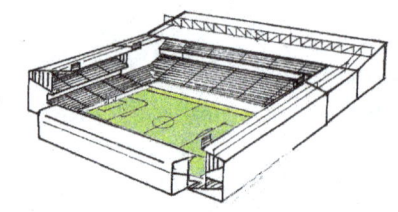

It was generally, street parking with a walk to the ground, which got more difficult with restrictions being extended. We were first housed at the end of the main stand, later in the street outside the away stand behind the

■ Upton Park. My first visit was in season 1958/59, a 4-1 loss.

goal without problems, though again the concourse was very tight. We'd often say hello to Tilly Vosburgh, and sometimes Nedum Onuoha's family. Stewards were once confiscating inflatables, deeming them racist, despite an article in

the programme on how the banana craze swept the country! Drinks were allowed on the concourse, as screens were in place in front of the entrance/exits to/from the terraces. Alfie Haaland was once hoisted shoulder high by City fans. Season 2008/09, we went on the Saturday and stayed over courtesy of R. and C. Fine day on the Sunday, decent place to visit, swapped with 'Over Land and Sea' fanzine number 456, which must come out for every home game? Bernard Manning Junior said hello,

Sven's first game of the season was in 2007, after numerous new signings. Pundits were filming Blues' responses to pics of City players shown, but told firmly to f*ck of, which they did, as they were "taking the piss", but returned later when the coast was clear. After the 2-0 win, I was regaled with "would you rather have Hughes now" or "what do you think of Sven now, hold your hands up" (I'd previously criticised the appointment). Well, you can't argue with a derby double, achieved later, which in those days were our Cup finals!

Season 2012/13 and a 5.30 KO, we drove down on the day. It was a squash on the concourse, Cult's 'She Sells Sanctuary" played, at half time, After the game I was made to sell outside. Sue was approached by a female steward who said how impressed she was with our support, "unlike some other teams" and although most Blues were drunk, they behaved like perfect gentlemen and had fun.

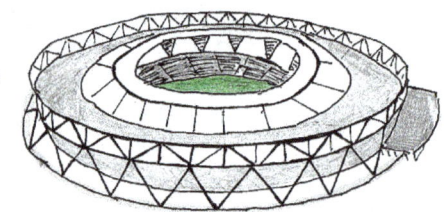

One of our best visits was in April 2018, when we were already Champions and could enjoy a relaxing weekend. We drove down on the Saturday, stayed with

■ The London Stadium, opened in summer 2016, A new ground with poor access.

friends R and C, and went to see the 42nd Street show starring Lulu at night. Taxi to St Pancras, then the train to Stansted International and the trek to the ground. We sold out of KK's pre kick off so we had a relaxing time watching the 4-1 win which put us in a good mood, even though we were made to walk round the perimeter of the ground before arriving at the station, then we drove home. Away days don't come much better.

We made further visits, (the Spirit of 1987 was always there), including the night match in 2018/19, a 4-0 win. We stayed over, but there was limited public transport and thus a trek to the ground. Steve and Tom managed a better route and parking. Results were very good, but in 2021/22 at 2-0 down, it looked dodgy, until we recovered to make it 2-2. Mahrez had a late penalty saved, which meant we would have to beat Villa at home in the last game of the season at The Etihad to clinch the title, what could possibly go wrong?

Awayday Zines *Fortunes Always Hiding, Over Land and Sea, On The Terraces, On A Mission From God, The Water in Majorca, The Ultimate Dream, Knees Up Mother Brown, East End Connection, Never Mind The Boleyn.*

19. SOUTH LONDON

Even worse than North, East and West, was South London, Charlton, Palace, Millwall and Wimbledon

CHARLTON ATHLETIC

First KK visit was in season 1989/90, November, 1-1 draw. We opted for the coach, entering Croydon via the M25, Dartford tunnel, arriving at the ground at 1.45 pm. Friendly coppers showed an interest in KK, so no problems selling. Journey home went well, and we found out from Blues on the train that they were advised by City Director Chris Muir, that Mel Machin had been given that one game before the sack.

The Valley, marvellous campaign by Addicks fans, after 7-year exile to Selhurst Park between Sept 1985 to May 1991, they returned to the Valley in December 1992.

September 2000 opening game of the season, full contingent of City zines selling which intimidated some Charlton fans, who thought they, not us, were at home! We lost 4-0!

■ The Valley, first visit was in season 1984/85, 3-1 win.

Not the easiest place to get to by car, it was a long journey. We once travelled in 'Flat Cap' Mike's car when the Blackwall tunnel was a nightmare, with a broken-down taxi causing chaos, and Mike shouting "w*nker" as we drove past (similar to the Inbetweeners bus w*nker sketch years later!) We had trouble parking, and said hello to actress and City fan Tilly Vosburgh, the latest addition to Eastenders "Let's hope we do it in the smoke for a change" she said!

The trick was to get there early, drive down the road next to the ground before the police closed it and park right next to the away end, behind the goal, to be able to pop back to the car when we needed more zines. Record away sales of

450 achieved with KK59.

We were not so lucky on another occasion, December 2005. We set off on the Friday night, staying at our daughter's in S. Wales, for a 4pm Sunday KO. We mistimed setting off, the south circular was a nightmare, had trouble parking, arrived at half time, missed the G. Best tributes, when a wreath was laid! Recovered, selling with Tom at half time, and at the end of the match in the exit alley with City fans having to pass by. After one game we took the ferry across the Thames (Could've been a Chas 'n' Dave song?) before heading North and home.

November 2006, we had an overnight stay in Greenwich, then an early trip to the Valley, parking in Sam Bartram close, brunch at the Valley cafe, alongside Les Chapman and a few of the City backroom boys. Lovely sunny day, 3 pm KO, nice! Older Charlton fan asked "is that the name of a player?" Which indirectly it is of course, Colin Bell. Sadly a 1-0 loss.

Awayday Zines *Voice of the Valley, Goodbye Horse, Forever Charlton, Addicted.*

CRYSTAL PALACE

After missing the 1988/89, 0-0 draw, first KK selling visit was the last game of the season in 1990, a 2-2 draw. Went by train with Danny, scorching day, arrived at half two, ground packed, most in fancy dress, mainly Blues Bros, further to Blueprint's commendable request. We wished Palace well for the F. A. Cup final v rags. Sadly, a rags win.

■ Selhurst Park. My first visit was in season 1984/85 a 2-1 win.

Certainly, the worst ground in the country to reach, having tried it all ways. Once bumped into Colin Shindler and Times correspondent Michael Henderson (wearing a cowboy hat) who slagged me off in a newspaper article penning "this is the calibre of the 'Fan on the Board'", after I referred to the swamp as 'Old Nafford' in my programme notes. Perhaps he had a point?

In 2004/05, Ged, who reckons all London clubs should move to Milton Keynes, drove. It was young Stephen Woodhouse's first away game with us, but we didn't arrive until 2.40.pm. I'd been on the radio on Ian Cheeseman's programme discussing the Kevin Keegan situation, plus City's problems, and was admonished by a Blue, who I managed to appease, after which he said I should be a politician. We won the game 3-1, to give Kevin some respite.

Eventually we chose an overnight stay, then being early enough to park in the supermarket car park next to the ground. Other occasions we arrived late, especially for issue 100 when the kick off was delayed, which helped sales.

We also opted for the official coach trip, with Liz Stones Blue podiatrist) and daughter Charlotte for company in season 2014/15, which set off later than we would have, for a Bank holiday Monday, evening KO, and we didn't arrive until half time, plus we lost 2-1. Selling was sometimes a pain, with Kevin Cummins once arguing on our behalf with a steward but to no avail, indeed he was refused entry, but still managed to see the game.

Most memorable, of course, was the visit in April 2014. The night before the game we attended KK top contributor John Burfield's 50th birthday bash. The following day we were selling KK as the City coaches parked up at the top of the hill, and Blues came running down excitedly as the news of Gerrard's "Slippy G" moment in Liverpool's home game with Chelsea came through. Before kick-off we learned that they'd lost 2-0, and we went on to beat Palace 2-0 to put us in the driving seat. A few games later Liverpool were beating Palace at Selhurst Park 3-0, and striving to improve their goal difference, but finished up drawing 3-3, and the title was within our grasp.

Awayday Zines Eagle Eye, Suffer Little Children, Eastern Eagle, One More Point, The Palace Echo.

MILLWALL

I missed out on our first visits due to work commitments, so it was up to Gideon to sell KK for the two F.A. Cup 3rd round replays, after the 0-0 draw at Maine Road, in season 1988/89. He travelled down on one of the four official supporters club coaches, and sold a few KK 8s. "It was rowdy until the river was crossed, but all was well as we parked in the away fans car park. We heard one of the other coaches was narrowly missed by a brick which shattered a local shop window! Kick-off was delayed due to Millwall's biggest gate of the season (17,696), as we watched City come back from a goal down to draw 1-1 after extra time, and the toss of a coin decreed we'd be back for the

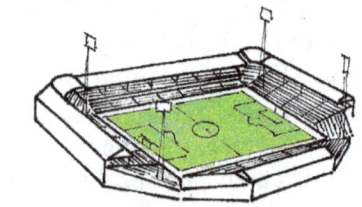

■ The Den (Cold Blow Lane).

second replay. This time there were six coaches laid on. A similar journey as before, with all banners and flags taken down when we crossed the river. It was a bigger City contingent in another bumper crowd of 17,771, but Sheringham and Cascarino tore us apart in their 3-1 win. Back at the coach we found it had been robbed, then about a mile and a half from the ground three young lads in a side street lobbed a brick which cracked the windscreen as a parting gesture. The incident passed unnoticed by the police escort".

The next KK visit, was later that season, a 1-1 draw. Danny and I went on the coach which halted temporarily before the Tower Bridge, (which was impressively painted in sky blue and white), until the other coaches caught up to form a convoy, with a police escort. We parked up on the bumpy, Telly Tubby type car park next to the away end and were amused by the 'Electric Blue' boys driving in and cheering as they went over the bumps. Selling was fine, no problems apart from a local scrote asking "why are you selling that shit rahnd 'ere? "Cos it's the last time we'll be coming here sonny" They were relegated that season.

For the 3rd tier game at the New Den in season 1998/99 I drove down with Ged, and we chose our car parking spot as carefully as we could, in South Bermondsey, after initially parking close to the ground. Selling was OK, we sold a couple of hundred, as the away end entrance wasn't accessible for home fans. West Yorkshire supporters club Chairman Ian Barton stopped for a chat advising that he didn't know what all the fuss was about Millwall fans, as the branch members had a good chat with them in the pub. However, many Blues complained about the abuse hurled at them, and some coaches were bricked on the way in.

■ The New Den, opened August 1993.

Sean Riley: "Roadworks around the Blackwall tunnel meant we chanced it off the M1/A1 right through London, sailing through with no delays. Parked up at 5pm near Tower Bridge, had a couple of jars and nosh at Wetherspoons, and left for the ground. The area round Millwall is the pits, we passed pubs full of nutcases, and were trying to find somewhere decent to park, eventually succeeding, then made our way tentatively to the ground. It was swarming with mobs of Millwall with not a Blue in sight. We reached our end entering via a 15-foot-high security gate, being relieved to see a good number of Blues, approximately 2,000.

As for the match, briefly it finished 1-1 with various pitch invasions. Vaughan and Shaw were red carded and we almost won it which would've caused a mass riot. Their Chairman, Dragon Den's Theo Paphitis, didn't know what all the fuss was about!"

However, it finished up as a scary night both on and off the pitch as City fans were kept in for an hour or more with Millwall fans rioting in the streets round the ground, having running battles with the police. As we waited patiently to exit the ground, we wondered what was in store, BTH's Steve Worthington comforted me saying "If you're gonna get it, you'll get it".

We had a tentative walk back to the car, adrenaline pumping, giving Ian Cheeseman a lift home. Drove off in relief, at a fast pace down the Old Kent Road, but was flashed by a speed camera, though luckily escaped a fine.

Further games were played in 1998 1-1 away, unattended by the KK sales team, 3-0 home, and 2001/02 when City fans were banned, but many made it including Sean to witness a 3-2 City win, when the KK team watched the game on TV in the 3rd tier Centenary Suite of the Kippax.

Awayday Zines The Lion Roars. No One Likes Us, Tales from Senegal Fields.

WIMBLEDON

First KK game was in season 1989/90. Div. One, and a 1-0 loss. I travelled down on the Mostonian coach, appreciating being plied with coffee there and back. I watched a Steve Martin video going and dozed off to a Rocky video on the way home. London was choc-a-bloc, but

■ Plough Lane, my first visit was in season 1984/85, first game of the season, and we didn't know what hit us with their style of play, going 2 nil down before we pulled it back to draw 2-2.

arrived at 2.45 pm which buggered up sales. As it happened Brian Spurrell, an FSA member and United fan took the bags of zines off me and kindly delivered them to Sportspages. It was touch and go for the 1990/91 September game with Chelsea (Saturday), Torquay (Tuesday), KK12 to get to the printers, then business trips to Norway, Denmark, Germany and Holland in the week. By 2am on the Saturday morning KK12 was far enough on to warrant the trip by train, to witness a 1-1 draw.

First KK visit to Selhurst Park was in season 1991/92, a 2-1 loss. On the Sunday before the game, I popped into work on site for the new T2 Terminal, and on the way spotted some of our players sitting on a grass verge awaiting

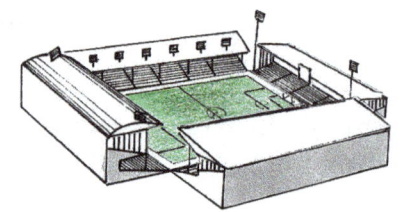

■ Selhurst Park, they ground shared from 1991 until 2003, staging a magnificent campaign becoming AFC Wimbledon after their then Chairman moved the club to Milton Keynes, as MK Dons.

the team coach. Naturally I had a chat with Steve McMahon, Fitzroy Simpson, Martin Margetson, Rick Holden, Terry Phelan, Mike Quigley and Gary Flitcroft. Not exactly a bundle of laughs, and the best they could muster was "Are you going down for the game tomorrow?" Must've thought I was some kind of nutter!

We lost the game, and If that wasn't bad enough, outside the ground we were greeted with Howard Yeats who informed us that the special train had crashed and we were to get service trains home, and possessions from the train were to be collected from the club the next day. My house keys were in my bag so I couldn't wait that long. Danny, Colin Lund and his son Darren from Soccer 2, and Scott from 'Singing the Blues' remained. Having retrieved our bags and salvaged some food from Alan Potter we returned to the station. British Rail had found a replacement train but all the City fans had gone by then. We managed to ride on this 'cattle truck' to Watford Junction, a whole train for five Blues. Prior to climbing on board, we met our least favourite referee 'gorgeous' George Courtney, waiting for a train to Newcastle. City fans hated him for once sending Coton off and another time awarding two pens. to Liverpool. He told us he'd received some dreadful letters from fans on his refereeing. We gave him a KK22 to read because he was actually a charming bloke out of the black gear. At Watford we rejoined the other Blues, the grub was distributed free to the City fans and surprised other occupants, some brownie points for footie fans gained on an eventful trip home!

Steve P: "In season 1998/99 January 2nd, we played them in the F.A. Cup 3rd round with Wimbledon in the Prem. Last day for selling the old KK, with 320 left to sell so I joined Dave and Ged for a bit of selling and a giant killing. Easy run M6, M40, M25, M4, Kew bridge, a pleasant detour through Richmond Park, then via Morden and Mitchum. Plenty of Blues, including spotting Sir Howard Davies one time head of the C.B.I., Erik and Maida from Norway. I did a personal best (128 KK's sold) but I did have a prime spot, Dave cursing that he'd left a further 20 pessimistically behind. We lasted until the 62nd minute when Cort scored, later sent off with Morrison. The final four zines were just a formality, Upper Norwood, Streatham, Wandsworth and the Kings Road, back to the M40 where we hit a traffic jam, otherwise a clear run home on the M40 then a meal at the Red Hen at Warwick. services."

Awayday Zines *Carlton, Carlton, Go Jack Go, Yidaho, The Grapevine, Roger Connell's Beard, There's Only One Mike Dziaddulwicz, Tenants Extra, Hoof the ball Up, Sour Grapes, Five All, Route One, The Big Tissue.*

20. SOUTH COAST

Off on the long haul to Brighton, Bournemouth, Portsmouth, Plymouth, Southampton and Torquay.

BRIGHTON AND HOVE ALBION

First visit was in season 1988/89, April. I took the early morning football special, meeting up for the first time with Ged Isaacs and Gideon Seymour. It was a 2-1 loss which dented our promotion hopes, and a middle aged ballboy was sacked after back heading the ball into the crowd to waste time, but we did finally go up. KK4 was on sale and we sweated over the front cover which predicted promotion! KK contributed to the 'Save the Seagulls' fund, and 'Attila the Stockbroker', amongst others, encouraged us to start the fanzine.

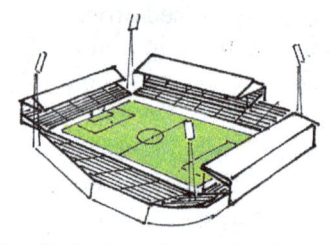

■ The Goldstone Ground, evicted in 1997.

■ The Wealdstone ground, vacated in 2011 Just the one forgettable visit in the Carling Cup September 2008, a 2-2 draw and 5-3 loss on penalties to League One Brighton. It was a good trip using the newfangled Sat Nav, and we stayed at a B and B. We visited the pavilion, museum, art gallery and shops. parked up near the ground (Athletics ground too awful even for a pic), said hello to Mark Ashton, and sold the few remaining KK162's. Near the end of the game a member of their back room staff caught the ball behind the goal and ran off towards the dressing room clutching it.

Kasper leapt over the railings, chased him, then snatched the ball, and took the goal kick. It was similar to the incident in 1989 at the Goldstone ground, but dunno if he was sacked?. Next day we had a stroll along the pier chatting and commiserating with fellow Blues before the drive home. We missed seeing the Moody Blues at the Apollo for this trip.

First visit was for the first game of the 2017/18 season, when we spent a pleasant pre-match time in a cafe on the promenade, before watching a 2-0 City win, though we didn't look like title winners.

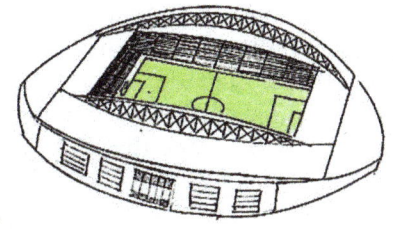
■ The Amex/Farmer's stadium, opened 2011.

Unforgettable visit was of course the final league game of 2018/19. It obviously necessitated an overnight stay. and it was not an easy ground to get too. We travelled from the hotel by train and bus after catching up with Tom and Steve, We were quizzed by the cops at the away end whilst selling and talking to our friend Raymond Ashton, ironically a barrister, plus Ian Cheeseman, as we queried the selection of Mahrez. City were not playing well, and went a goal down, Murray (27) giving us palpitations, but Aguero (29), Laporte (38), Mahrez(63) (justifying his selection) and finally Gundogan (72), gave us an unlikely, relaxing, last twenty minutes. Brighton did us proud with the post match trophy presentation and celebrations. I was asked to go on Talksport post match, but after hanging on for ages, they ran out of time.

Awayday Zines Gull's Eye, Brighton Rocks, Come Over The Dyke, Keep The Faith, Dogma, And Smith Must Score, Scars and Stripes, The Seagull Live Review, Nine Nil, On The Up, Seasick Saga, The Tommy Cook Review, Build A Bonfire.

WEMBLEY 2019, F.A, CUP SEMI FINAL 1-0

It was there and back in a day, for us, on the official City supporters club coach, the Mostonian. Tickets for the coach were subsidised by the club by a fiver so down to £25 each for us. £10 each if we'd known about booking on one of the Thos Cook coaches!

Pierre, a journalist from the French newspaper "L'Equipe" asked to meet with us to chat about the zine and what City fans thought of the effects that Brexit may have on our club.

Whilst advising that the zine was not political, (unless it does affect the club and/or the zine) and, strangely, many friends and KK readers are Brexiteers, personally I was with Remainer Vinny Kompany, and many others, on this. I disagreed with Noel Gallagher, reported as not voting, but claiming it to be fascism if it wasn't actioned. I thought it was the daftest thing we've done since sending the 600 into the wrong valley in the Crimean war, and basing the biggest post war decision on a 52/48% vote without a recount just seemed silly. It was a sentiment confirmed later by my hero, William Keegan in The Observer Sunday newspaper. Let's face it, referendums are stupid, people are mischievous, Cameron was the modern day Pontius Pilate.

For the fanzine it meant extra bureaucracy, having to fill in a form for every bloody zine sent abroad.

Anyway, there was a bit of an altercation outside the ground which needed police intervention, so the distraction enabled us to sneak in with our bags of zines. Inside the ground our end was sparse and worrying, but it filled up nicely before kick off. Wow, we'd only just entered, when Kev's wicked cross was glanced in by Jesus and that was that, with just the one scare. Surprisingly we exited the car park fairly easily and were soon on our way home.

AFC BOURNEMOUTH

First KK visit should've been in season 1988/89, a 1-0 win which I missed, future City Mag editor Mike Barnett doing the match report honours. Then it was the 1998/99 season 0-0 draw, in the 3rd tier, most famous for Kevin Horlock being sent off for "aggressive walking"! by referee Brian Coddington.

■ Dean Court. My first real visit was in 87/88 a night match which we won 2-0, although I did visit in 1959 aged 15, when I was on holiday in Southbourne.

We'd travelled by car with Steve and Cath Knott, and parked in the park next to the ground. It was a great selling place, with a narrow alley to the open away end, behind the goal. Ged was positioned on one side of the alley, and I stood opposite him as we sold about 400. We stayed for two nights, and on the night before the game we relaxed in the hotel amongst (non City fans) sporting scarves proclaiming love for Daniel O'Donnell who had a gig there the next night!

KK subscriber Geoff Watts went for a walk on the Prom with his wife on the morning of the game, bumping into Jamie Pollock, Danny Tiatto, Shaun Goater and Gerard Wiekens, posing for photos. Unfortunately a scrawny ginger haired scrote wearing a sweater over what turned out to be a United shirt tried to spoil the photo. Jamie Pollock then took hold of the little runt and threw him into a nearby bush. Pure class from Jamie!!

On the evening of the game Bernard Buckley from the City Chadderton supporters club had arranged a Medieval banquet evening which was brilliant.

The ground had been upgraded and turned through 90 degrees by the time we revisited in season 2015/16. We were housed at one end of the stand down the side, with a limited allocation. It was also an opportunity to visit my cousin Derek in Christchurch. A remarkable man, in his 80s, who, after a career as a merchant

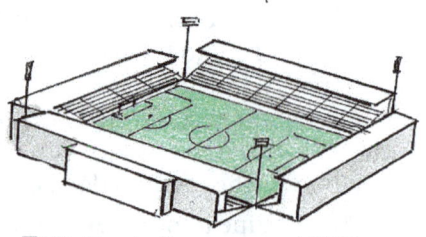

■ Vitality stadium, opened 2001.

banker in the city, turned his hand to becoming a successful professional poker player, who regaled us with fascinating stories of his achievements.

Parking was easy in the Kings Park next to the ground for a quid, but sales were poor in comparison with the previous successes, also considering our low allocation.

In August 2017, the 3rd game of the season, (Brighton A 2-0, Everton H 1-1) we were still unconvinced about Pep's managership, despite the 2-1 win, with a late Sterling goal. Whilst selling, post match, I was accosted by an irate Cherries fan, who thought they'd been robbed. The next week we defeated Liverpool 5-0 at home and we had lift off.

Awayday Zines Community Service, Exiled, Not the 8,502, Out Of Court.

PORTSMOUTH

First KK visit was in season 1988/89 a 1-0 win, which I think I missed, the Young Govs. selling KK on our behalf! Years later I bumped into Frankie of the YG's at the Vitality, now matured into a fine fella!

■ Fratton Park, My visit was in 1984/85 season a 2-1 win. (Although we did visit in the summer of 1983 when we holidayed in Portsmouth, visiting the ground on Alan Ball's first day as assistant manager under Bobby Campbell).

In season 2001/02 I had my aching tooth patched up by the dentist (United fan) who advised me not to go, but I said "needs must" so he gave me antibiotics etc. Went to Southsea promenade past the Blue Oasis bar/restaurant, surely an omen? It was Karaoke night too, so thanks to all the young kids who kindly invited us back, on the Saturday night. City lost 2-1. CD and record fair on the Sunday morning, I bought Kansas's *Carry On My Wayward Son* CD,

It was usually an overnight stay for us. On one occasion we arrived on a foggy Friday night in 2006/07. I managed a few songs on karaoke, had an early breakfast, with Blues Barry and Yvonne, referee Mike Dean was on an adjacent table. We then heard that the game was off, so I toddled off to the ground and inspected the pitch, which was in fact, quite frozen. I picked up a few programmes from the shop to pass on later to Karl Madden. As it happens we had a lovely day in Portsmouth, though Ian Cheeseman in his book 'Best Job in the World' found it amusing that he'd found out that the game was off before setting off, whilst we were stuck in Pompey after a fruitless journey. Barry and Yvonne, stayed on for a few more nights to take in the Youth Cup game on the Wednesday.

When the match was eventually played, I travelled with the 'Blue Watch' boys in a hired mini bus which set off from Huddersfield in the snow, with various pick up points and smoking stops, meaning we arrived in Pompey too near to kick off to sell. I also missed the chance to say hello to Pompey fan and KK subscriber Ian Cunningham, and it was a 3-0 loss.

Awayday Zines *Frattonise, Blue n White, January 3rd 88, Pisces, Not The 8,502, Out Of Court, True Blue, Park Life, The Greatest City.*

PLYMOUTH ARGYLE

In the KK years, we played them in the 1988/89 season, winning 6-3 in the 2nd round of the League cup.

The following Saturday it was a 1-0 City win, and I somehow managed to miss both games. The latter game was postponed for a day, making it four long trips in a week for Blues, Ipswich Saturday, Plymouth mid week twice for the League cup, then again in the League on the following Saturday. Those that travelled with the supporters club were presented with a certificate, but not me obviously!

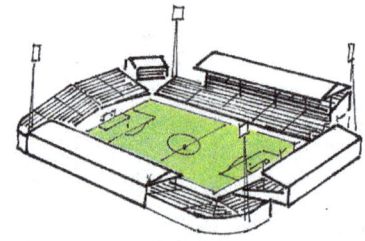
■ Home Park, and my first visit was in season 1987/88 a 3-2 loss after being two goals up.

Awayday Zines *Storming With Menace, The Guzzler, One Team in Devon, Rub of the Green.*

SOUTHAMPTON

First KK visit was in season 1989/90, December a 2-1 loss. Mel Machin had been sacked, Joe Royle turned us down and Howard Kendall was lurking. Eldest son Danny and I travelled down on the train, selling was OK.

Boxing Day 1990, drove down with Danny and Noel Bayley, stopping at

Strensham services. We arrived at 1pm, sold, and. City lost 2-1. We had a cup of tea, post match at Saints fan Ged O' Brien's house round the corner from the ground, and arrived back home at 10.30 pm. Richard and Louise went on the official supporters club chartered plane!

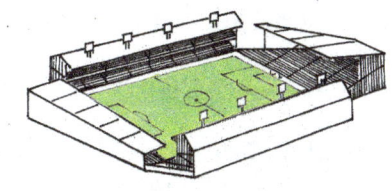

■ The Dell, and my first visit with the family was pre season 1983 when we were on holiday in Portsmouth, and the Saints club kindly agreed to give us a ground tour.

November 1991 we set off from Leigh in the KK mobile, when the warning lights came on, as the car was overheating. We limped along to Bootle street police station where the cops kindly provided us with enough water for the radiator, to enable us to drive to the train station. We got an urgent telephone message to Noel Bayley that we couldn't pick him up in Wythenshawe. We boarded the train just in time, and made it to the ground, to watch a rare 3-0 win. Noel watched the reserves at Maine Road and sold a few KK20's, as well as his own Electric Blue.

On another occasion, May 1st 1993 we were planning to stay for the weekend, but I had an accident at work, cornering a filing cabinet at speed, and pulling a muscle. After a quick visit to A. and E, I was patched up and provided with a set of crutches. I couldn't drive, so Sue booked us on a supporters club coach, thanks to Howard Yeats, so we made it to the ground and sold a few KKs. Result was a 1-0 win, but our coach was greeted with friendly waves, V-signs, wanker signs, and the one finger as we left Southampton, which amused us, arriving back in Manc at 9 pm

The iconic KK 50 was on sale at the 1999/2000 League cup tie. We've seen the front cover emulated many times on different fanzines/publications, but I think we were the first with the idea? I drove down with Ged, the game went to extra time and I was allowed out to collect more zines to sell at the end, though we lost 4-3.

First KK game at St Mary's was in season 2002/03 when we were moved from selling, which was never a problem at the Dell. Season 2003/04 we had a good run with Ged driving. The stewards tried their best, but failed to stop us from selling. Home fans comments included - " Is that the Autotrader, you shouldn't be selling pornography here, you should

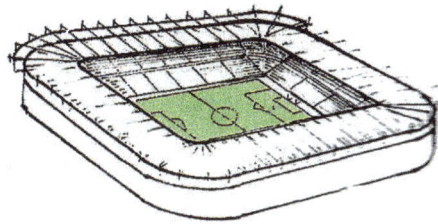

■ St Mary's, opened in 2001.

use that as toilet paper, It's a long way to come to lose". I'd also written a grovelling letter to the club asking if it would be OK to sell, but to no avail, and the stewards were still the unfriendliest in the league. I told one of them so, and he didn't even care, but we still sold out despite the 2-0 loss.

The high was the last game of season 2017/18, when we travelled down in Tom's car. We didn't have the usual hassle selling, as we'd already sold out of KK's, and after about 89 minutes wondered why we'd bothered, it was such a poor game. We didn't look like scoring if we'd played all night, until Gabriel Jesus latched on to Kev's through ball and lobbed it into the net. All was right in the world, City were Centurion Champions, first team ever to do it.

Awayday Zines The Ugly Inside, On the March, Devalued, Red Stripe, Beautiful South.

TORQUAY UNITED

Just the one meeting in the League Cup 2nd rd 1st leg, in season 1990/91. There and back in the day by car, bit of a difference from 1960. A mate, Kevin Gorton, had sussed out and booked in at the hotel where the team were staying, which we visited pre match to collect autographs and chat with players and backroom staff. We followed the team coach to the ground and City coasted to a 4-0 win. On the way home I was doing the ton on the deserted Motorway, then checked into a service station which was closed. On the way out we passed a parked police car which was lying in wait for speeding motorists, so it was a lucky escape! Return leg was a 0-0 draw.

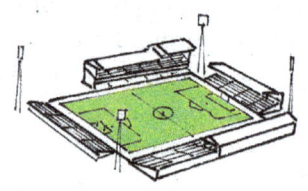

■ Plainmoor, and my first visit was for a friendly game when I was on holiday in 1960. We went on a Yelloway's coach, which took all day to get there.

Awayday Zines Mission Impossible.

21. EUROPE 2003/04 TO 2011/12

European competitions, re-commenced in season 2003/04 via the Fair Play rules, after a 24 year absence, with just the 1970 European Cup Winners' Cup nestling in our trophy room.

So here we go, covering a selection of the away games where we sold KK. We started off quite humbly playing TNS, (see chapter 15) Lokeren, Groclin, Schalke, Copenhagen, Aalborg, Hamburg, Salzburg, Juventus, Bayern Munich, Napoli, Porto and Sporting Lisbon.

SEASON 2003/04
LOKEREN
Wednesday September 24th 2003 UEFA Cup 1st rd 1st leg City 3 - (Sibierski,11, Fowler 77, Anelka 80P) Lokeren 2 - Zoundi, 14, Kristinsson, 40) 29,067 (910 LVK)

Wednesday October 18th 2008 1st round 2nd leg Lokeren 0 City 1 (Anelka, 18P)

■ Dakman Stadium.

We travelled with Flight Options/90 minutes, flew out at 08.35 from T1, arrived at Ostend, then took a coach to Lokeren arriving by lunchtime. We spent a pleasant day in the town, with Dave. Miller, his son Alex and his mate, with plenty of Blues, free and easy. Cheesy told us that on the way out Jimmy Wagg said disbelievingly, that on one previous European trip David Oates of GMR had to broadcast the game from a bus, adding "at least we won't have that", but guess what?

The meeting point compound idea, mooted by our club, to prevent City fans supposedly ransacking the town, never materialised. Sean Riley and John Burfield, thought it was a smokescreen to get fans onto official packages. We sold KK116.

Kevin Keegan reckoned that the fans were better than the game. There was only one blackspot, the trouble in the stand to our right in what looked like City fans in amongst the Lokeren fans, who got upset about our soft penalty, and waded in. Turns out they were fans of the Antwerp club wearing City shirts? Some Blues were quick to try and help fellow Blues in trouble, but luckily nothing much materialised. No hitches with the trip, so thanks to Spike and co. We were home by 01.30 Thursday morning, just in time to watch most of the re-run on BBC3, the 1-0 win enough to take us through to the next round.

GROCLIN

Thursday November 6th 2003 UEFA Cup 2nd rd 1st leg City 1 (Anelka, 6), Groclin 1, (Milka, 66) 32,506 - (583 Groclin)

Thursday November 27th 2003 2nd leg 4.15KO, - Groclin 0, City 0 (City exit on away goals)

The official party flew out on the Wednesday and I was able to wish them Bon Voyage in Terminal One at Manchester Airport. Ged and I (wearing thermals) opted for the Thomas Cook one day trip, flying out at 7.45am and arriving back at 9.15pm. We were provided with a copy of the glossy City news magazine issue 9 - for City card and ISC members (which took about five minutes to read), as we boarded. The coach dropped us off in the pleasant city of Poznan, where it was warmer than Manchester and we met up with fellow Blues, David Bookbinder, Nigel, Sean and Jane etc. We sold KK117.

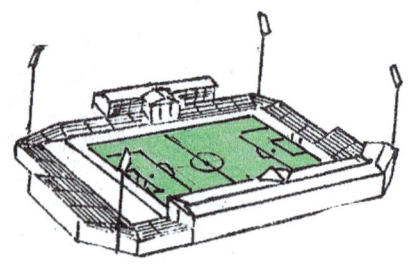

■ Daknamstadion.

We then boarded the coach, which took about an hour to arrive at the ground, as it was 'in the back of beyond'. Entry to the ground was dreadful, duly observed by City chairman John Wardle and Director Alistair MacIntosh. The view was OK where we were, behind the goal, but there were a few dickhead Blues knocking about. At half time one lad was having a pee in the Portaloo when a couple of City lads decided to push it over for a laugh. Not funny.

Second half there were a couple of Polish lads messing about and after a few warnings one received the finest right hook I've seen since the '70s. So our European adventure came to an abrupt end, but leaving us thirsty for more. After the game one Blue (Paddy Godfrey?) ran on the pitch, and had a go at Keegan, who wondered what the problem was? The players didn't come over to acknowledge the fans, and were therefore berated at the Airport by some Blues.

There was a raffle on the plane home, which had to be redrawn a few times as some of the winners were on the other flight! We were late arriving back and were given a City calendar on landing. Overall a well organised trip but disappointing result.

SEASON 2008/09

SCHALKE 04

Thursday November 27th 2008 UEFA Cup GS 1st leg Schalke 04 - 0 City 2, (Benjani, 32, Ireland, 66) 54,142 (2,710 Blues)

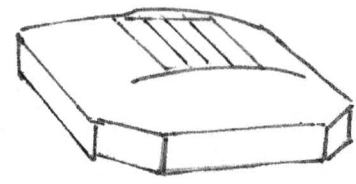

■ Veltins Arena.

Sue and I plumped for the two day official Thomas Cook trip, arriving in Cologne by early afternoon. Time was taken to revisit the magnificent cathedral, then the Chocolate factory, followed by a meal, after meeting up with Tom and Steve P (Ged and co. drove separately), then the Christmas markets, finishing with a late night session with a couple of chatty Blues, Vinny and Morgan. Thursday, and it was a visit to the chilling Nazi museum, then a stroll round Cologne before boarding the coach to Gelsenkirchen at 4pm, an estimated hour's drive away.

The traffic was horrendous, due to a couple of bumps, a twenty minute stop to line up the convoy of coaches to await the police escort, which never turned up, due to riots in Gelsenkirchen by Schalke fans, which was just a lame excuse. We arrived at the Veltins arena at about 7.10 pm, coaches parked ten minutes walk away from the turnstiles in the dark, with poor lighting and no proper paths.. It was chocker at the turnstiles, then we were searched. and inside the ground at 7.25.

We sold KK164. Chaos again, and the stewards were dis-interested. No programmes were available for us, but Steve P. got one which included a feature on Bert but with a pic of Frank Swift! Jethro Tull's Locomotive Breath was played at half time.

Great 2-0 win, but the inevitable crush at the end, though fairly well organised travel home after wandering around in the dark and mud to find the coach. "Good luck against the dirty rags on Sunday" announced the pilot. Nice one. Took about one hour to get through passport control at Manchester Airport as we serenaded the boys on the way through. On the mini bus (parked behind the City coaches) which drove us back to the car park, we sat next to a respectable looking couple coming back from holiday. They spotted the City players and the bloke came out with - "the only good thing about City is their manager (Mark Hughes)", followed by "run over him", as the bus pulled past a City player, Jo maybe. "Twice as bitter rags" - Dontcha just love 'em? No.

Overall a good trip, disappointing at the Veltins, but maybe we'll visit again and enjoy better treatment? (we lost 1-0 at the swamp on the Sunday)

FC COPENHAGEN

Thursday February 19th 2009 UEFA Cup stage 32 FCK 2 (Almeida, 56, Vingaard, 90) City 2 (Onuoha, 29, Ireland, 61) 30,159 (1805 + 130 Sc/Blues)

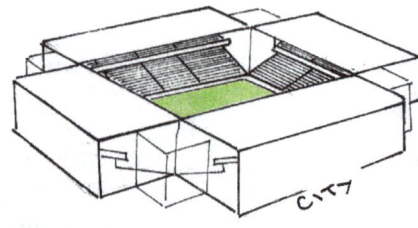
■ The Parken Stadium.

Pre match their boss, Stale Solbakken agreed that "City are ruining football", according to the delighted Daily Mirror, though this may have been a response to a loaded question?

Early start to the Airport at 5am for the 7.30 am flight. Bar was packed at 5.30,am, the beer flowing freely. A rag fan was jeered as he walked through the bar area, but no noticeable vitriolic abuse. Benjani was spotted going through to the departure gates. I was indebted to John Leigh and his bro-in-law Craig, along with KK contributor Neil Shaw, for helping me with a fanzine delivery to the Scandinavians. The Thomas Cook flight arrived roughly on time and there was plenty of snow around. The coach dropped us off in the middle of the city and we wended our jovial way to Bloomsday's to meet Tor and the Scandinavians, who duly received their KK167's. Big Alan Potter was in there also, and we did visit a few other bars bulging with familiar Blues. Then it was off to the match, where we entered the ground without incident. It was disappointing that we didn't secure the win, but the highlight was the City 'Spiderman' on the netting in front of us.

There were delays at the airport whilst the wings were de-iced and we had to circle Manchester a couple of times whilst they supposedly finished a job on the runway, before we landed. We couldn't use the 2nd runway due to the weather conditions, though it wasn't even snowing, although rumour had it that we were preparing for a crash landing? So it was a 24 hour day, pretty tiring, but enjoyable and I didn't see any trouble.

Thursday February 26th2009 2nd leg City 2 Bellamy (72.80) FCK 1 Vingaard (90) 26, 018

AALBORG

Thursday March 12th 2009 UEFA Cup stage 16, 1st leg City 2 (Caicedo,7, SWP, 30), 24,586 (404 AB)

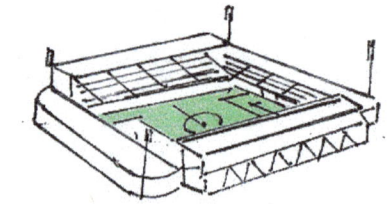
■ The Energi Nord Arena.

Early start and flight over with no complications.. What a lovely place Aalburg is with its bars, cafes and restaurants in which to meet fellow Blues. We sold KK168. It was a cold night. Pre KO, the locals put on an impressive display of flag waving, the flags changed from red to white as a giant flag was passed along the home support for the length of the stand. Plan A was to get an early goal and coast it, but we opted for plan B which was, of course, in true City style ; concede two late goals, then extra time and penalties. Their English chant of 2 nil up and you f*cked it up gave me a chuckle, but thankfully we gave it back to them after the penalty shoot out.

Thanks to Shay (2 saves) , Ched, SWP, Elano and Dunney for staying strong and putting us through. You had to smile at the sight of Dunny charging up to take his penalty like a white Rhino in full flight. Cheers to the Blue who gave me a City belt he'd made up in Thailand cos "I'm a top bloke" he said. Makes a nice change. Got back to bed at 3.45 am so it was a complete day. Hamburg next, tough draw, but another good trip. Either our name's on the Cup or we've used up all our luck already.

Thursday March 19th 2009 2nd leg, 0-2 aet 4-2 pens. Aalburg 2 (Shelton, 64, Jacobsen, 89P), 10,735 (700 Blues)

HAMBURG

Thursday April 9th 2009 UEFA Cup Q/F 1st leg Hamburg 3 (Mathijsen, 9, Trochowski, 63P, Guerrer 79) City 1 (Ireland, 1). 50.500 (2614 Blues)

Early start, up at 3.30am Thomas Cook flight to Hanover. (with night time flight restrictions from Hamburg) then a coach to Hamburg, beers and snacks with Roger Reade, Ian and Mark, soaking up the sun. Open bus trip round the impressive city, then a few more beers in the Reeperbahn before boarding the coach to the ground.

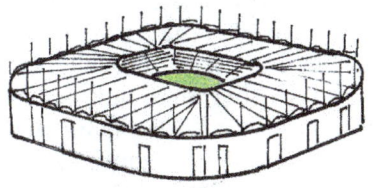
■ The HSH Nordbank Arena.

Like Schalke, the away coach park is a good walk away from the ground, but we were soon inside soaking up the atmosphere. We sold KK169. What a start and what a stadium with the roof keeping in the noise, whilst our announcer could learn a thing or two from theirs, as he roused the crowd, to chant in their gutterral but effective language. 1-1 at half time, then yet another woeful second half to put the tie almost out of reach at 3-1.

I finally bumped into youngest son Alex, in the bogs, after the game. For some strange reason, he had opted not to travel with his dad, but drove with his mates to Hull, the driver having only one arm, caught the ferry to Rotterdam, then drove to Hamburg.

Pity they forgot the map, pre Sat Nav days, going 100 miles out of their way, nearly running out of petrol, having scary moments, but made it for kick off.

Their journey back was via Amsterdam. I didn't ask!

Having lost Roger and co. I had a panic trying to find the coach, but luckily made it for an uneventful and downbeat flight home, though we knew 2-0 would do it in the return leg.

2nd leg Thursday April 16th 2009 City 2 Elano (17P), Caicedo (50) Hamburg 1 Guerrero (12) 3-4 agg. 47,009 (2,528 HG) Slashed ticket prices, flag day, club provided inflatable bananas to help create a fantastic atmosphere.

SEASON 2010/11

R B SALZBURG

Thursday September 16th 2010 Europa Lg GS MD 1 Salzburg 0 City 2 (Silva 8, Jo 63) 25,100 (798 Blues)

Usual early morning start for the Thomas Cook flight and I arrived at the Airport at 3.45 am whereas son Alex, his mates and loads of other Blues flew out to Munich at the more reasonable time of

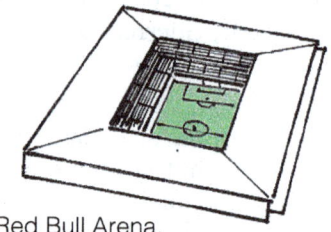
■ Red Bull Arena.

9.30am then took the train to Austria. Strangely, again, I didn't think he wanted me on this trip with him? Salzburg was enjoyable, we arrived at the picturesque town, yodelling away, at about half nine, so plenty of time strolling around in the bright sunshine, frequenting the bars and cafes, meeting up with the usual fellow Blues, though we missed Noel G. and Mike P. etc. Personally I spent the day alongside Roland Griffin RIP, ex fireman (once with workmate and future City Chairman John Wardle), programme collector, and Stretford Labour councillor. Great bloke, massive Blue, and excellent companion.

Locals were tipping us to win by a couple of goals, which always makes us wary, but it was very complimentary nevertheless. We sold KK181. The game itself was a bit of a stroll, it was good to see 'Hi-Ho' David Silva get his first goal (8) and for Jo (63) to clinch it. Everyone was happy, and the home supporters seemed to take it fairly well. The flight home was uneventful to round off a successful trip.

Wednesday December 1st M/D5 2nd leg City 3 (Balotelli 18,66), A. Johnson (60), Salzburg 0. 37.552 (208S/B)

JUVENTUS

Thursday September 30th 2012 Europa Lg GS MD 2 - City 1 (Johnson 37), Juventus 1 (Laquinta 10) 35,212

Thursday December 16th 2010 KO 7pm 2nd leg MD 6 Juventus 1 (Giannetti 43) City 1 (Jo 75) 6,998 (1476 Blues)

■ Stadio Olympico.

6.45 am flight, flying in over the snow-capped mountains, and a pleasant, but cold day was spent by Sue and I in the grand and elegant city of Turin. All went smoothly with an impressive police escort to the ground. We were searched three times on entry and had to show our tickets with our names on the back, with our passports. Toilets consisted of Portaloos. We sold KK 184. Good turn out of Blues in a small crowd (Juve fans not keen on going to Torino's ground) who had an entertaining time. Pre match music included AC/DC's Thunderstruck, chant of "Thunder" replaced by me with "City" yup that old chestnut of mine, everybody's doing it now. We could've been first if Chris Bird, as I've often reminded him, had been a bit more 'with it' all those years ago when I handed him the tape, though I suspect as it was my idea, it was turned down just on that basis!?.

There was, inevitably, a 1985 banner "don't they know it was Liverpool, not us", Neil Shaw said to me afterwards? We fielded a weakened team and came away with a creditable draw, though we should have had a couple of stonewall penalties. After the game we were swiftly driven back to the Airport, where the plane's wings were de-iced and missing nuts and bolts replaced (?) before take off, as the temperature plummeted to -15 degrees. It sounds like we were a bit lucky there, as the team, who were flying out a little later, were held back until Friday morning due to the mechanical problems and arctic conditions. It had been very low key with the police and it was good to meet up with Neil Shaw, Graham Brine, Nigel Gregory, Sean Riley, Worthy, and many other familiar faces and solid Blues. City fans who had driven from Milan and other areas encountered snow blizzard conditions, resulting in cancelled rail and plane journeys, adding an extra day or two journey time.

SEASON 2011/12
BAYERN MUNICH

Tuesday September 27th 2011 Champs Lg G/m 2 Bayern Munich 2 (Gomez, 38,45) City 0 - 65,000 (3000 Blues)

Usual early start, all went smoothly. I was pleased to see that the club took up my proposal of a few weeks ago, after the draw was made, of doing something for the 1958 Munich victims and Frank Swift at the memorial at the old Airport. I'd suggested they provided a coach for fans who wished to pay

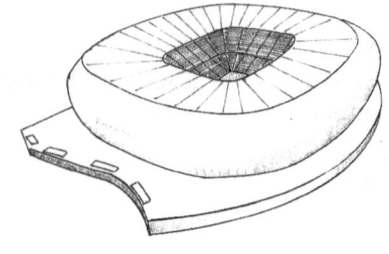
■ Allianz Arena.

respects. OK, it's possible that the club had something in mind already, but those that I spoke to in this regard were generally enthusiastic to my suggestion. I wasn't surprised though that no such coach was provided, and only club officials, apparently, visited the site. How much credibility did that have? Fanzine editors eh?

We took advantage of the tour bus, on a sunny day, then repaired to the Augustinerteller where we mingled with fellow Blues, the Woodhouses, our son Alex and his mates etc, who were having fun and singing the songs. Some Germans sitting close to us took exception, and were unimpressed when I told them it was just working class Mancs enjoying themselves. The German sense of humour eh! Off to the match then, and we had a great sing song on coach 4 to the ground. We sold KK190 Again, as per Schalke and Hamburg, we parked a good way away, and when we got to the stadium there were no signs for away supporters which meant tramping all the way round the ground before finding our entrance.

Then followed a Newcastle-type trek up the stairs to the top tier. Away fans located up there, not in a prime spot like at Eastlands, and home and away fans mixing on the concourse. As for the game, and what a great occasion, we

should have had two penalties before it was 0-2. Edin wasn't happy about being taken off, with Nige shoring things up. We were surprised that Carlos wasn't brought on, but we were soon informed by Blues on their phones to home, that he'd refused to come on.

We got to bed at 3am, then I was mithered to death by the media, and finished up doing a midday interview on Channel 4 before picking Alex and his mates up at the Airport after their lengthy trip via Zurich. It turned out Mancini repeatedly asked Carlos to get ready, but kept changing his mind, and eventually Carlos got miffed and refused to go on. He then left to play golf on 'gardening leave' in Argentina, and didn't return until April/May at Norwich, (6-1), "to help City win the title", which we did.

Home leg - Wednesday December 7th 2011 - City 2 (Silva 36, Yaya Toure 52) B. Munich 0 46,002

NAPOLI

Wednesday September 14th 2011
Champs lg m/d 1 - City 1 (Kolarov 75)
Napoli 1 (Cavani 69) 44,026 (2523 Naps)

Tuesday November 22nd Cg Lg M/D 5
Napoli 2 (Cavani 17,49) City 1 (Balotelli 33) 57.575 (1072 Blues)

■ Stadio San Pauli.

Up at 4am on the Monday morning for the 7.30 am flight to Naples on Spike's trip, which included plenty of seasoned City travellers, arriving at mid morning. after a short delay, (someone had lost their wallet). We were coached to Sorrento with a police escort, which included an incredible piece of manoeuvering and driving by our coach driver, through three solid lanes of traffic, which were opened up miraculously by the Police, to enable the coaches to steam in, out of, and through, as though it was a Sunday morning breeze oh a leafy Cheshire lane.

We holed up in the majestic Hilton hotel and found that our room was next to that of Barry and Yvonne, who we last met up with in Portsmouth for the ill fated postponed game a few years previously. We love Sorrento, had a nice meal outside in one of the many cafes then strolled through the town, chatting and nodding to fellow Blues, most of whom we've met over many years. "Better than that rainy night in Lincoln eh!" Sorrentorians specialise in inlay and marquetry and the display in the shops was breathtaking. I bought one as a memento, then when I arrived back home, found out I'd made a similar one myself years ago. We took a further stroll up to the cliff top area, where we looked over the harbour towards Capri (where United fans according to the song, shovel shit). We met a couple of tremendous Blues, Steve, who now lives in Bristol, and Ian, who now lives in Edinburgh.

There was a group of American girls who asked us to take their photos for which Ian obliged. One asked where are you from? - when we said Manchester, the inevitable reply was " whenever I think of Manchester, I think of Manchester United" We nearly threw her over the cliff.

We went back to the hotel where we crashed out, then had a snack before intending to head off into the town later. However we were advised against it as there were reports of trouble between the locals and City fans. Blues were herded back to the hotel where, on police advice, the bar was closed. So it was an unhappy end to the day.

At breakfast the next morning, Sue and I were ushered by the staff into a separate area from the City fans. They were obviously thinking that such a respectable looking couple couldn't possibly be football fans! Once again, little did they know!

5 live rang me up for an update on the previous night's events, then it was off to (Hiyo!) Pompeii (not Pompey!) bumping into KK contributor, Dave Ansbro, with Steve and Ian, plus fellow Blues, all wearing City colours, despite the club's ill advice to avoid wearing colours at all costs. It's seen better days of course, but it's a fascinating place, and we entered the auditorium where Pink Floyd

once played live. We met some more Americans but this time one of them said he liked Manchester City because of Oasis. Then we returned to Sorrento and boarded the coach, which was accompanied by the Police escort, for the drive to the stadium, which was interesting and well organised.

We sold KK192 Tremendous atmosphere in the ground, despite the running track, but the place was crumbling.. Stewards wearing hard hats weren't a comfort and the ladies toilets (I'm told) were a disgrace, plus the City fan letting off fireworks was embarrassing. Roberto's team selection was a surprise and we paid the price with a 2-1 loss, with Napoli fans booing our every touch.

Tony Dempsey told us he and his Yorkshire mates had drank in the city's bars and were subjected to confrontations with 'The Mastiffs' which they laughed off. After the game they were attacked by crash helmet wielding bikers who they also saw off, but, after drinking in a bar, they were advised to return to their hotel, as "they're coming to get you". Tony was safe and sound when he related the incidents to us at the next City home game.

We were coached back to the airport without much bother despite a fracas at the Terminal , and home at 4am, after a great trip spoilt only by the result, which could have been even worse.

THAT result relegated us to the Europa League, and, whilst we were gaining valuable European experience, and enjoyed eventful trips, we needed to 'up our game' on the pitch.

PORTO

Thursday February 16th 2012 Europa Cup rd of 32 1st leg Porto 1 Varela (27) City 2 Perreira (55og), Aguero (85) 47,717

■ Estadio Do Dragao.

We opted for the one day Thomas Cook trip, so arose at 4am, parked up at T1, even though our flight was from T2. We walked past the ads proclaiming Turkish airlines in partnership with Manu.

Everything went smoothly, the coaches dropped us off in Porto by the river, and we enjoyed the bars, then a river cruise, followed by the cable car. bridge walk. We shared the Funicular lift with Bryan Hince in his wheelchair. Met up with Steve Mingle and his lady Lindsay, and were joined by Steve and Ian from the Napoli trip. It was nice and warm and sunny, so we had a laugh when we found it was snowing in Amsterdam where the rags were playing.

After exchanging pleasantries with many hardened and loyal Blues, we went on to the impressive stadium, where annoyingly, ladies' bags were banned. We sold KK194, then swapped scarves with a couple of Porto fans, watched the colourful display in the stands from Porto pre kick off and observed a few fireworks from City fans. 1 -0 down at half time, and pleasingly their fans, situated close by, didn't turn on us after they scored. Great second half performance from us and a 2-1 win. We didn't hear the disgusting monkey grunts aimed at Mario and Ya Ya, so we awaited developments on that score.

We were kept in after the game, but the TVs were switched off, though the bars were open so no probs. We had a smooth flight back, then drove home (M56 shut), through Manc, which seemed fairly drab compared to Porto, and were in bed by 4.30am, which gave us the feel good factor to finish KK195, at the weekend.

Thursday February 22nd 2012, 2nd leg, City 4 (Aguero 1, Dzeko 76, Silva 84, Pizarro 86) Porto 0 39,538 (1171 Ps)

SPORTING LISBON
Thursday March 8th 2012 Europa Lg Rd 16
1st leg S Lisbon 1 (Xandao 51) City 0, 34,371 (878 Blues)

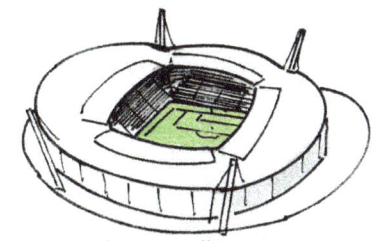
■ Jose Alvalade stadium.

Sue and I travelled on Spike's trip with Blues' comedy duo Steve and Ian again on a lovely day, for once. We finally met up with long time KK contributor and now Lisbon resident Simon Curtis, and had a catch up chat outside a cafe by the Bull Ring. We then enjoyed the splendours of Lisbon, the sunshine, including spotting Radio Manc presenter Ian Cheeseman, (Nice mention for us in his column in the return leg programme). For the first time, and hopefully the last, we were serenaded by a spaced out lad with a didgery doo, but we didn't take advantage of the many drugs (Charlie) on offer. We sold KK195, and had good craic with the Lisbon fans who don't like United (who does?) but love City and Oasis. The stadium was great with a Lidl's and a cinema and I particularly liked the multi coloured seats which made it look full even when half empty.. The game showed that whilst Edin continues to struggle, and his reported remarks fired up Sporting before the game, (and they booed him off) we're probably going to need Carlos for the Prem. count down. On reflection we've probably forgotten that the game in Munich was already lost when he was finally asked to come on. Outrageous time wasting by their goalie, who fell over with a few minutes to go, feigning injury, as we lost 1-0..

All went well until we arrived back at the 'World's best airport' along with a big flight from the Middle East. No automatic passport control centres available, and only a couple of desks open, causing a long wait, particularly difficult for those with young kids who'd endured an eight hour flight. However, it was another great trip clocked up, as usual more memorable for the camaraderie than the game itself. "Boring, boring City, we'll score when we want", well not always.

Thursday March 15th 2012 2nd leg - City 3 (Aguero 60,82, Balotelli 75P) S.Lisbon 2 (Fernandez 33, Van Wolfswinkel 40) 38,021. Going out on away goals.

22. EUROPE 2012/2013 TO 2022/2023

Continuing in season 2011/12, we visited Real Madrid, Ajax, Barcelona, Sevilla, Glasgow Celtic (see chapter 5), Basel, Lyon, Chelsea in Porto and Inter Milan in Istanbul. Again these are a selection of European games we attended where we sold the fanzine.

SEASON 2012/13

REAL MADRID

Tuesday September 18th 2012 Champs league Group D MD 1 Real Madrid 3 (Marcelo 76, Benzema 87, Ronaldo 90) City 2 (Dzeko 69, Kolarov 85) 70,381 (3,504 City)

Last time we went to Spain in the summer it was to visit our friends, City fans Colin and Margaret Brinkley, when we did the 'meet and great' thing at Manc Airport. However the 'greeter bloke' turned up with our car on our return with a smirky look on his face and was wearing a rag bob hat, so obviously they've been binned, and I told them why. Sue thought I was being churlish but you have to have some principles in life.

■ The Bernabeu.

Today Sue and I opted for Spike's trip and were well looked after as you'd expect, as a pair of old timers. It was nice and hot so we headed for the Major square with Colin Savage, where we met, ate, drank and mingled with fellow City fans. Front cover of KK 200 shows the KK 'Spice Boys', average age 21 (!), holding up the KK flag. Meanwhile, someone had produced the inevitable football, which was kicked around the square with gusto (a fine lad!), even the waiters joining in on the act, though the shoe coming off as the ball is kicked, always amuses. The Police confiscated the ball, not the shoe, but a new one appeared immediately and the fun continued to roars of approval.

Then it was off to the Bernabeu, Colin convincing us that the tube was a better option than a taxi (?), Hm. We had a snack outside the ground where Gary Owen and Kevin Parker's crew were ensconced, then made our way in after hearing about cops battering City fans, (for not leaving a bar when told), including Charlton Athletic Chairman (a City fan) who officially complained to the club.

We also heard of a group of Blues teaching Spaniards the Ya-Ya song, with City fans on one side and the Spaniards on the other, much to everyone's amusement. We sold KK199. Great support for the Blues, we so nearly did it. Watching the game, high up on level 5 behind the netting. We were kept in after the match, then herded down a narrow exit lane, which could have caused problems, but City fans were patiently looking out for each other. Next day we made a swift visit to the Palace, and the beautiful Cathedral (by taxi). Time for home and a fairly uneventful return trip, even passport control being well organised, though having to walk past portraits of United players and their logo on the walkways was unimpressive, and annoying.

Wednesday November 21st 2012 2nd leg M/D 5 City 1 (Aguero 74P), R. Madrid 1 (Benzema 10) 45,740.

AJAX

October 24th 2012 Champs Lg GS 1st leg M/D 3 Ajax 3 (de Jong 45, Moisander 57, Eriksen 68) City 1 (Nasri 22), 46,743 ,2694 Blues.

We plumped for the Hull to Rotterdam ferry organised by friends Joe and Dolly O'Neill with a two night stay. We had a reasonable starting time, with a good drive over the M62 to Kingston upon Hull by driver Dolly, and

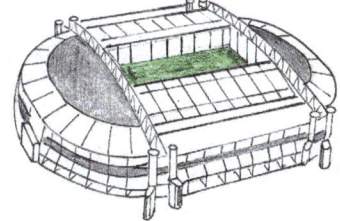
■ Johan Cruyff Arena.

a few pleasant hours were spent in the city, bringing back memories of when we lived there for a couple of happy years in the late 70s.

We boarded the ferry, along with plenty of Blues, including Gary Brough and the South Yorks contingent, (who later had a panic when one of them lost his passport!) plus Dave Griffiths RIP who championed the City connection with the Sierra Leone branch. There was an excellent evening meal provided plus entertainment, before we woke up the next day, in Rotterdam, then we travelled by coach to Amsterdam. We enjoyed the city sights, viewing the Anne Frank house, visiting the Jewish museum, and a canal trip when the guide pointed out a carving of "some saint on a creature", which turned out to be St George and the dragon! We didn't see any City players or media folk.

There were reports of one or two incidents around the 'Old Sailor' pub later in the afternoon where the amount of beer consumed and funny cigs smoked had led to problems.

We arrived at the ground and marvelled at the escalators. Only four turnstiles were open, so there were long delays, crushing, slow heavy searches by stewards, no escalators or lift for us, so it was up the stairs to our level, but no stewards to show us to our seats. Some City fans didn't arrive in the ground until half time, it was a complete shambles.

We made a token effort to sell some KK 200s which had been out for a few weeks but typically for European away games there wasn't much interest. We started off well in the game, going ahead but finally went down 3-1.

The next day we visited the cafes and enjoyed more sight seeing, chancing another river cruise, before making the trip home. All in all it was one of the best trips we'd had, so far, but just attending for the occasion was beginning to wear a bit thin, and it was about time we achieved some results.

"A win at last " was the headline in the Dutch press, the next day, as Ajax, had been in poor form. It just had to be us!

November 6th 2012 2nd leg City 2 (Toure 22, Aguero 74) Ajax 2 (De Jong 10,17) 40,222, 1800 Ajax.

SEASON 2012/13
BARCELONA

Tuesday February 18th 2014 Champs League rd 16 M/D 1st leg City 0 Barca 2 (Messi 53, Alvez 89) 46,030 (2,725 Barca)

Wednesday March 12th 2014 2nd leg Barca 2 (Messi 67, Alvez 90) City 1 (Kompany 89) , 88,626 with 4626 Blues.

We plumped for the two night stay on Spike's (Sports Options) trip. Usual early start but pleasant flight and smart hotel, finding City fans in relaxed

■ The Nou Camp.

mood. We managed to visit the Sagrada Familia which was breathtaking, after bumping into the MacKinnon gals Clair and Cath from the Swinton branch. Later we visited son Alex and friends Rik, Danny, Natalie etc in the Place Real, but Sue was unwell so we retired to the hotel by taxi and missed KK 'ers we were hoping to meet up with. We did manage to spot young City fan Don in his Borat suit! We arrived at the ground in good time so enjoyed a bite to eat, caught the lift up to our level, then we were herded into one of the sections, but not the one on our ticket. What a dump. No drinks allowed, so naturally I took in a bottle of water out of cussedness. The game was uninspiring, and not without incident; we weren't embarrassed, but easily put out 4-1 on aggregate. We had a comfortable journey back home, unlike the Thomas Cook trip the previous night, which was diverted to Newcastle because of fog, but not on the Tyne!!

SEASON 2015/16
SEVILLA

Wednesday October 21st 2015 Ch lg GS M/D 3 City 2 (Rami 36 OG, KDB 90+1) Sevilla 1 (Konoplyanke 30) 45,595 (1300 SV)
Tuesday November 2nd 2015 2nd leg M/D 4 Sevilla 1 (Tremoulinas 25) City 3 (Sterling 8, Fernandinho 11, Bony 36) 39, 261 with 2,509 Blues.

The result meant that despite losing our first game in the group 2-1 at home to Juventus, City had qualified for the round of 16 with two games left.

Early foggy start for Sue and I on Spike's two night trip. There was a slight delay, lots of familiar faces, and a fairly mature plane load, arriving in the early afternoon.

■ Ramon Sanchez - Pizjuan Stadium.

We had a bit of a roam around, went for a meal in the pouring rain then had an early night. Text received from the kids at home regarding trouble in the Irish bar being attacked by Sevilla fans, who ran off when City fans came out in force. Maybe this kind of incident caused the attack on Sevilla fans by Poles before the home game.

Tuesday was nice and warm, hot even. We strolled around, bumping into, and chatting with City fans, and had a smile watching four Priests exiting the Irish bar. We had a look round the magnificent Cathedral (our last Cathedral visit, always welcoming, and free, apart from a donation!) before being laid low for a while after a dodgy Lasagna. We thought that Blues were meeting up in the Plaza Espana but we were late due to the effects of the Lasagna, so found ourselves on our own, to make our way to the ground. Mackies was the least risky foodwise, and we sat with a couple of Blues, having a chat, and munching on a hamburger! We sold KK227.

Into the ground after a search "Is that your phone in your pocket?", I resisted saying " no I'm just pleased to see you", then up the many stairs where the stewards told us to sit anywhere. resulting in total chaos. Thanks to Graham Brine and his daughter Siobhan we managed good seats at the front of the second tier. Some City fans had A4 posters with the words BOO on them, maybe inspired by my recent KK blog post. Tremendous noise from Seville fans pre-match for their anthem. Plenty of booing for the Champs League anthem and it was a dominant display from the Blues in one of our best away performances in Europe. We were kept in for an hour and entertained by Fabian Delph and others doing warm downs, playing to the crowd with cart wheels and roll overs We then made our way back to the hotel for a good night's sleep. Wednesday, and it was a leisurely morning, before heading back to the Airport, then home sweet home.

SEASON 2017/18

FC BASEL
Tuesday February 13th 2018 Champs Lg rd of 16 1st leg Basel 0 City 4 (Gundogan (15, 53) B. Silva (18) and Aguero (23), 36, 000 (1,789 Blues.

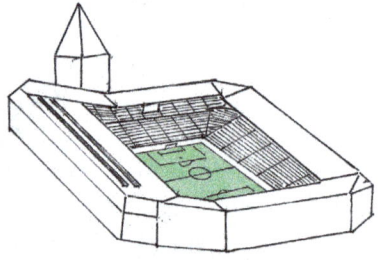

■ St Jacob-Park.

7.30am flight for us on Sports Options. We arrived in Basel mid morning and were dropped off in the city for some sight seeing, including visiting the impressive cathedral, before partaking of a Mackies! Then it was a stroll down the main street, dropping off at cafes, bars, and restaurants. One of the beauties of these European trips is bumping into and chatting to fellow Blues who we've not seen for ages. without the pressure of selling the zines, although we did sell KK249 at the ground. The locals were very friendly and many wished us good luck for the game with the rider "It'll be tough".

Dodgy start to the game on a cold night, when Basel looked more than a handful, and we survived a couple of tricky decisions in a non City vintage display. However, Gundo's early header settled the nerves, but Ederson's quick thinking prevented an equaliser. Bernardo and Sergio made it 3-0 at half time, after clinical and ruthless finishing. Ilkay scored a stunner for 4-0, then we admired Eddy's scorpion kick, as we saw the game out.

It was something of a trek to the coaches after the game, before the transfer to the airport and the flight home, arriving back in the early hours, after a tiring but very enjoyable day, very well organised by Spike and the team.

Wednesday March 7th 2018 2nd leg City 1 (Jesus 8) Basel 2 (Elyounoussi 17, Lang 71) 49,411, but City were through to the Q/F.

SEASON 2018/19

LYON

Wednesday September 19th 2018 Champs League Group stage MD 1 1st leg City 1 (Silva 67) Lyon 2 (Cornet (26), Fekir (43) 40, 111 (445 Lyon)

Tuesday November 27th 2018 2nd leg M/D 5 Lyon 2 (Cornett 55, 81) City 2 (Laporte (62, Aguero 83) 56,039 (2566 Blues)

All went smoothly on Spike's Sport Options flight. We were sitting next to Worthy and Bibby ex of BTH, Sue and I both had a bad cold, and the cabin pressure affected our hearing which lasted all day, and night, and was very painful.

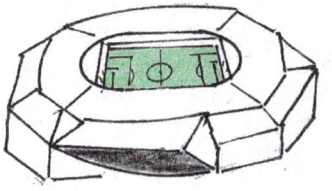
■ Anchor Stake.

It was a nice bright day in Lyon and we were bussed to the city centre, going past the ground on the way. We bumped into friends Keith, and Cath and Steve Knott, whilst witnessing the protest march of the Firemen. We had a chat with one of them who spoke excellent English, and he told us that they were protesting for pay, and against reduction of numbers.

Then we eventually managed to hail a taxi which took us to meet our friend Chrissie at the Marriott hotel, where, co-incidentally, the team were staying. We didn't fraternise, even though Laporte was wandering about in his City kit, as we didn't want to pass on our germs to Pep and the boys. We were joined by Phil and Amanda, an amazing couple who we've known for some years and the conversation flowed..

Then it was time for a stroll, and back to the hotel to book a taxi. But we were kindly offered a lift on the executive coach, which we gratefully accepted, and we spent the journey to the ground sitting next to Mike Pickering. Unfortunately we were both almost completely deaf, so didn't take the opportunity for a chat. He must've thought we were a right pair of miserable bastards. (If, in the unlikely event you read this Mike, apologies!)

We were kindly escorted to the City end by the super efficient Tommy Cook rep, searched twice, and were guided through a private entrance, with a few other Blues, up the lift and onto the concourse, where I had a cold hot dog and chips.

Into our section, and we were advised by the stewards to sit anywhere. They were replaced by another steward who hadn't a clue, so a bit of chaos ensued. We were in the top tier and watched the game through perspex panels and a safety net. Not much booing of the anthem, with Blues chanting 'City' throughout. We were outplayed in the first half but went in 0-0 at the interval. We perked up second half and against the run of play, ironically, they went ahead. The equaliser soon arrived through the impeccable Laporte. They went ahead again and this time Sergio did the biz. Who says we've no plan B?

Lyon were very impressive, (they looked a better team than PSG who beat Liverpool the following night). We exited the ground, boarded the coaches, back to the airport, annoying searches by security, shoes off and everything, and back to Manc on time, with ears still ringing.

We got a taxi back to Leigh, and the driver knew Lyon as he'd played for the volleyball team there for a few years. He was full of praise for the owner. One of his sons is in the Liverpool Academy and is doing well at only 15. Second son is in the Wigan Academy, Third son is into music, fourth son is only 4!.So we were back to bed at about half three, knackered, then woke up at gone twelve on the Wednesday, feeling very old!!

CHAMPIONS LEAGUE FINAL

Saturday May 29th 2021, Estadio Do Dragao stadium, Portugal, Chelsea 1 Havertz (42) City 0. (P/L 3-1 A, 1-2 H. FACS/F 0-1)

I received the all clear to go, although I knew it would be a major physical effort, and I could suffer afterwards. All the necessary tests and paper work were sorted and tickets plus free flight secured, thanks to Sheikh Mansour, a magnificent gesture. Unfortunately, Sue had only four months left on her passport, so couldn't go due to the stupid Brexit idiocy. I bumped into Geoff Homer, who worked for the club, and his daughter and grandson, so spent an enjoyable day with them. We arrived in sunny Porto early afternoon, and after spending a pleasant time, bumping into Blues, I boarded the bus to the ground and made my way to the top tier, where I sat gazing at the view, looking down to the right, where the few Chelsea fans were gathered, and from where we watched City beat Porto 2-1 a few years ago. It was a lovely evening and I was here, about to watch Manchester City in the Champions League final. Pinch me! The drunken Blue in front of me then fell over into the seats in front of him and had to be helped to his feet! Pep's selection of the out of form Sterling, instead of defensive midfielders Rodri or Fernandinho, surprised many, and it proved to be disastrous.City just weren't at it, and the horrific injury to KDB by Rudiger, who was not red carded, was the final straw. The game was a devastating loss, and it was particularly galling to see ex Blue Willy Caballero, celebrating with the Chelsea team at the full time whistle. Then it was a long trudge down the steps, but confusion as to where the coaches were parked. I felt very alone, then luckily bumped into long term KK subscriber Pete Roberts (top right in pic)n who helped me back on the long trek to the coach, as by now my legs had completely gone.

The final ignominy was losing a tooth as I bit into the in-flight meal, on the flight home! So, it wasn't the season's end we'd hoped for, but we did finally win it, and the Treble later in 2023. Chelsea have yet to beat us after that final.

That concluded our European away days.

CHAMPIONS LEAGUE FINAL

Saturday June 10th 2023 – Ataturk Olympic Stadium, Istanbul, (Kick off 10 pm local time) City 1 Rodri (68) Inter Milan 0 , 71,412 (including 19,926 Blues officially

We settled down in front of the TV, when we suffered a power cut, so had to dash to grand daughter Heather's in Blackrod with grandson Joe to watch it! At times the win didn't look possible, as we struggled against a determined Inter team. Eventually the winning goal came from Rodri, and we rode our luck in the closing minutes, with miraculous defending. The final whistle came, and we realised we'd finally done it. Not only winning the Champions League, but also pipping Arsenal to the Premier League title, and beating United in the F.A Cup final to complete the best ever TREBLE.

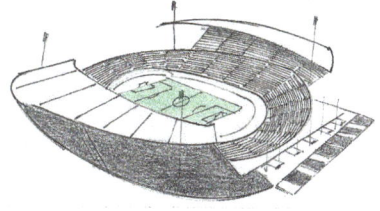

■ Ataturk Olympic Stadium.

After a couple of days in London and Brighton, our eldest daughter Marnie and husband Andy flew out to Istanbul and suffered the same problems encountered by most Blues, Andy even having his wallet nicked. Alex was there with a mate who didn't get in as he arrived late, and the stadium doors were locked. The win made it all worthwhile of course! Congratulations to Marnie and Andy who were celebrating their first wedding anniversary, so spent another couple of days in Istanbul, whilst Alex flew off to Athens. This meant they both missed the parade, and it was too much for us.

Watching the parade on the TV, how wonderful it was. The start was postponed as the heavens opened but it did not affect the parade and full marks to everyone, players and fans alike for the rain soaked celebrations. Special mention for Jack, who has now picked up two titles, an F.A. Cup and Champions League medal, fully justifying his move from Villa, and deserving of his celebrations, despite what the miseries in the media might have tried to make of it.

The Treble, is celebrated in the special + which is in colour throughout, sized between A4 and A5, 28 pages, lavishly illustrated, and sells for just £5. Front cover shows Ruben, Kyle, Kev, Bernardo and Rodri smartly clad.

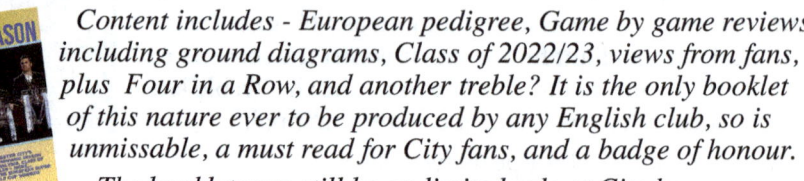

Content includes - European pedigree, Game by game reviews including ground diagrams, Class of 2022/23, views from fans, plus Four in a Row, and another treble? It is the only booklet of this nature ever to be produced by any English club, so is unmissable, a must read for City fans, and a badge of honour.

The booklet may still be on limited sale at City home games, subject to the weather, but can be purchased direct from (cheques to) King of the Kippax, 25, Holdenbrook Close, Leigh, Lancs, WN7 2HL for a mere £5 inc p&p. Bacs details can be arranged if required by email, and paypal is to kotk.fanzine@gmail.com.

Note: *I haven't sung a single song on Karaoke at any European venue!*

23. OUTLETS & DISTRIBUTION

In tandem with producing the zine, whilst at the printers, A4 envelopes were bought, stamps purchased, address labels collected (from Steve P), and both fixed to envelopes, plus compliment slips written.

Zines (required for British Library, contributors, subscribers, apologies, other zines, freebies, outlets), with relevant compliment slips, were bagged up and delivered to post boxes, all over the locality, including Culcheth, where I'd park in the car park next to the post box. Luckily I wasn't present when the police shot an innocent suspect.

For foreign subscribers they were delivered to the Tyldesley Post Office, who did us proud, but Brexit complicated matters, as we were no longer in the EU, so then had to fill in and stick customs labels on every single zine. (Goodness knows how this bureaucracy affected proper companies?) Delivery notes and invoices for the outlets were also produced.

Zines were bagged up ready for issuing to KK sellers, with estimated quantities for home and away games established, based on the opposition, selling history, how far into the run we were in. Unfortunately we couldn't predict the weather, which always affected sales.

Main Outlets included:

SPORTSPAGES London, were the first promoters of fanzines, highlighted by an article in the Observer Sunday newspaper. Football Supporters Association monthly meetings were held in Coventry, when we were able to hand over quantities of KK's to London based supporters of other clubs, who kindly delivered them to the shop in Charing Cross Road. On occasions, when City played in London, QPR in particular, we were able to pop in and deliver, otherwise it was parcelling up and posting. Christmas time, without warning, they would clear the shelves of zines, to make room for books and videos. Eventually, sadly, they went bust owing us a lot of money.

PICCADILLY RECORDS, surprisingly, initially in Piccadilly, then Brown Street, and later in the Northern Quarter, were brilliant, taking various quantities. It was always a pleasure to visit and have a football chat with the sales team, even "John the Red". Phillipa often joined us on the Kippax for City games.

NEEDBEST, on the corner of Cross Street/Market Street, were eventually sold to Simply News/Aleef, but payments weren't forthcoming. Indeed we had to visit their headquarters in Bolton, where they were very, very nice. However, they needed two signatures on the cheque from the partners, and guess what? One of the partners wasn't in that day, so they would have to send the cheque on later, which in fairness they did!

ARNDALE NEWS, then took over, and eventually Bhaji, when we entered into a new era of deviousness regarding payments. We'd often have to make two or three journeys to their shop in the Arndale where the proprietor usually attended, but was often back "in business" (?) in Turkey. When we did finally catch up with him, he'd write a cheque……..forward dated!

When we delivered in August on a nice sunny Friday, just before the Community Shield game with Liverpool, they weren't stocking them anymore, the clueless shop assistant thought? However, the bonus was that we bumped into Bernardo Silva, who was buying some sweets (?) and was pleasantly surprised when he saw KK 261, asking incredulously - "You do this?" We had a little chat, and he corrected me when I asked if he was playing in the game tomorrow. "Yes, Sunday" he said, putting me in my place. They did carry on stocking later,

They also had a couple of shops in Mersey Way in Stockport, who paid up, there and then, in cash, for sales of about ten each, The shops were about 50 yards apart, and one would sell out, whilst the other one didn't, and they never thought to check with each other to even up. By the time we'd paid for petrol, parking, the buskers, and a snack, it was hardly worth the effort, but it was a trip out I suppose!

Also in Stockport, was the **HARLEQUIN** shop owned by big Blue Fred Follows, where parking was tricky. Fred eventually sold the shop, to a strange bloke who wasn't very helpful and sales petered out. Fred became a KK subscriber until issue 300 when we finally called it a day. Also **KING BEE RECORDS** in Chorlton.

SPORTSPAGES MANCHESTER, had a shop in Barton Arcade, with the fanzine section in a cramped corner, always rammed, whilst the rest of the spacious shop was allocated to minor sports, and usually empty. They closed in December 2005, when it became a Gents Outfitters. John Rowan said "I went in for a fanzine, but came out with a cravat!"

BARNEY FOOTBALL CHIC, was a short-lived venture, based in Affleck's Palace. Sadly they had to finish trading as, I believe, they were threatened by the local scrotes who wanted protection money, but I could be wrong?

For a short period Eddie Phillips, owner of the **CITY SOUVENIR SHOP**, stocked KK, and did very well until the club forced him to cease selling, as we'd become quite critical towards the end of the Swales era. I did receive a nice letter from director Ian Niven with an explanation to that effect!

The **NATIONAL FOOTBALL MUSEUM**, which became Urbis, stocked until Covid hit. It was OK initially with a QPR, then a Liverpool fan in charge, but then relapsed into a new era of incompetence. We'd check the shelves which were empty, no KK zines on show, meaning they'd sold out, but then they'd then find they had another stack in the drawer, under the counter. Other times, when they'd proudly announce they'd sold out and paid up, the next time we'd visit with a new delivery, they'd sheepishly advise they'd found some more of the old copies, so would have to reduce payment by that amount! No doubt under new management, the situation has improved?

W.H. SMITHS at Manchester Airport stocked for a while and sold exceptionally well. As I worked there at the time it was fairly easy to deliver large quantities. Unfortunately, despite repeated requests, payments weren't forthcoming, and I had to use the influence of 'those up above' for action. I was invited to their office at roof level of the Terminal, with windows adjacent to roof access. It was a sitting target for any one fancying a break in, as there were mountains of cash stacked on the tables, but I never heard of any such thefts.

Their main outlet in Manchester refused to stock the 'Century City' book as they said it would "get stolen off their shelves!" **BORDERS** in Stockport went bust, owing monies.

OMEGA RECORD SHOP in Northwich was owned by massive Blue, and Charlatans manager at the time, Steve Harrison (pictured here with son Martin). I was then working on site at Kelloggs Wrexham, so it was convenient for me to call in, on the way, for deliveries, and enjoy a coffee with Steve, who was great company and support. He had no time for ageism, but he'd joke that he'd love me to come to a Charlatans gig, when I could "sit at the back with my headphones on, listening to Jethro Tull if I liked!" I would never do that of course, but did attend gigs, which were always a great experience, with my kids. I did, though, get queried looks from young ageist punters, who found my presence acceptable when I lied about being Tim Burgess's dad! I admitted this to the bloke sitting next to me, who said "actually, I am Tim's dad!". Tim, incidentally, before the family moved to Northwich, lived just

around the corner from Sue in Pendlebury, as did actor George Costigan. Ben Kingsley, plus City fan, the great L.S Lowry, and my dad, lived on the famous Station Road, where Swinton Lions RFC resided. Steve's book, 'Dead, Dead Good' is now out so buy it!

There were other short term outlets with similar problems which aren't worth recounting here.

AND THERE'S MORE...

Once the local outlets were serviced it was just a matter of parcelling up and posting to the following outlets -

SELECTADISC in Nottingham (I once delivered after daughter Kaye had gone for an interview at Nottingham Uni, and was waiting for her and Sue outside the toilets in the city centre, and must have had my miserable face on because a bloke walked past and told me to "cheer up!" Which still makes me laugh!) **CARDIFF CITY SUPPORTERS CLUB SHOP, NOSTALGIA AND COMICS, SEAN WATTERSON IOM, GOOD VIBES, JUMBO RECORDS LEEDS, FOOTBALL FEVER, STRATHCLYDE PROGRAMME SHOP, ARCHWAY, AFN DISTRIBUTION, SCOTTISH ZINE SCENE, MIDDLESBROUGH PROGRAMME SHOP, MCFC SUPPORTERS CLUB IN DUBLIN, SCANDINAVIAN SUPPORTERS CLUB.**

SUPPORTERS CLUBS Along with the cool guys, Jason Manford, Ricky Hatton RIP, Noel and Liam from Oasis, Billy Duffy from the Cult, and Johnny Marr from the Smiths, amongst many others, (Pete Maclaine, later Elbow, Doves, The Blossoms) It was the City supporters clubs who helped keep morale up in the dark times, and we salute the thankless task that the Chairman and Secretaries perform. As a fanzine editor and for a short time 'Fan on the Board', 1994/95 season, I was often asked to visit and talk at Supporters club meetings, which was the primary object, but we did also sell a few zines.

These included Warrington, Astley and Tyldesley, Irlam & Cadishead, Prestwich and Whitefield, Swinton, Droylsden, Reddish, Bredbury, West Yorks, South Yorks, Rochdale, Chorley, Blackley, Blackpool, Morecambe, Gorton, Stretford, Costa Del Sol, Cookstown, Guernsey etc.

Other zines we swapped with included all the City zines plus When Skies Are Grey (Everton), Follow, Follow (Rangers), The Fox (Leicester, Give us An R (Tranmere), Those Were The Days (Ipswich), Half Magpie, Half Biscuit (Newcastle), Dribble (Ipswich), Chelsea Independent (Chelsea), Follow The Yellow Brick Road (Mansfield), My Eyes Have Seen The Glory (Spurs), Through the Wind And Rain (Liverpool, Heroes and Villains (Villa), Leyton Orienteer (L.Orient), plus, especially, United We Stand (ManU) and The Gooner (Arsenal), who still swap with us even though we now have no longer any KKs to exchange!

Finally, we regularly posted to famous and celebrity City fans, including Eddie Large (who invited us to various shows backstage and in hospitality), Billy Duffy (who's invited us to enjoy gigs in hospitality), subscribers John Henshaw and John Stapleton RIP, Fred Eyre, Ian Cheeseman, Susan Bookbinder, James H

Reeve, Nick Leeson, plus many others, all very supportive.

CONCLUSION Whilst in the main the outlets did a great job, at times they could be a pain! I'm exhausted just reading the above, and frankly, at my age now, I wonder how on earth we did it, but we did, somehow!

24. SOME HIGHS & LOWS

Alan Rainford, takes us through some of the Manchester City highs and lows, from season 1988/89 until season 2023/24, highlighting incidents, generally on the pitch, achievements, and major signings, complementing homegrown talents such as Weaver, Lake, Brightwells, White, Hinchcliffe, Edghill,etc right through to Foden, Lewis and O'Reilly. Obviously, if we were a United book, we wouldn't mention any lows, as 'the legendary Man. United selective memory syndrome' would kick in, and every low would be deleted from the memory and record books, as there must be no "negativity of the brand". We are City, from Maine Road, (and the Etihad), warts an 'all, read on...

MAINE ROAD 1988 TO 2003, 15 KK YEARS

(88/89) Dibble, Biggins, Taggart, Cooper, Gleghorn, Oldfield, Megson, Bradshaw signed; KK1's home debut v Plymouth Lg Cup 1-0 win; 1-4 loss to Oldham, 3-3 draw, after 3-0 with Bournemouth; promotion achieved with a late equalising goal by Trevor Morley at Bradford the following week. (D2 2nd 82 pts)

(89/90) 'Blue Moon' first sang; 5-1 win over United; Machin sacked, Kendall appointed; Quinn signed (£800M) (D1 14th 48 pts)

(90/91) Coton signed (£900K); 3-3 draw v United after 3-1; Kendall off to Everton, Reid appointed; Coton sent off v Derby – Quinn goes in goal and saves a Saunders penalty in 2-1 win; (D1 5th 62pts)

(91/92) Curle signed (£2.5M); 4-0 April win against eventual Champions Leeds. (D1 5th 70 pts)

(92/93) Phelan signed (£2.5M);Premier League starts – City's opening game v QPR is first live Sky TV match; New Platt Lane stand opened for 6th rd FA Cup 4-2 loss to Spurs with pitch invasion; 2-5 home loss to Everton in last game of season. (PL 9th 57 pts) .

(93/94) Rosler, Walsh, Beagrie signed); Maddock appointed; Reid sacked, Horton appointed; 3-2 defeat to united after 2-0 upn, at H/T; Ipswich FA Cup game abandoned at 2-0 up due to waterlogged pitch; 'Swales out, Franny in' new Chairman; 'The Kippax Last Stand' v Chelsea 2-2. (PL 16th 45 pts).

(94/95) Burridge signed on loan 43 yrs, 5 months, the oldest player to appear in Prem). Build of new Kippax stand commenced and opened (in stages); 5-2 win v Spurs; Rösler scores 4 in 5-2 FA Cup 3rd rd replay win v Notts County; Horton sacked. (PL 17th 49pts).

(95/96) Kinkladze signed (£2M), & Symons (£1.5M); Ball appointed; 3-2 loss v united despite going from 0-2 to 2-2; Kinkladze's 'mesmeric' goal v Southampton in 2-1 win; Relegated against Liverpool, despite another 0-2 to 2-2 fightback, but mistakenly playing for a draw. (PL 38pts rel on GD).

(96/97) Dickov signed (£700K); 5 managers in first 28 games; Ball resigned after just 3 games; Hartford appointed caretaker (8 games); 1-5 aggregate League Cup defeat to 3rd-tier Lincoln; Coppell appointed and resigned after 6 games (transfer money promised did not materialise ?); Neal appointed caretaker (10 games); Clark appointed permanent manager.(D1 14th 61pts).

(97/98) Bradbury (£3M & Goater signed (£400K); 6-0 win v Swindon; Home defeat to Bury – fan rips up season ticket on pitch – protests outside main entrance; Clark sacked, Royle in; Franny out, David Bernstein in as Chairman; Pollock's OG V QPR in last home match; Relegation to 3rd tier (despite last day 5-2 win at Stoke).(D1 22nd 48 pts).

(98/99) Cult hero Morrison signed £80K); 7-1 League Cup victory over Notts County; 1-2 home defeat to 4th tier Mansfield in Auto Windscreen Shield before lowest-ever Maine Road crowd of 3,007; 12th place at Christmas, but Wrexham 1-0 away and Stoke home 2-1 turning points; Millwall 3-0, seats ripped out and riots in Moss Side; 3rd tier play-off v Wigan – 1st leg away, but shown on big screen at Maine Road – Goater disputed goal in home leg secures place in final v Gillingham (D2 3rd 82pts).

(99/2000) 1-2 home defeat to Stockport; 1-0 win v Birmingham in final home match – mass pitch invasion by fans -promotion achieved in the next and final match at Blackburn 4-1. (D1 2nd 89 pts)

(00/01) Hat-trick for Wanchope in first home match back in Premier League (4-2 v Sunderland); Dunne signed £3M); 0-1 defeat at home to United; 0-4 home loss to Arsenal who are 4-up after only 36 minutes; Ultimate relegation 8 points from safety; Royle sacked. PL 18th 34 pts).

(01/02) Keegan appointed; Benarbia signed; Shock 0-4 home defeat to Wimbledon; 6-0 League Cup win over Birmingham; 3-2 win at 'no away fans allowed' Millwall, screened to fans at Maine Road; 5-1 home win over League leaders Burnley puts City top; Another 5-1 home win over Barnsley secures the Championship and promotion again; Last day 3-1 win over Portsmouth, but in his last-ever game Stuart Pearce misses the last-minute penalty that would have given him his 100th career goal. (D1 1st 99 pts)

(02/03) Anelka £13M, Schmeichel, and Distin signed; United beaten 3-1 (first games since 1989) – The Goat dispossessing Gary Neville for the second goal and then scoring his 100th City goal for the third; 1-5 home defeat to Arsenal who were 4-nil up after 20 minutes; David Bernstein resigned over Fowler signing, John Wardle new Chairman; Marc-Vivien Foé RIP scores two in 3-0 home win over Sunderland – his last goals for City, his second being the last City goal scored at Maine Road; 0-1 loss to Southampton in last game at Maine Road on 11th May 2003; Tributes laid at Maine Road for Marc-Vivien Foé RIP; (9th 51 pts).

THE ETIHAD 2003 TO 2024, 21 KK YEARS

(03/04) Barcelona friendly 2-1 win, Total Network Solutions 5-0, 6-2 win against Bolton, 4-1 win against United, 5-1 home win against Everton on the last day, but 7 wins out of 24 home matches, one of the worst in City's history.

(04/05) Lazio 3-1 win (Inaugural Thomas Cook Trophy); 7-1 win against Barnsley in League Cup; Keegan resigns, Stuart Pearce taking over; Final day 1-1 v Middlesbrough, David James up front, miss out on European qualification. (16th 41 points)

(05/06) Samaras signed (£6M); T/C Trophy 3-1 win over Olympiacos, Ya ya Toure scores their goal);3-1 victory over united; 1-2 FA Cup Q/F defeat to West Ham; FA Youth Cup Final 2nd leg City beat Liverpool 2-0 but lose 2-3 on aggregate. (8th 52 pts)

(06/07) Hart's debut; Porto, win 1-0 in the T/C Trophy; Thatcher sent off v Portsmouth; Only 15 goals scored in the 21 home games with no goals at all scored in last 7 home games; 1-0 defeat to united, last home game; Stuart Pearce sacked. (14th 42 pts)

(07/08) Thaksin Shinawatra, take over; Sven-Goran Eriksson appointed manager; 8 new players signed; Valencia win the T/C Trophy 1-0, D. Silva goal); 1-0 win over United, Stephen Ireland revealed his 'Superman' underpants after 1-0 Sunderland winner; In the FA Youth Cup Final home 2nd leg City beat Chelsea 3-1 to win the Cup by a 4-2 aggregate; Lose 3-2 to Fulham; after 2-0 up; Eriksson sacked. (9th 55pts) UEFA final Rangers v Zenit.

(08/09) Mark Hughes appointed manager; 6 new players signed inc Jo (£18M),

Kompany (£6M), Zabaleta (£6.5M) SWP (£6.5M), ADUG takeover;Robinho (£32.5M) scores against Chelsea, but City lose 1-3; 6-0 home win v Portsmouth; January Bridge, de Jong, Bellamy, Given signed; City beat Hull 5-1 with Phil Brown H/T lecture to his players; 3rd Round 0-3 defeat by Championship team N. Forest; City 2 Hamburg 1 in UEFA Cup, with great atmosphere but lose 4-3 on aggregate. (10th 50 pts)

[09/10] 8 players signed inc K Toure, Barry, Santa Cruz, Tevez, Adebayor, Lescott £118 total); 4-2 victory over Arsenal, Adebayor, 90-yard run back down the pitch celebration; Hughes sacked, Mancini appointed; 2-1 victory over united in League Cup S/F, but ends in ultimate 3-4 aggregate defeat; last home match 1-0 defeat to Spurs. they, not us, qualify for Ch Lg. (5th 67 pts)

[10/11] FA Cup winners. Six players signed Boateng, Yaya, Silva, Kolarov, Balotelli, Milner (£116M); Sheikh Mansour attends his first game – a 3-0 win against Liverpool; January Dzeko signed £27M); City 3 Lech Poznan 1, but Poznan fans' celebration steals show; City 1 Reading 0 - FA Cup Q/F; City 1 Spurs 0, Ch Lg qualification. (3rd 71 pts)

[11/12] Premier League winners. Six players signed inc Sergio Aguero (£36M) who scores 2 goal in debut v Swansea, 4-0 win; Garry Cook resigned; FA Cup 3 - City 2 United 3; 1-0 defeat to Liverpool in League Cup S/F 2-3 on aggregate; Kompany heads in for 1-0 win over United; 4-1 win v Villa; The QPR 'miracle' last game with two goals in injury time from Dzeko and Aguero to turn defeat into a 3-2 victory and the League title. (1st 89 pts)

[12/13] Premier League runners-up; FA Cup runners-up. 3-2 loss to United; Tevez hat-trick in 5-0 FA Cup Q/F win over Barnsley; Mancini sacked, Brian Kidd caretaker for last two games; Last match shock 2-3 defeat to mid-table Norwich City. (2nd 78pts)

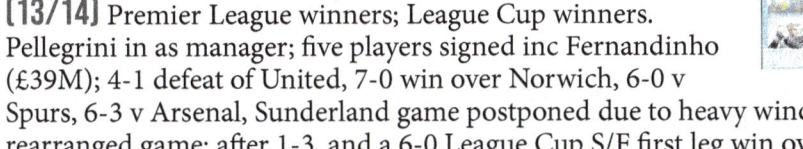

[13/14] Premier League winners; League Cup winners. Pellegrini in as manager; five players signed inc Fernandinho (£39M); 4-1 defeat of United, 7-0 win over Norwich, 6-0 v Spurs, 6-3 v Arsenal, Sunderland game postponed due to heavy winds, 3-3 in rearranged game; after 1-3, and a 6-0 League Cup S/F first leg win over West Ham, 3-0 2nd leg; Shock 2-1 FA Cup Q/F defeat to Uwe Rosler's Wigan; City beat West Ham 2-0 on the final day to lift title. (1st 86pts)

[14/15] Premier League runners-up. Six players signed inc Mangala (£42M); Sheffield Wednesday beaten 7-0 in League Cup, Aguero nets all four in 4-1 defeat of Spurs – and misses a penalty!; 1-2 defeat to CSKA Moscow in C/L: City beat Bayern Munich 3-2 after 2-1 down in C/L, 2-0 FA Cup 4th round loss at home to Championship team Middlesbrough; Bony signed (£25M); In FA

Youth Cup Final City lose 1-3 at home and 2-5 on aggregate to holders Chelsea; 6-0 defeat of QPR in penultimate home game. (2nd 79pts)

[15/16] League Cup winners. Five players signed inc KDB(£55M), Sterling £44M), Otamendi (£28M); South Stand extension completed raising capacity to 54k in time for use at first home game v Champions Chelsea and 3-0 win; 6-1 win against Newcastle; Heavy 4-1 defeat to Liverpool; 3-1 win over Everton in League Cup S/F to overturn 1-2 first leg loss; Statement 3-1 win by Leicester, who go on to win title; Youth Cup Final loss to Chelsea again after 1-1 draw at home (2-4 aggregate); 0-0 home draw with Real Madrid in CL S/F, followed by 0-1 defeat away. The Ed, with grand daughter Ellie (15), finally gets to hear Thunderstruck blasted out by AC/DC in the summertime gig. (4th 66 pts)

[16/17] Pep takes over light weight, ageing team as manager; Seven new players inc Stones £47M), Sane (37M), Gundagon £20M); Borussia Mönchengladbach C/L game called off due to 'tropical' rainstorm – 4-0 win next day; 3-1 win v. Barcelona in CL; 5-3 win over Monaco in C/L last 16 1st leg but out on away goals. 1-3 away loss; Youth Cup Final loss to Chelsea for 3rd year in a row – 1-1 home draw, but 1-5 away defeat. (3rd 78 pts)

[17/18] 'Centurions', Premier League winners, League Cup winners. Five new players inc Bernardo (£43M), Ederson (£35M), Walker (£45M), Mendy (£52m), Laporte (£57M Jan). Second home game 5-0 win over Liverpool, followed by another 5-0 against Palace and then a 7-2 against Stoke; Bristol City beaten 2-1 in 1st leg of League Cup S/F, 2nd leg 3-2; Aguero nets 4 goals in the second half of match against Leicester for a 5-1 win; 2-1 home loss to Liverpool in 2nd leg of C/L Q/F, appalling refereeing decisions, 1-5 on agg; 3-2 loss to United after 2-0 up puts off title win for a week. (1st 100pts)

[18/19] 'Domestic Treble', Premier League winners, FA Cup winners, League Cup winners. Mahrez signed (£60M); 6-1 v Huddersfield; Shock 2-1 home defeat to Lyon in CL; 6-1 v Southampton and 6-0 v Shakhtar Donetsk in CL; 3-2 defeat to Crystal Palace; 7-0 win over Rotherham in FA Cup 3rd round, 9-0 against Burton in the League Cup S/F 1st leg and 6-0 over Chelsea; 7--0 win over Schalke in the C; 4-3 CL Q/F win over Spurs, late goal disallowed by VAR, 4-4 on agg, but out on away goals Youth Cup Final is lost to Liverpool on penalties (3-5) after a 1-1 draw; – "Don't shoot Vinny" 1-0 win against Leicester. (1st 98 pts)

[19/20] The 'COVID Season'Premier League runners-up, League Cup winners. Rodri (£63M), Cancelo (£60m) signed; 51,000 attend testimonial/charity match for Vinny - City Legends v All Star XI; 8-0 v Watford; 5-1 win v Atalanta in CL; 1-0 defeat to United in League Cup S/F 2nd leg, but 3-1 1st leg win puts City through; Season suspended on 13th March due to COVID – restarts on 17th June with City beating Arsenal 3-0 in empty stadium; Champions Liverpool beaten 4-0 to stop their charge to 100 points; Norwich beaten 5-0 in last League match; C/L restarts on 7th August with 2nd leg 2-1 home win over Real Madrid to add to 1st leg away win

back in February for a 4-2 aggregate; August 15th season ends with 3-1 loss to Lyon in Lisbon. (2nd 81pts)

(20/21) The 'No Fans Season' Champions League runners-up, Premier League winners, League Cup winners. New signings inc Dias (£62M), Ake (£40M), Torres (£20M); Season starts 12th September with all games played in empty stadiums; Shock 2-5 defeat to Leicester; 2019/20 held-over Youth Cup Final sees City beat Chelsea 3-2 at St George's Park; 'King of the Kippax' Colin Bell sadly dies on the 5th January; City lose 2-0 to United at the Etihad; 1-2 home loss to 10-man Leeds; Chelsea 2-1 home loss; CL S/F 2nd leg 2-0 win (4-1 on aggregate) against PSG; Final League game 5-0 home win against Everton in front of 10,000 'lucky' fans who see Aguero come on for last 30 minutes in his final appearance and scores two goals, before the PL Trophy is awarded. 1st 86 pts)

(21/22) Premier League winners. Grealish signed (£100M); 5-0 against both Norwich and Arsenal and a 6-3 CL defeat of Leipzig; A 6-1 win over Wycombe in the League Cup sees no less than 6 debuts given to Academy players; Shock 2-0 home defeat to Crystal Palace; 2-1 win over PSG in CL Group; Two big home wins in December – 7-0 v Leeds and 6-3 v Leicester; 3-2 loss to Spurs, 4-1 defeat of United; 1-0 win over Atletico Madrid in C/L, 0-0 away; 5-1 win over Watford; 4-3 home win over Real Madrid in the 1st Leg of the CL S/F but lose 3-1 away aet.after late goals; City win 3-2 over Villa, after 2-0 down, with just 15 minutes left, to bring back memories of Agueroooooo!! 1st 93 pts) Alvarez signed (£14m) loaned back to R Plate.

(22/23) The 'World Cup Season' 'THE Continental Treble', Champions League winners, Premier League winners, FA Cup winners. Haaland (£51m), Phillips (£42M), Akanji (£15M) signed; 4-2 win over Palace after 2-0 down; 6-0 defeat of Forest; 6-3 demolition derby with hat-tricks for both Haaland and Foden; 2-1 loss to Brentford before the World Cup break; City beat Liverpool 3-2 in League Cup 4th Round; 4-2 win over Spurs, another, 0-2 at H/T; FA Cup 4th Round 1-0 win over Arsenal. Leipzig beaten 7-0 in CL last 16 2nd leg; 6-0 trouncing of Vinny's Burnley in FA Cup Q/F; Convincing 3-0 win over Bayern in CL Q/F 1st leg; 4-1 win over table toppers Arsenal; Haaland's goal against West Ham is his 35th league goal to break the PL record; First leg 1-1 away draw in the CL S/F then Real Madrid are blown away 4-0 in the second leg; City beat Chelsea 1-0 in a carnival atmosphere at the last home game and are presented with the League trophy for the 3rd year running. (1st 89pts)

(23/24) FIFA World Club Cup winners, Premier League winners, UEFA Super Cup winners, FA Cup runners-up. Signings inc Gvardiol (£77M), Doku (£55M), Nunes (£53M), Kovacic (£25M). Bournemouth beaten 6-1, Bell, Lee and Summerbee statue unveiled; City 3 United 1, 0-1 down at H/T; After 3-3 in Madrid in C/L, City draw 1-1 at home (first time away goals don't count) lose 4-3 on pens; 5-1 win over Wolves; Youth Cup Final City 4 Leeds 0; 3-1 win over West Ham for a 4th successive League title.

Alan Rainford

25. MANCHESTER CITY FANZINES

■ City fanzine team, 'King of the Electric Blueprint' at the Stoke fanzine fair 1989, and 5-a-side competition, comprising - (L to R) Noel, Pete Gregory, Frank Newton, Mike Kelly, Dave. (We didn't win?)

Blueprint was the first City fanzine, followed by our very own King of the Kippax, then Electric Blue/Bert Trautmann's Helmet, Wig Out (one off), Main Stand View, Singing the Blues, Blue Murder, The Fight Back, Chips 'n Gravy, This Charming Fan, A Million Miles Away, and the wonderful aptly titled City 'Till I Cry. It's fair to say there was much rivalry between City fanzines, who'd nicked whose articles, vying for position when selling on the streets etc. not helped by fans advising "this one's by far the best fanzine, your's is crap!" We are all City fans so you wouldn't imagine us all to have the same views on who played well, who was poor, who we've signed, who we should've signed etc. You'll also find there are rivalries between authors, radio and TV presenters, pop and rock stars, film stars, radio DJ's, managers, mechanical and electrical engineers, Politicians, and players etc. Emotions run high before, during, and especially after matches, the performances on the pitch often affecting sales. We're generally all good friends now, and can laugh at the previous goings on, though becoming successful has helped enormously.

With respect to all the fanzines the big ones were:

BLUEPRINT, "OFTEN COPIED, NEVER BETTERED!"

Emerged in the winter of season 1987/88, 27 issues until Spring 1994. A pot pourri of strands; critical and left-field, satirical and surreal (a nod to FOUL Magazine). Diverse contributors, mainstay, included Mike Kelly (founder), Rob Dunford, Frank Newton, "Jocky" Wilson, and, in early days Dave Wallace.

Milestones and achievements include a prime role in fancy dress at Stoke 1988, the Kippax flag, Blues Brothers at Palace 1990, aeroplane over Ragworld May 1991 and, dubiously, interview with Peter Swales! Later, editor Bill Borrows went on to greater things with mainstream Loaded and 4-4-2 magazines. Rob became a regular contributor to KOTK.

■ Rob Dunford

ELECTRIC BLUE/BERT TRAUTMANN'S HELMET - "THE ONLY CITY 'ZINE TO COME FROM MANCHESTER"

Covered in Noel's foreword. Some contributors also produced articles for KK. Various superb issues of 'The Helmet Rides Again' have been produced on line, contact - noel_bayley@yahoo.co.uk

■ Noel, hogging the limelight with Sue and Alex in the background (Pic from G James' 'Farewell to Maine Road' book.

CITY TILL I CRY, "THE QUINTESSENTIAL MANCHESTER CITY FANZINE"

The summer of 1998 was one of reflection and the birth of CTIC. Tom Ritchie, after contributing to EB/BTH and KK, was the leader and driving force, me, Steve & Sean were the muses, the sounding board. Our aim, to compliment our fellow fanzines, stamping our own experiences. Seven years of fun, misery, cold, wet afternoons and long away trips. Good Times... Gary (Gazzor)

■ Gary Phillips

THE FIGHTBACK - "FREE THE 30,000"

Born 8 December 1993 v Everton 1-0. 20 hand made & stapled copies and brought out printed copies in following seasons on and off until May 1998. Best sales 1,500 - Daft Donald Special ! Born out of complete frustration as to the way the club was being run under Swales and just felt I had a lot to say. Came off the back of the 3-2 November 1993 derby when Utd fought back against us. I thought we should start Fighting Back. Some of the content was quite naive and reads as quite embarrassing now. But it made an impact during the Lee Out campaign. Also contributed to KK.

■ The Ed & Dante

MCIVTA

Not strictly a fanzine, but the longest running City newsletter, is currently produced and issued by ex KK and CTIC contributor, Phil Banerjee, available on - editor@mcivta.com.

■ Phil Banerjee

THE ROLE OF THE FANZINE ?

As 'letters to the editor' declined, or weren't published, and the views of fans were ignored, the fanzines arrived to give City, (and, indeed, fans of all clubs, as there was a camaraderie between the fanzine fraternity), a voice in print and in the media. The aim being to cover fans' views on games, players, running of the club, football in general, to make fun of the totally biased media regarding their darlings United and Liverpool, and to take to task the FA, Uefa and Fifa.. Also to support campaigns, cover day to day events, interviews with City managers, players, ex players, Chairmen, club officials, and City supporting celebrities, and review away day fanzines, and City books. Basically to "have a laugh", and act as a vehicle for fans to support the club of their choice, not necessarily the biggest or the best. 'For the fans, by the fans'.

26. CHANGES BY IAN CHEESEMAN

Ian has travelled on a similar journey to KK, certainly through the same period from 1988 to 2024, and beyond. We asked Ian if he would include a contribution reflecting on the changes he's personally encountered during this period…

When I started attending City games, during the Bell, Lee, Summerbee era, football wasn't as fashionable as it is now. It was a working-class sport and as a shy council house kid, growing up in Radcliffe, being a City fan helped me gain some credibility among the school bullies. They were impressed that I attended games and knew what I was talking about.

In those days, if you didn't go to games there was relatively little coverage of my club. I had posters on my wall of my hero Colin Bell, and bought Shoot and other football magazines. My Dad worked for British Rail, so while I was young I could take advantage of free or subsidised train tickets. I could get match tickets through the supporters club or just pay at the turnstiles. Life was less complicated back then. I collected tokens from programmes or reserve team sheets, and I queued early on Sunday mornings at Maine Road for the big games.

I collected the matchday programmes and then, when independent fanzines came along, I read them and saw the other side of being a fan. Real fans wrote their uncensored opinions and it was a refreshing change from the ever more sanitised content being created in the programme.

I fully embraced my passion for the club, and the joy I got from being part of the City family. I became a steward on the Supporters club football special trains which meant I started to mix with City directors, who occasionally travelled with us. I started to see both sides of my ever-changing club.

I hosted the Junior Blues meetings, was the clubs first commentator on video, and had a few seasons as stadium announcer at Maine Road. I got to know people like Club Secretary Bernard Halford, Directors Ian Niven & Chris Muir.

I met Chairman Peter Swales on several occasions at Supporters Club functions, and he even presented me, along with other fans, with a certificate for travelling to Ipswich and Plymouth twice in a week. I had the chance to buy a few shares in the club, giving me access to the Annual General Meetings, which became quite fiery during Francis Lee's takeover.

Having spent twenty years travelling everywhere, to follow my beloved Blues, I made the transition into the media and lived my dream as the BBC's City commentator/reporter/correspondent. I travelled with the team on their European flights, passing through customs late at night, with Sergio Aguero behind me, handing his passport over to a giddy official. It became normal for me to be among players, managers and famous fans. I hosted a few lunches for the club and my favourite memory was travelling with Tony Book and Patrick Vieira in a limousine for an hour each way to a restaurant on the bay of Naples. I had rare privilege, and was was very lucky.

Alongside these unique moments, too many to mention here, I saw all the ups and downs, like losing at York, Lincoln and at home to Mansfield Town in the AutoWindscreens Shield; just over 3000 (officially) of us were at Maine Road that day.

I was at Stoke on the last day of the season when we won, but still went down to the third tier of English football. I was alongside my son at Wembley when we scraped past Gillingham to start climbing back up via the play offs.

Within a year or two I was interviewing Kevin Keegan after promotion back to the top flight. I was behind the microphone when we beat United at Wembley to confirm our resurgence, and when Aguero scored THAT goal, in 2012.

Slowly but surely I could see changes to the club I loved and football in general. Press Officers started to control what could be asked and how questions would be answered. Access to players and behind the scenes became ever more restricted, and as the Sky riches came in, players moved further and further away from the fans. VAR took away the spontaneity of goal celebrations, new fans, with more disposable income, suddenly latched on to football and City's success. Working class fans felt more and more alienated.

I left the BBC and became a YouTube vlogger, giving a voice to matchgoing fans as I tried to stay connected to the club I love. In 2023 I saw it all. The Treble, Supercup and Club World Cup, travelling to every game and sharing those special moments with fellow fans I've got to know throughout my life.

We saw, during the pandemic, that football without matchgoing fans felt sterile and soulless. City won the Premier League the season that only the lucky few thousand, including me thankfully, could be there for the trophy lift against Everton.

King of the Kippax represented the soul of Manchester City fans, honestly and passionately. Players come and go, as do owners, all the contributors to Dave and Sue Wallace's passion project did it from the heart and for the love of our club, just as I have done throughout my life and career. Has City and football changed for the better? That's for you to judge, but I'm so glad that we've all been part of the most wonderful ride of our lives. It is, and always will be, "Great to be a Blue!"

27. EPILOGUE

"Just look where we've come from!"
Is the line often trotted out by City fans, usually referring to York away. Well it's not where I came from, though I WAS there. I came from an era when we reached cup finals, played in front of 70,000+ crowds, won FA cups, the League, League Cups, and a European Cup, so that one season in the third tier is certainly NOT where I came from.

MATCHDAY

Seventy years on from my first City game in 1955, 57 years for Sue since 1968, and 37 years on from the start of the fanzine, two years since we stopped producing KK, (though we've since done a Colin Bell and a Treble special), it's a very different match going experience.

We don't travel to away games these days, so we'll just concentrate on home games. We usually set off about two and a half hours before kick off, which can be any time from morning, until evening, Sometimes, Tom and/or Steve drive, through parts of the Manc suburbs we never knew existed! I love it when we drive up Ashton New Road, past all the Blues heading to the stadium, wearing the colours, proud to be Blue. We park up about an hour and a half prior to kick off, and make our way to the stadium, past the merchandising stalls, to our entrance D in the East stand (after picking up a programme) and are searched by the stewards, always helpful and friendly. The Etihad would shut down but for the stewards, and the only one I've had a problem with was a pasty faced incompetent toe rag.

Season card (so much for the 'No to Id cards' campaign, although the technology wasn't there in the 80s) checked, (never worked on my phone) approved, then up in the lift, to the 2nd tier, then via the 'Kits Bar', with the odd half 'n half scarf on show and onto the concourse, for a pie, a Bovril, and a hot chocolate, which the staff happily transfer into our special rigid-lidded containers.

Up we go to our padded seats, then we gaze round at our surroundings, a green pitch all year round, we check out the progress on the North stand extension, hotel construction, fanzone etc.. The ground starts to fill up, familiar faces around us, sometimes new fans, who we welcome. Away fans are a long way away in three tiers of the South stand, so we miss the banter. We listen to the DJ, watch Nat and 'Fanzone Danny' interview whichever City celebs are in town. The goalies come out to practise, encouraged by a ripple of applause, then later the players appear, before they all troop off back to the dressing room. Stadium logistics mean we don't meet up with other family members, who prefer the South stand, but we do give them a wave.

Kick off approaches, sometimes there's a feature by the 1894 group, chants are exchanged between opposition fans in the South stand, the teams come out to the strains of *Hey Jude*, and up tempo *Blue Moon*. We kick off, generally towards the South stand, and the players look resplendent in the Sky Blue, although these days there's a choice of three new kits every year. On a Champions League night we are entertained by an impressive light show. Half time breaks now last for quarter of an hour, (sometimes not long enough for Pep), we don't bother trying to get drinks. Teams are allowed five substitutes, the game is cleaner these days, ball and boots lighter, and we are blessed with VAR, which we thought would rule out poor decisions. It hasn't.. At the end of the game the players do a lap of honour, win draw or lose, and we make our way back to the car park, (we're grateful for a spot) after having a chat with Margaret Henshaw, waiting for John, and it takes forever to exit (worse now if there's a Co-op gig on), before wending our way home via all the tedious roadworks. We usually listen to Talksport, as I find Cundy quite entertaining, and Jacky often comes on, talks up the Blues, with a lot of humour and sense.

MEDIA WATCH

Saturday mornings are a waste of space on Sky TV since *Soccer AM* was dropped. We generally just pick up the Guardian, which has gone down the nick with its football coverage, and absence of the brilliant little Guide, saved only by John Crace, and Adrian Chiles. We don't get the Mirror any more, despite it being the only decent 'red top' paper, (sorry Kevin Maguire) the sycophancy and regular three page coverage of the Rags and Dippers has become too much. As for the MEN, they gave us a nice send off when we finished the fanzine, but the letters page dedication to United fans - "Rashford is better than Haaland, United's treble was better than City's, Will Foden ever get a game", and other such nonsense, without usually printing my responses, is exasperating.

MOTD is eagerly awaited at night, win or not, and congrats to Gary Lineker for winning 'best presenter' award this year after years of Ant and Dec dominance. Of course, Carragher and Neville are never off the telly, but I don't mind Neville.

Sunday mornings, I eagerly awaited Sunday Supplement, a group of journalists discussing regular soccer topics. My particular favourites being Henry Winter, John Cross and Martin Samuel, who regularly went against the tide, by talking sense and bigging up City. It has recently returned, but without the previous impact so far. We usually buy the *i* these days for £1, the MEN is £2.40, half the paper taken up by adverts. I must confess to enjoying Sam Luckhurst's reports on the rags, reflecting fanzine style reports including fan chants etc. How refreshing to read marks of two given to each and every United player recently. No David Meek, United style reporting such as; "United involved in 7-goal thriller, after a 5-2 defeat, for Sam, or a seat on the team coach, presumably? (Ironically, at time of writing, Sam has just been replaced by West Ham fan David McDonnell!)

The general media? Oh dear. These are grown up, "in the know", pundits and journalists, on TV and in the newspapers, usually red team sycophants, seething with jealousy, about City's success, searching for clickbait, and too bitter to be objective. Far too much to cover here but typically, when the 'dirty oil money' came in: "Failure is in City's DNA; Team of individuals; Money can't by success; City have bought the league; City are a pantomime, they bought David Silva not David Villa; The Sheikh should've taken over FC United; The game has gone mad, they've signed Chelsea flop Kevin de Bruyne for £55M; They're signing full backs (Walker £45M) for what clubs sign forwards (United £90M for Lukaku); How many hospitals could you build with the money City spend?; Not in my lifetime; When you've got money you spend it willy nilly; and the two Daddy's of them all, Simon Jordan with his "City are a manufactured club", and Ian Herbert with his "Grubby club with under-the-table dealings", who are both unbelievably bitter and twisted. But if it's United or Liverpool spending like there's no tomorrow? Well that's just wonderful. Hypocrites.

FIT FOR F-ALL?

Then we come to the F.A, FIFA and UEFA, all of whom have been after City since day one, 1904 in fact, then 2008. Remember Platini's "We can't have clubs spending money they've not got " (we've got money) re FFP, and so far all have been seen off, though 'the 115' is their last shot, unless they lose, when they'll trump up something else.

Apologies if I've missed anything out!

THAT'S ALL FOLKS

So that's it, the end of an era. Thanks for staying with us. The world is in a bad place right now, but matchdays enable us to forget the woes, for a brief period. Remember though, that nasty people can always be nastier than nice people, so cherish your friends, and loved ones.

Dave and Sue

SUBSCRIBERS & SPONSORSHIP

Thanks to Dr Raymond Ashton for sponsoring this book.

Raymond was brought up in Guernsey, but finished his secondary education in the North of England, bunking off school to watch City! A passionate Manchester City fan, home and away, since the age of eight, Raymond's love of football extends to clubs and individual players at all levels. He has been a KK subscriber, and contributor since the first issue and would like to dedicate this sponsorship to fellow Channel Islander Billy Spurdle, who played for City in the 1955 Cup Final, moving to full back after Jimmy Meadows went off injured, in the 3-1 loss. In 1956 he gave up his place, through injury, to Don Revie. Billy also played for Oldham and Port Vale.

We are also grateful to the following people for subscribing in advance to this book. Numbers 1 to 40, sellers and contributors, as listed in the relevant chapters.

41) M. Freeman, 42) P. Denny, 43)B. Garnett, 44) J. Pickton, 45)C. Darvill, 46) H. Quinn, 47) J. Dinsdale, 48) P. Chappell, 49) G. Waite, 50) B. Petyt, 51) A. Nolan, 52) J. Peach, 53) P. Mansell, 54) B. Cronshaw, 55) I. Allcroft, 56) S. Rigby, 57) D. Lee, 58) T. Douch, 59) P. Quinn, 60) D.Clarke, 61) M/K. Chidgey, 62) N. Hurll, 63) L. Mcdonough, 64) K. Gooch, 65) E.Broome, 66) M. Theobold 67) C. Robinson, 68) M. Charnley, 69) A. Zuill, 70) D. Allison, 1) P. Goldstone, 72) T. Faulkner, 73) F. Parsons, 74) R. Holmes, 75) D. Hinchcliffe, 76) W. Cooke, 77) D. Ansbro, 78) P. Roberts, 79) Tony Frost, 80) R. Foster, 81) R. Gerlach, 82) R. Reade, 83) S. Pears, 84) S. Bell, 85) I. Cunningham, 86) A. Webster, 87) S. Davenport, 88) J. Wood, 89) Johnny D, 90) R. Parkes, 91) S. Haseldon, 92) S Mingle, 93) B Moreton, 94) J Schulman, 95) R. Bullock, 96) K. &I. Pattinson, 97) G. and L. Millar, 98) G.Ford, 99) D. Grundy, 100) L. Stones, 101) W. Mitchell, 102) M.Short.

www.ingramcontent.com/pod-product-compliance
Lightning Source LLC
Chambersburg PA
CBHW071700170426
43195CB00039B/2394